Lost Souls of Horror
and the Gothic

Lost Souls of Horror and the Gothic

Fifty-Four Neglected Authors, Actors, Artists and Others

Edited by ELIZABETH MCCARTHY
and BERNICE M. MURPHY
Foreword by SIR CHRISTOPHER FRAYLING

McFarland & Company, Inc., Publishers
Jefferson, North Carolina

LIBRARY OF CONGRESS CATALOGUING-IN-PUBLICATION DATA

Names: McCarthy, Elizabeth,, 1971– editor. | Murphy, Bernice M. editor.
Title: Lost souls of horror and the gothic : fifty-four neglected authors, actors, artists and others / edited by Elizabeth McCarthy and Bernice M. Murphy ; foreword by Sir Christopher Frayling.
Description: Jefferson, N.C. : McFarland & Company, Inc., Publishers, 2016. | Includes bibliographical references and index.
Identifiers: LCCN 2016039148 | ISBN 9781476663142 (softcover : acid free paper) ∞
Subjects: LCSH: Gothic revival (Literature)—Bio-bibliography. | Horror tales—History and criticism. | English fiction—20th century—Bio-bibliography. | American fiction—20th century—Bio-bibliography. | Horror films—History and criticism. | Motion picture actors and actresses—United States—Biography—Dictionaries. | Motion picture actors and actresses—Europe—Biography—Dictionaries.
Classification: LCC PN3435 .L57 2016 | DDC 809/.9164—dc23
LC record available at https://lccn.loc.gov/2016039148

BRITISH LIBRARY CATALOGUING DATA ARE AVAILABLE

ISBN (print) 978-1-4766-6314-2
ISBN (ebook) 978-1-4766-2653-6

© 2016 Elizabeth McCarthy and Bernice M. Murphy. All rights reserved

No part of this book may be reproduced or transmitted in any form or by any means, electronic or mechanical, including photocopying or recording, or by any information storage and retrieval system, without permission in writing from the publisher.

Front cover: (top inset) Aleister Crowley, 1906; background illustration © 2016 Yaroslav Gerzhedovich

Printed in the United States of America

McFarland & Company, Inc., Publishers
Box 611, Jefferson, North Carolina 28640
www.mcfarlandpub.com

Acknowledgments

The editors would like to thank the School of English, Trinity College Dublin, for supporting this project, and in particular for facilitating the award of a Patrick Kavanagh bursary which aided us in meeting editorial costs. We are also very grateful to Dr. Kate Roddy for her tireless and astute fact-checking work. The support and encouragement of our friends and colleagues at *The Irish Journal of Gothic and Horror Studies* and the M.Phil in popular literature program is, as always, much appreciated. This book simply would not have been possible without the work of our many contributors, and we cannot thank them enough for the work and thought that they put in to their individual entries. We are also very grateful to Sir Christopher Frayling for kindly agreeing to write the foreword. Bernice M. Murphy would like to thank her family for their continuing support and encouragement. Elizabeth McCarthy would like to thank Paul Cronly for respecting the deadlines she has to meet while making sure wine, song, and dance are never left off the schedule for too long: "I'm thinking that it must be love."

Table of Contents

Acknowledgments   v

Foreword: "Welcome to the Island of Lost Souls"
    Sir Christopher Frayling   1

Introduction   5

Evelyn Ankers
    Elizabeth McCarthy   11

Morris Ankrum
    Bill Warren   16

Theda Bara
    Maria Parsons   20

Ralph Bates
    Peter Hutchings   26

Charles Beaumont
    Edward O'Hare   30

Ingrid Bergman
    Mark Jancovich   34

Guy Boothby
    Ailise Bulfin   38

John Buchan
    Anna Powell   43

Susan Cabot
    Tom Weaver   46

Oscar Cook
    Darryl Jones   50

Marie Corelli
    Caitriona Kirby   54

Aleister Crowley
    Clive Bloom   58

Danielle Dax
    Catherine Spooner   63

Dulcie Deamer
    Jim Rockhill   68

Maya Deren
    Wendy Haslem   72

The *Erkenwald* Poet
    Brendan O'Connell   76

John Farris
    Xavier Aldana Reyes   80

Nicholas Fisk
    Katherine Farrimond   83

Charles Fort
    Tania Scott   86

Dion Fortune
    Kristine Larsen   90

Charles Gemora
    Mark Cofell   94

Gregory of Tours
    Peter Dendle   100

Victor Halperin
    Murray Leeder   104

Edward Jerningham
    Peter N. Lindfield
    and Dale Townshend   107

Jerome K. Jerome
    William Hughes   114

Skelton Knaggs
    John Exshaw   117

Alfred Kubin
    Tracy Fahey   121

Francis Lathom
    David Punter   124

Ira Levin
    Bernice M. Murphy   127

Jeff Lieberman
    Jon Towlson   130

Stephen Mallatratt
    Madelon Hoedt   135

Carl Mayer
    Jim Rockhill   139

Robert R. McCammon
    Neil McRobert   142

Shinji Mikami
    Eóin Murphy   147

Joseph Minion
    George Toles   151

Paula Modersohn-Becker
    Wendy Mooney   155

Fitz-James O'Brien
    Kevin Corstorphine   160

Sandy Petersen
    Rachel Mizsei Ward   165

Leonora Piper
    Dara Downey   169

Edogawa Rampo
    Colette Balmain   174

Charlotte Riddell
    Clare Clarke   178

Philip Ridley
    Douglas Keesey   182

Regina Maria Roche
    Christina Morin   186

Vincent Schiavelli
    Sorcha Ní Fhlainn   190

William Buehler Seabrook
    Roger Luckhurst   193

Sidney Sime
    Maria Beville   197

Tod Slaughter
    Jarlath Killeen   200

Lionel Sparrow
    James Doig   204

Montague Summers
    Frank Furedi   209

Team *Silent Hill*
    Ewan Kirkland   212

Peter Van Greenaway
    Edward O'Hare   215

Stephen Volk
    James Rose   220

Tom Waits
    Jenny McDonnell   224

Fredric Wertham
    Sarah Cleary   227

About the Contributors   231

Index   239

Foreword: "Welcome to the Island of Lost Souls"

SIR CHRISTOPHER FRAYLING

Ever since the rise of Gothic studies as an area of serious academic endeavor half a century ago, in pushback against the accepted "tradition" of literature, most books about the Gothic have been merrily trusting each other's judgment about who should be saved and who should be lost. Even though academic specialists in this area often liked to position themselves as in opposition to establishment methods of literary criticism, in a beleaguered way, some age-old assumptions were carried over. In particular, an apostolic succession—or canon as it came to be known—of key Gothic writers soon emerged, the ones who should be saved: a great chain of heroes and—importantly—heroines which began with Horace Walpole, matured with Ann Radcliffe, was popularized by Jane Austen's "horrid novels," diversified with Monk Lewis, Mary Shelley and Charles Maturin and then went multimedia. The links in the chain were left largely unexamined, as were examples of the Gothic in other art forms. These were Lost Souls. What happened during the many years between Walpole and Radcliffe? What were young painters and sculptors up to, in the same period? What became of those many writers whose tales of wonder failed for one reason or another to enter the cultural bloodstream? And so on. It took a long time for such questions to be asked, and in some cases they are still in the process of being answered.

Parallel studies of horror films were also surprisingly quick to establish an apostolic—or should that be diabolic?—succession of key stylistic moments: German Expressionism, Hollywood's Universal horror, Technicolor costume dramas with Hammer, domestication and radicalization by independents in the 1970s, then the move from guilty pleasure to mainstream entertainment. Each moment had its own director-heroes. It was as if a kind of "natural" selection was at work. Studies of what was happening between these moments, and by whom, were also a long time coming.

What of the writers and film directors, the books and the films, the visualizers and the performers who fell between the cracks in the floorboards, many of them having lost their footing in the mists of literary or film theory? Were they to be consigned to a purgatory of neglect, waiting to be promoted to the paradise of academic respectability or demoted to the inferno of oblivion? Or were they to be kept alive only in the blotchy pages of fanzines lovingly assembled by hard-line buffs and collectors, well below the taste threshold of most academic commentators? Who would have the energy and interest to dig deep enough to resurrect them from the enormous condescension of posterity?

I first saw Erle C. Kenton's *The Island of Lost Souls* (1932) in the mid-1960s, as part of a season of transgressive horror films organized by a student film society, in a double bill with Mark Robson and Val Lewton's *Isle of the Dead* (1945). The program notes owed a lot to the then-untranslated theoretical writings of Georges Bataille. These particular "Lost Souls" on their remote island had fallen foul of the British Board of Film Censors on three separate occasions—1933, 1951 and 1957, which may be a record—but the film had finally and reluctantly been passed with cuts in summer 1958. The hint of bestiality, the vivisections, the cross-breeding of the species, the implied cruelty to animals in the House of Pain, the Panther Woman sinking her claws into the all-American hero, the emphasis throughout on un-natural selection—not to mention Charles Laughton brandishing a whip and (presumably) asking the creationists in the audience, "Do you know what it means to feel like God?"—were all thought to be well beyond the pale, and so banished from the mainland just like Dr. Moreau himself. Laughton's bio-anthropological experiments with "plastic surgery, blood transfusions, gland extracts and ray baths"—of necessity more explicit on screen than in H.G. Wells's short novel of 1891, *The Island of Dr. Moreau* (Wells himself was disgusted by the film, rightly feeling that his theological implications had become somewhat sidelined in all the excitement)—still seemed transgressive some thirty-five years later, and the film's reputation as a subversive horror movie was intact. But it had all but disappeared from view, where British audiences were concerned, between 1932 and 1958. Nowadays, *The Island of Lost Souls* is classified PG (Parental Guidance) for home viewing, and that's with the cuts restored. The borders of transgression are shifting ones, as Bataille often pointed out.

The point is that since first seeing *The Island of Lost Souls*, I have always associated Arnold Boklin's painting of 1880 *The Isle of the Dead* with Dr. Moreau's other island—partly because the supporting feature screened that evening was directly inspired by it and the painting actually appeared behind the opening credits; partly because Dr. Moreau's island in the Kenton film has a similarly creepy atmosphere albeit with a different, South Seas, ecology. Boklin's isolated, rocky island—with its tall cypress trees, rock-tomb entrances, and mysterious white-clad figure arriving in a rowing boat on a wine-dark sea—became in my mind's eye the place where lost souls went. And after that, the painting kept appearing in films I subsequently saw: Skull Island in *King Kong* was copied from it, and the great wall of Skull Island was recycled as the burning wall of Atlanta, Georgia, in *Gone with the Wind*; Norman McLaren animated the painting in *A Little Phantasy* in 1946 and it became one of Hein Heckroth's sets in Michael Powell's *Tales of Hoffman* (1951). A number of Northern European emigres to Hollywood and Hollywood England brought their aesthetic with them, Arnold Boklin included, and they referred to his best-known painting, to them a visual cliché, all over the place. Then *The Island of Lost Souls* started surfacing in the Gothic and Metallic reaches of rock 'n' roll: "What Is the Law?" "Are We Not Men?" And the painting itself kept popping into my line of vision too: in museums in Basel, New York, Berlin and Leipzig. It transpired that there were four surviving versions made by the artist. But this was beginning to resemble a real-life version of a story by Edgar Allan Poe. Lost Souls everywhere. Or was it me, looking for them?

With this book, some of the lost souls of horror and the gothic have at last been rescued from that remote island, and from the purgatory of scholarly neglect. Not before time. About half of the lost souls are authors, matched by an assortment of actors, artists, designers, directors, mediums, musicians and occultists—dating from medieval times to the present, with an emphasis on the modern, all ripe for acknowledgment or re-appraisal. The book takes the form of a collection of short essays by leading scholars, artists and experts, assembled—with wit and enthusiasm—by Elizabeth McCarthy and Bernice M. Murphy. By resurrecting so many lost souls, it expands the cast of characters in Gothic studies, deepens the research pool and maybe even questions the very definitions of "Gothic" and "horror." And it evidently involved a lot of digging…

Sir Christopher Frayling is an educationalist and writer. In 2001, he was awarded a knighthood for services to art and design education. His publications on literature, art, film, and history include the recent On Craftsmanship: Towards a New Bauhaus, The Yellow Peril: Dr. Fu Manchu and the Rise of Chinophobia, *and* Inside the Bloody Chamber: On Angela Carter, the Gothic and Other Weird Tales.

Introduction

What do the following have in common?

A Classic-Hollywood-era "gorilla man"; an English occultist, ceremonial magician, and author; an early twentieth-century German expressionist painter; a nineteenth-century medium from Boston; an English experimental musician working in the late 1970s and mid–1980s; a sixth-century French bishop.

Well, if you guessed that Charles Gemora, Aleister Crowley, Paula Modersohn-Becker, Leonora Piper, Danielle Dax, and Gregory of Tours—for it is they who are being described—are all the subject of short essays contained within this volume, you'd be absolutely correct. But what they also have in common, in the eyes of our contributors, is that they have yet to be fully appreciated for the ways in which their work has interacted with the horror and gothic genres. And this brings us to the purpose of the collection you are reading at this very moment.

It is our intention to shed light upon the lives and work of individuals whose contribution to the macabre, the morbid, and the monstrous has at best been underappreciated, and at worst, been forgotten about or overlooked entirely. While we anticipate that some of you who are reading this introduction will likely be long-standing fans of all things horror and gothic related, we also hope that the eclectic range of subjects and entertaining nature of the essays will also capture the interest—and the imagination—of the general reader.

Lost Souls of Horror and the Gothic began life as a feature in *The Irish Journal of Gothic and Horror Studies*, an online, free-to-access academic publication, which was launched in 2006, and is, happily, still in operation. As the founders, and, until 2012, the co-editors of the journal, we felt that it was important to have, in addition to the expected peer-reviewed articles and reviews, at least one regular section which would allow us to expand our consideration of the horror and gothic genres beyond conventional academic avenues.

6   Introduction

Lost Souls grew out of a lively post-editorial meeting conversation in the pub (which is of course the venue where many of the best ideas in life originate), during which those assembled—all knowledgeable genre enthusiasts—began to debate one particularly pressing question: who were the individuals, to each of our minds, who had made important and yet often unacknowledged contributions to horror and the gothic? Indeed, it was thanks to a lengthy discussion about the impression made upon one of our number by the small but unforgettable roles that veteran character actress Una O'Connor (an Irishwoman, like the editors of this volume) played in the Universal horror classics *Bride of Frankenstein* (1935) and *The Invisible Man* (1933) that the premise behind *Lost Souls* emerged. In short: in order to qualify for inclusion, the subject must be a real-life person who has, in the eyes of the author of the essay in question, made a notable, if underappreciated contribution to the horror or gothic genres.

You will find all walks of life represented. Some of the subjects featured have played what was at the time a very visible, if subsequently neglected, role in shaping the horror and gothic genres, and will as a result have been prominently associated with these genres during their careers and lifetimes. Others may not be readily associated with the dark side of literary and popular culture. As a result, they would not usually keep the company that we have placed them with. We have not made any distinction between the broadest manifestations of popular culture, whether it be on the cinema screens, in the pages of gothic novels and sensation fiction, 1970s mass-market horror fiction, or computer games, and the work of architects, musicians, painters and visual artists. The Church of the Lost Soul is a broad one, happy to accommodate any and all, provided their advocates can make a compelling case for inclusion, and perhaps even play some small part in delivering their subject from the purgatory of current obscurity or lack of appreciation.

Perhaps inevitably, given the prominence of the big screen and the original impetus for this project, many of the subjects are actors, from behind-the-scenes stalwarts such as Charles Gemora to now sadly neglected stars such as Theda Bara, Skelton Knaggs, and Tod Slaughter, as well as more contemporary character actors such as Vincent Schiavarelli and Ralph Bates. However, we are just as interested in behind-the-scenes talent, as entries on screenwriters Joseph Minion, Stephen Volk, and Carl Mayer indicate. Directors are also well represented, as the entries on fascinating and diverse talents such as Philip Ridley, Victor Halperin, Jeff Lieberman, and Maya Deren will testify.

As a perusal of the table of contents suggests, however, it is authors— including fiction writers, journalists and playwrights—who make up the majority of entries. While some of the names cited are indisputably still well known among genre enthusiasts in particular—including writers such as Ira

Levin, John Buchan, and Charles Fort—other writers were prominent during their lifetimes, but have latterly been relegated to the sidelines as the tides of public taste have shifted. We include in this category authors John Farris and Robert R. McCammon, to cite two beneficiaries of the 1970s horror boom who, subsequently, and unfairly, we believe, fell out of public favor; as well as much earlier writers such as Marie Corelli, Regina Maria Roche, Guy Boothby, and Charlotte Riddell. Other authors featured who we feel have yet to receive their proper due include "Colonial Gothic" proponent Oscar Cook, important early gothic author Francis Lathom, Australian writer Dulcie Deamer, American writer and journalist William Buehler Seabrook (who brought the concept of the Haitian zombi to a Western audience for the first time), Irish-American journalist and author of the fantastic Fitz-James O'Brien, Australian author Lionel Sparrow, 1950s horror author Charles Beaumont, Japanese master of the macabre Edgowa Rampo (still largely unknown in the West), playwright Stephen Mallatratt (who has paradoxically been overshadowed by the immense success of his *The Woman in Black* [1983] adaptation), and the fascinatingly idiosyncratic 1970s British authors Peter Van Greenaway and Nicholas Fisk.

We are also immensely pleased to be publishing entries on musicians (Tom Waits and Danielle Dax), painters and visual artists (Sidney Sime, Alfred Kubin, and Paula Modersohn-Becker), architect/playwright/poet Edward Jerningham, the medium Leonora Piper, no less than three occultists/ writers (Aleister Crowley, Dion Fortune and Montague Summers), and three figures associated with the world of video games and gaming: Shinji Mikami, Sandy Petersen, and the team behind the immensely influential *Silent Hill* series. Fittingly perhaps, given the tantalizing eccentricity of some of the individuals cited, our subjects also include one psychiatrist, the *bête noire* of the 1950s horror comic industry, Dr. Frederic Wertham.

We should make it clear at this point that we are of course well aware that it may seem like a real stretch to classify some of the subjects in this volume as "Lost Souls," in that to describe them as obscure or forgotten about is not just inaccurate, but ridiculous. After all, Ingrid Bergman, to cite one obvious example, is one of the most famous and beloved actresses of the late twentieth century. Ira Levin wrote multiple bestsellers—including *Rosemary's Baby* (1967) as well as many successful Broadway plays—and his death was reported in most major newspapers. Tod Slaughter was one of the most successful actors of his day. John Buchan will forever be famous as the author of *The Thirty-Nine Steps* (and was also the governor general of Canada). Marie Corelli, like Guy Boothby, was one of the bestselling authors of the late nineteenth century and helped create our present day idea of the writer-as-celebrity. Tom Waits has long been one of the most respected singer/songwriters in the world. It may therefore seem inappropriate—and indeed, disingenuous—to place them alongside subjects whose talents are, for whatever reason, currently appreciated only by a relatively small number of enthusiasts.

And yet, it is our considered opinion that all of the figures just cited—in addition to the dozens of other subjects discussed (some of whom will likely be familiar to even a mild genre enthusiast, while others will likely only ring a bell with the most thorough genre scholar)—deserve more recognition than they have previously been afforded for their contributions to the horror and gothic genres. As the authors of the entries cited make clear, while several of these subjects could certainly still be called high profile in many important respects, what has, to a greater or lesser extent, been overlooked is the unique way in which they have lent their talents to our chosen genres. Bergman may often have been associated with wholesomeness and warmth, by both audiences and critics during the 1940s, but, as discussed in the entry devoted to her, the many paranoid and tormented women she played during this period meant that her work at the time was also frequently associated with horror. Two film adaptations of Ira Levin's work in particular remain very well known (*Rosemary's Baby* and *The Stepford Wives*), but academics and scholars have, to date, written very little indeed about his fiction, and his monumental influence upon modern horror fiction remains underappreciated as a result. Tod Slaughter was for many years one of the leading onscreen exemplars of the gothic villain, but today, his name and his work are generally recognized only by avid fans of early British cinemas and by historians of film and of the melodrama. Buchan's adventure and spy stories made him famous, but his use of gothic tropes and the supernatural and his powerful interest in oral folk narrative is now much less well known. The work of Corelli and Boothby is today usually only read by students of popular fiction and late Victorian literature. And as the entry on Tom Waits outlines, his work has frequently provided critically underexplored evidence of his distinctively gothic inclinations.

One of our main aims is to make the work of talented scholars working within the field of gothic and horror studies available to as wide a reading audience as possible. Many of these essays are written by contributors who are acknowledged experts on their subject and have happily seized this chance to communicate their knowledge and appreciation of their subject in question to the wider reading public. As the contributor biographies also indicate, quite a few of our contributors are independent scholars and highly informed genre enthusiasts from outside the world of academia who have for years lovingly researched the individuals they write on here. We are very proud indeed of the work that our contributors have done, and are grateful for their contributions, all fifty-four of them. Readers will note therefore that while we do have suggestions for further reading appended to many of the entries, we have also done our best to make sure that the essays are jargon-free, entertaining, and accessible.

As editors, we have found the process of assembling this volume to be immensely enjoyable, not least because both of us so often ended up so being pleasurably sidetracked by individual entries. It is our sincere hope that the effect upon readers of this volume will be the same—to provide fresh insights into the work of familiar names, to rejuvenate the moldering reputations of the once acclaimed, to bring together the reputable and the disreputable, the has-beens and the never-weres. In short, we have set out to resurrect as many of horror and the gothic's "Lost Souls" as we can, and to celebrate the depth, diversity, and endless imaginative possibilities of the Dark Side.

Bernice M. Murphy and Elizabeth McCarthy

Evelyn Ankers
(1918-1985)

Elizabeth McCarthy

No screen actress has been pestered and pawed by a more impressive cast of monsters and ghouls than 1940s Scream Queen extraordinaire, Evelyn Ankers. The Wolf Man, Frankenstein's Monster, Dracula, the Invisible Man, the Mad Ghoul, the Ape Woman and the Creeper have all at some point made Ankers the object of their pitiable lusts and infantile aggressions. Fay Wray may have been mauled by the biggest of the silver screen's brutes but Ankers was harassed by the most varied assortment. Born in Chile, to British parents, she moved to England in the 1920s and by the mid-1930s began appearing in small parts in British films. Like many actors of the time, Ankers relocated to the United States, where she found a career in Hollywood. Her association with horror films began when she co-starred with Abbott and Costello in the comedy *Hold That Ghost* (1941), which also featured Joan Davis as a professional radio screamer, and a musical number by the Andrews Sisters.

Later that year Ankers starred alongside Lon Chaney, Jr., in *The Wolf Man*, a film that would define her as the 1940s' leading horror heroine. In this sadly underrated Universal monster movie, which also features Claude Rains, Bela Lugosi, and Maria Ouspenskaya, Ankers' intelligent and sensitive heroine is perfectly suited to Chaney's somewhat bumbling yet gregarious character, Larry Talbot, and his pitiful alter ego, the Wolf Man. A nice everyday girl working in her father's antique and bric-a-brac shop in a small Welsh village, Gwen Conliffe (Ankers) sells Larry an ornate walking stick. Correcting Larry's mistaken identification of the figure on the stick's sliver handle as a dog, she explains that it is actually a wolf's head. Pointing out the sign of the pentagram engraved on the stick, she then tells Larry about the folkloric tale of the werewolf. Thoroughly modern and level-headed, Gwen is surprisingly knowledgeable about such matters and can even recite an old proverb about the werewolf: "Even a man who is pure in heart and says his prayers by night may become a wolf when the wolfbane blooms and the Autumn moon is bright."

The unfortunate Larry will experience all this firsthand when he is bitten by a wolf (gypsy fortune-teller Bela Lugosi), which he clubs to death with the silver handle of his walking stick while trying to save a woman from its savage attack. But of course, like so many ill-fated heroes when first informed of such things as the werewolf myth, Larry simply laughs, his only concern being to get a date with Gwen. "What big blue eyes you have..." is his reply. Ankers and Chaney would appear together again in numerous Universal horror movies, including *The Ghost of Frankenstein* (1942), *Son of Dracula* (1943), *The Frozen Ghost* (1945), and *Weird Woman* (1944), part of Universal's "Inner Sanctum Mystery" film series.

The exact lineage of the term "scream queen" is not easy to trace. In many ways, the busty heroines of the 1960s cult horror movies were the first, at least the first to be given the title of scream queen. It seems that this term was then retrospectively applied to all those horror actresses of earlier times who greeted each crisis with an ear splitting shriek. Perhaps Gary J. Svehla says it best in his introduction to *Classic Scream Queens of the 1930s* (2000):

> Even if the male icons were the legends in the making—Karloff, Lugosi, etc.—the women, less identifiable, less recognizable, became the impetus for the horror and its resolution; the actresses who helped make the male performances so classically memorable. For far too long the women remained in the shadows, posing in provocative shots with their more easily identifiable male counterparts.

Undoubtedly, Fay Wray is the most famous of these, her lung power being tested to the full alongside her mute co-star Kong. She headed an illustrious line of high voltage horror heroines such as Mae Clarke (*Frankenstein*, 1931), Gloria Stuart (*The Old Dark House*, 1932), Valerie Hobson (*The Bride of Frankenstein*, 1935), and Frances Drake (*Mad Love*, 1935).

By the 1940s however, there came a decided shift in the scream queen formula. Replacing the usually frail, passive and somewhat aristocratic horror heroines of the 1930s, the horror films of the 1940s presented a new kind of leading lady: intelligent, quick witted and more often than not, working class. Enter Ms. Ankers. Of the twenty-seven or so features she made with Universal, eleven would have distinct horror elements. Along with her four co-starring roles with Lon Chaney, Jr., cited above, these included *Captive Wild Woman* (1943), in which mad scientist John Carradine injects an orangutan with a dying woman's blood, turning it into a beautiful she-creature (Acquanetta) that turns back into her murderous ape state when her jealously is aroused. *The Mad Ghoul* (1943), mad scientist George Zucco exposes apes and then his assistant to an ancient nerve gas, resulting in the latter's transformation into a ghoul who must have human hearts to live. In *Jungle Woman* (1944), Ankers, once again, finds herself the object of a murderous ape woman's jealousy. *The Invisible Man's Revenge* (1944), where (you guessed it) mad scientist John Carradine tests his invisibility formula on an escaped convict with calamitous results, involves murderous revenge, an invisible parrot named Methuselah, and an invisible dog who answers (presumably) to the name of Brutus.

Among the most notable of non-horror ventures Ankers starred in during her time at Universal were two films in the Sherlock Holmes series, staring Basil Rathbone and Nigel Bruce, *Sherlock Holmes and The Voice of Terror* (1942) and *The Pearl of Death* (1944). The latter is based on the Arthur Conan Doyle story "The Adventure of the Six Napoleons" (1904) and is one of the best in the Rathbone/Bruce series. In it, Ankers plays Naomi Drake, a charming and brilliant criminal, adept at bravura disguises, who, working in cahoots with Giles Conover (Miles Mander), attempts to steal a priceless and ill-omened pearl. Yet, even in this film, Ankers' monster magnetism is at work, as she finds herself the unwilling recipient of the adoration of Conover's hulking henchman, The Creeper, played by none other than Rondo Hatton; who, when he's not snapping people's spines at Conover's command, can be found prowling around her room "making wistful little noises like a dog" and stroking her make-up compact.

Rondo Hatton, another Lost Soul in the making, subsisted on uncredited bit roles as a thug/monster assigned to him primarily, if not wholly, based on his disfigured appearance, which was caused by acromegaly, a hormonal disorder resulting in an excessive growth of the brow, lower jaw and hands and feet. Hatton's role as the Creeper in *The Pearl of Death* would change this however, as Universal capitalized on his looks (no make-up department budget required) with a series of films in which he reprised his Creeper role, *House of Horrors* (1946) and *The Brute Man* (1946). Sadly, as a result of health problems caused by his acromegaly, Hatton died of a heart attack soon after making these films. Curiously, Hatton did feature in *The Jungle Captive* (1945) as Moloch the disfigured assistant of mad scientist Otto Kruger. This was the third in Universal's Ape Woman series, the first two installments, as mentioned, featuring Ankers. This third venture did not feature Ankers, however, and for once, she was spared the advances of a hulking admirer.

Ankers' monster magnetism makes her a classic Scream Queen without the epistemological confusion which surrounds certain other horror actresses such as Gloria Holden (*Dracula's Daughter*, 1936) and Simone Simon (*Cat People*, 1942), who are called Scream Queens but are actually the baddies, and more likely to elicit a scream than emit one. Clearly a cover-all term for women in horror films, Scream Queens may be goodies or baddies but they are rarely both. An interesting exception is Elsa Lanchester, who, in *The Bride of Frankenstein* (1932), blurs these boundaries by playing both Mary Shelley and the female creature. Indeed, even as the creature Lanchester is both monster and damsel in distress, hissing like a snake but also emitting a terrified scream when she sees her intended mate.

Another more recent term associated with women in horror film is the "final girl," coined by Carol J. Clover, in her seminal work on gender and modern horror cinema, *Men, Women, and Chain Saws* (1992). Like the "final girl" of modern horror Scream Queens of the past survive their attackers. However, while the final girls of slasher films such as *Halloween* (1978; Jamie Lee Curtis) survive by facing off with the killer and appropriating his methods and weaponry, the classic Scream Queen's methods of survival are quite different. Although some peripheral squared-jawed hero may engage in fisticuffs with the monster, in truth, the heroine's survival is more often than not brought about by her relationship with said monster. Her empathy or simply lack of aggressive behavior towards the creature is often enough to ensure that she, at least, will not be harmed. Rather than appropriating the violent methods of her male counterparts, as the slasher film heroines do, horror heroines such as Ankers, older than final girls and infinitely wiser than their own male counterparts, are perhaps best described as "final women." Not only final women in their tendency to survive the attentions of a brutal monster, actresses like Ankers were final women of an era of horror films. Already fading considerably since the halcyon days of the early '30s, by the mid–'40s and the end of wartime hostilities, monster movies had lost much of their potential to shock or excite. Increasingly associated with juvenile delinquency and psycho-sexual problems, the monster would once again raise its ugly head in a slew of 1950s teenage drive-in horror movies. At the same time, more mature audiences were invited to consider the threat their beautiful homes and good jobs faced from a surprise attack of atomically mutated giant ants or large-brained invaders from Mars.

With the demise of the more traditional monster Ankers' career in Hollywood was soon over. In 1942 she married B-movie hunk Richard Denning (*Creature from the Black Lagoon* [1954], *Creature with the Atom Brain* [1955]). By 1945 her time with Universal Studios had ended, and after free-lancing in the odd mystery and adventure movie (most notably *Tarzan's Magic Fountain* [1949], the first Tarzan film to feature Lex Barker in the title role) she went into semi-retirement in 1950 to raise her daughter, with occasional appearances on TV. Ankers and Denning moved to Hawaii in the 1960s. There, Denning was offered the role of Governor Paul Jameson on the television series *Hawaii Five-O*, remaining with the series for its entire 12-year run. Sadly, Ankers died of ovarian cancer in 1985 at the age of 67. As one of the last, and certainly one of the most talented heroines of the Classic

Horror movie era, Evelyn Ankers truly deserves to be remembered. May her blood-curdling scream ring on in the ears of horror fans for many years to come!

SUGGESTED FURTHER READING

Berenstein, Rhona J. *Attack of the Leading Ladies: Gender, Sexuality, and Spectatorship in Classic Horror Cinema.* New York: Columbia University Press, 1996.

Skal, David J. *The Monster Show: A Cultural History of Horror.* New York: Norton, 1993.

Svehla, Gary J. *Classic Scream Queens of the 1930s.* Baltimore: Midnight Marquee, 2000.

Morris Ankrum
(1896–1964)

Bill Warren

Morris Ankrum was instantly recognizable, with or without his characteristic mustache. His head was large and blocky with a square chin, a broad and furrowed forehead, and piercing pale eyes staring out from under heavy brows. He was a man who looked and sounded like he knew what he was doing, a figure of authority—a judge, a doctor, a military officer, a district attorney, an Indian chief—and over his long career, Ankrum played all of those head honchos and more. He had a deep, commanding voice and a strong physical presence. He was born to play the Man in Charge.

Morris Ankrum may be best known today to those familiar with 1950s science fiction movies, as he was a figure of authority in several of them. He appeared as Colonel Fielding in the original *Invaders from Mars* (1953), one of the most emblematic science fiction movies of the era, as well as *Rocketship X-M* (1950), arguably the first 1950s SF movie of all.

There was something reassuring about Ankrum's presence, especially when clad as a military officer, battle ribbons bedecking his chest. He was broad-shouldered with a wide chest, one seemingly made for mounting those medals. He seemed to be a large man, an immovable man, the man who would set things straight. Latter-day SF movie fans most likely come upon Ankrum's movies out of chronological order, and there's a good chance they'd see his most emblematic roles, in *Invaders from Mars* and *Earth vs. the Flying Saucers* (1956) before the rest. So it was unusual to see him as a bad-guy Martian (in colorful, flowing garments) in *Flight to Mars* (1951); he didn't seem to fit his scientist roles in *Kronos* (1957) and *Giant from the Unknown* (1958). It was peculiarly disturbing to see a helpless, remotely controlled Ankrum with his brain visible in *Earth vs. the Flying Saucers*. But even when defeated, he was usually a stalwart presence in 1950s science fiction movies.

However, over his thirty-year movie career, his roles in Westerns, theatrical and for television, far outnumbered his science fiction movies; he played sheriffs, bad guys, townsmen, ranchers and a lot of Indians, mostly chiefs. His origins, however, were anything but flavored with the frontier: he was born Stephen Morris Nussbaum, August 28, 1896. (Note: the IMDb cites his birthdate as August 27, but Ankrum's own notes, prepared for MGM, give August 28.)

He was active in television during the 1950s, primarily in Westerns. Sooner or later, he turned up in most Western series: *Maverick* (1957–60), *Sugarfoot* (1957–9), *Lawman* (1959), *Bat Masterson* (1959), *Rawhide* (1959–61), *Gunsmoke* (1960) and many others. In 1957, he began appearing occasionally as a judge on Raymond Burr's much-loved *Perry Mason*; his judge was never given a surname, but Ankrum appeared in more than 15 episodes of the long-running series. He ended when it did: *Perry Mason* was cancelled in 1964, and on September 2 of that year, Ankrum died of trichinosis. His son David is also an actor—and multi-Oscar winning effects maestro Dennis Muren grew up across the street, appearing with the Ankrum kids in home movies.

In those biographical notes prepared for MGM, Ankrum claimed to have wanted to be an actor since childhood, but he got a law degree from USC, later becoming an associate professor of economics at UC Berkeley. But he always acted; he was on stage in New York as early as 1924—with Lillian Gish—having walked there from California, was the "Jew lead" in a revival of *Sweet Nell of Old Drury* with Laurette Taylor in 1925, and among other theatrical ventures, appeared as King Henry IV in *The Five Kings* with Orson Welles in New York in 1938.

On that MGM questionnaire, he listed his residences as Berkeley (1924–27), New York (1928–1936) and Pasadena, from 1938 onward. He also lived in Tacoma, Washington, for one unidentified year. He was active in baseball and swimming while at college, and studied economics, history, English and sociology; he was involved in college theater at UC Berkeley.

However, his most significant endeavor was at the prestigious Pasadena Playhouse; he was involved in that influential organization from 1934 until his death in 1964; among his students were Robert Preston and Raymond Burr, and his son David is still associated with the Pasadena institution. He worked hard to support his family; the Playhouse was not rich enough to pay him an adequate salary, so in 1934, he began appearing in movies, although there is a citation for his appearing in *Reunion in Vienna* in 1933. By 1946, he was a regularly featured (in different roles) in many low budget Westerns. He made more than a dozen of them, including appearing with Jack Benny in *Buck Benny Rides Again* (1940). From 1936 through 1937, he used the screen name Stephen Morris, perhaps to separate his somewhat disreputable movies from his work at the Pasadena Playhouse. He appeared in no movies released in 1938 and 1939; he was in New York *directing* plays. He'd previously written

The Mystery Man which had a short run in January 1928, but now was back on Broadway, after his Pasadena Playhouse experience, as a director. *Prologue to Glory* ran from March 17 to November 5, 1938; *The Big Blow* blew from October 1, 1938, to February 1939. After that, he returned to movies; in *The Light of Western Stars* (1940), he was Morris Ankrum.

He began working in more and more movies, often now in A-level features, such as *I Wake Up Screaming* (1941), in which he played an assistant district attorney, an early example of his propensity to be cast as stern figures of authority. In 1942, he played Confederate President Jefferson Davis in *Tennessee Johnson* (1942), the role which he cited in his MGM questionnaire as his favorite to date (1943). He remained busy on through the 1940s, now occasionally being cast as high-ranking military officers; he was a colonel in *The Cross of Lorraine* (1943) and again in *See Here, Private Hargrove* (1944), a captain in *Thirty Seconds Over Tokyo* in 1944. And he began playing steely eyed professionals in other areas as well: he was a doctor in the "Crime Does Not Pay" short *Purity Squad* (1945) and again in *The Cockeyed Miracle* (1946).

But in 1950, he played a central role, Dr. Ralph Fleming, in the popular and influential *Rocketship X-M*. Even though Ankrum also appeared in several major movies that year, including Humphrey Bogart's *In a Lonely Place* (1950), as well as *The Damned Don't Cry* (1950), and *Chain Lightning* (1950) (also with Bogart), it seems to have been *Rocketship X-M* that struck a chord with at least casting directors. In that film, he was the scientist in charge of launching the rocketship, which was intended for the Moon but accidentally landed on Mars instead. Ankrum stayed on Earth.

But in *Flight to Mars* in 1951, he was one of the scheming Martians who, briefly clad in *Destination Moon* spacesuits, hoped to force the arriving Earthmen to build a rocket allowing the Martians to invade the Earth. He wasn't done with Mars; in *Red Planet Mars* (1952), the almost hysterically anti–Communist Earthbound tale kept Ankrum, and everyone else, firmly on planet Earth. And of course, there's *Invaders from Mars* in 1953, with Ankrum stalwart and heroic as Colonel Fielding taking on the title intruders.

For the next couple of years, Ankrum was involved in other kinds of movies, playing Indian Grey Eagle in the 3-D *Taza, Son of Cochise* (1954), Chief Tall Horse in a couple of episodes of the *Hopalong Cassidy* TV series, and Red Cloud in the Victor Mature vehicle *Chief Crazy Horse* (1955).

In 1955 and 1956, he appeared in four episodes of the TV series *Science Fiction Theatre*, then made what's probably his second best-known science fiction movie, *Earth vs. the Flying Saucers* (1956). He's Brigadier General John Hanley, father of the heroine, who's kidnapped by aliens. The Ray Harryhausen-activated flying saucers have a gadget inside that reads victim's minds by candling their skulls so their brains are visible—and it's Morris Ankrum's brain we see.

After that, science fiction movies became increasingly routine, though *Kronos* (1957) had its moments, including when Ankrum, as Dr. Stern, is electrocuted by alien-possessed John Emery. Ankrum has lesser roles in *The Giant Claw* (1957) and *How to Make a Monster* (1958), but had a bit more to do, and scenic Big Bear Lake locations on which to do it, in *Giant from the Unknown* (1958). In this same period, he also appeared in one of the rare fantasy-horror movies of the time, *Zombies of Mora Tau* (1957).

He had what amounted to a showy cameo as President Ulysses S. Grant in the tepid *From the Earth to the Moon* (1958); that film was shot largely in Mexico, perhaps explaining why Ankrum turned up in another Mexican-shot science fiction thriller, *Most Dangerous Man Alive* (1961). Around this time, he did relatively little in two Roger Corman-directed outings, *Tower of London* (1962) and *X: The Man with the X-Ray Eyes* (1963).

But the end was drawing near for Morris Ankrum. He appeared in only one theatrical film after *X*, the little-seen *Eagle Rock* (1964); the rest of his time was spent on television, winding up with the *Perry Mason* episode "The Case of the Sleepy Slayer."

More than most supporting players of the 1950s science fiction thrillers, Morris Ankrum is memorable; he had strong features, an intense screen presence, and could deliver even ludicrous dialogue with conviction and sincerity. He's well-liked by fans of those films, including prominent ones; Fred Holliday played Colonel Ankrum in *Lobster Man from Mars* (1989), written by the late Bob Greenberg; an Ankrum fan in the Mant scenes in Joe Dante's *Matinee* (1993), Dante regular Kevin McCarthy played General Ankrum. A doff of the military hat then to 1950s SF movie icon Morris Ankrum.

SUGGESTED FURTHER READING

Parish, James Robert. *Hollywood Character Actors*, New York: Arlington House, 1978.
Pitts, Michael E. *Horror Film Stars*, Jefferson, N.C.: McFarland, 1991.
Warren, Bill. *Keep Watching the Skies! American Science Fiction Films of the 1950s: The 21st Century Edition*. Jefferson, N.C.: McFarland, 2009.

Theda Bara
(1885–1955)

Maria Parsons

Infamous in the annals of the history of the "vamp" and the changing nature of the vampire is the actress Theda Bara, who came to fame in Frank Powell's silent film *A Fool There Was* in 1915. A graduate of the Biograph motion picture company, Powell had recently completed *The Stain* (1914) for Pathé, written by Forrest Halsey. It was while working on *The Stain* he came into contact with the then relatively unknown actress Theodosia Goodman, who had some previous stage experience under the name of De Coppett. Having impressed Powell with her audition she was given a minor role in the film, classified as an extra. A year later, Powell was chosen to direct the film *A Fool There Was* with the lineup for the casting of the central female role including leading actresses of the silent movie era such as Valeska Surratt, Madlaine Traverse and Virginia Pearson. However, Powell, trusting his instincts, decided upon the unknown Goodman and so began her rise to stardom. It was also Powell who was responsible for her screen name Theda Bara, with Theda an obvious contraction of Theodosia, and Bara taken from a relative's name of Barranger.

A Fool There Was, released in January 1915, was an immediate box office hit with both audiences and critics alike, catapulting an unknown Theda Bara to stardom, with a cast that included Mabel Frenyear, Victor Benoit, May Allison, Clifford Bruce and the child actress Runa Hodges. Bara's performance was lauded by critics who claimed it was her "sterling acting of the role of Satan's ally that started the vampire craze in motion pictures" (*The Chicago Defender*, 20 July 1918). Another review commented that "Miss Bara's interpretation is remarkable for intense dramatic realism, while her wonderfully seductive beauty serves to enhance the illusion created by her art" (*The Atlanta Constitution*, 7 November 1915). Or, as an article in *The Chicago Trib-*

Theda Bara in *Cleopatra* (1917).

une in October 1945 noted, "Theda, when she played the character for the movies, became so popular that she made the verb 'to vamp' a much used American slang term. But the old Fox company made Theda vamp in all her films thereafter, and in each one she literally ruined dozens of men." Thus followed successive roles in films such as *The Devil's Daughter, Sin, Carmen* (1915), *Her Double Life, The Vixen* (1916), *The Tiger Woman, Cleopatra, Her Greatest Love, Heart and Soul, Camille, The Rose of Blood* (1917), *Salome, The Soul of Buddha, When a Woman Sins, The She-Devil* (1918), *The Siren's Song, The Light, A Woman There Was, La Belle Russe, Kathleen Mavourneen* and *The Lure of Ambition* (1919).

Powell's film was an adaptation of the previously successful stage production of the same name, written and directed by the playwright and novelist Porter Emerson Browne. Browne's stage production in 1909 owed much to the art and literature of the previous decades. Early influences ranged from paintings such as Henry Fuseli's *The Nightmare* (1781) to Arthur Symon's poem "The Vampire" (1894). In Symons' short poem woman is described as an "intolerable" creature of the night, who "Would fain pity, but she may not rest / Till she have sucked a man's heart from his breast / And drained his life-blood from him, vein, by vein."

However, the work which had the most influence on Browne's play was Philip Burne-Jones' painting *The Vampire* (1897). The painting included a set of verses written specifically for it, by the artist's cousin Rudyard Kipling, and was also titled "The Vampire." (The model for Philip Burne-Jones' painting was the actress Mrs. Patrick Campbell.) Kipling's poem opened with the line which was to become the title of Browne's play "A fool there was." In Kipling's poem the woman is a gold-digging, merciless harlot, who "To a rag and a bone and a hank of hair / (we called her the woman who didn't care) / But the fool he called her his lady fair." The poem concludes with the fool "stripped to his foolish hide." It was the success of the stage production of *A Fool There Was* which led first to its novelization and then its adaptation for the screen. Across its manifestations, from the stage to the screen, the success of Browne's work reflected the cultural climate in these opening decades of the twentieth century, which were marked by an insatiable public appetite for popular representations of financially ruinous women. The film visualized a middle-class, married man's hapless infatuation with the "Vampire" and his eventual downfall at the hands of her ruthless gold-digging and morally degenerate ways. It also contained the infamous predatory kiss which horrified audiences, with Bara's "Vampire" sibilantly hissing, "Kiss me, my Fool, Kiss me, my Fool."

Such was the success of Bara in the role of the "Vampire" that it wasn't long before the studios started building on the exoticism of the screen persona that Bara had created. Crucial to the building of the Bara myth were the press agents Johnny Goldfrap and Al Selig. Earlier in his career, Selig had worked alongside the now Fox general manager Winfield Sheehan as a reporter for the *New York World*. The columns of the press were dominated with the fabulous fabrications of typewriters, claiming that Theda Bara (an anagram for Arab death) was of foreign birth and possessed supernatural powers. She was said to have been born in the Sahara, to a French artist and his concubine. A press release in *The Atlanta Constitution* in 1915 claimed, "Theda Bara, leading woman at the Theater Antoine, Paris, has been cast as the 'Vampire,' one of the most fascinating, though revolting female characters ever created." Her costumes for the film were also said to have been "designed by the leading costumers of her native Paris." Bara contributed to such myth-making by wearing an Egyptian head piece and allowing herself to be photographed with snakes and skulls. Most of the images of Bara photographed in this style of oriental mysticism were taken at Underwood & Underwood studios. As Terry Ramsaye in *A Million and One Nights* (1926) notes, "This deadly Arab girl was a crystal gazing seeress of profoundly occult powers, wicked as fresh red paint and poisonous as dried spiders. The stronger the copy grew the more it was printed. Little girls read it and swallowed their gum with excitement." He also observes how the "motion picture public went to the theatre to see about all this promisingly snaky stuff and found that the effect on the screen was up to the advance notices. Theda Bara of the screen, working her willowy way with me, became the vicarious and shadowy realization of several million variously suppressed desires." However, Bara's actual origins were much less exotic than her studio persona suggested—she was born in Cincinnati, Ohio, in 1885 and contrary to her femme-fatale status was happily married to the director Charles Brabin. Despite these facts having been readily available for many years now, Bara's silent screen image as a mysterious and exotic seductress remains the pervading one. All of which testifies to the power of the media and, more significantly, the power of the movie screen to invent potent and enduring myths.

By 1919 Bara's contract with Fox Studios had expired and her screen career came to a halt—whether this came about because Fox felt her popularity was waning or because Bara herself, was tired of being typecast is still not entirely clear. Nevertheless, utilizing her success and infamy as the original screen vamp she undertook a successful and lucrative tour of the movie houses of America. As was stated in an article titled "Look Who's Here! It's the Movie Vamp Again" in *The Atlanta Constitution* (23 April 1922), "Theda's retirement from the screen for the footlight stage left the film world destitute of a vampire." While on tour Bara, feeling the pulse of cinema going audiences, conducted her own personal survey asking the public the following: "Do you want to see me on the screen again? (Much applause from the audience). Do you want me to return in vampire parts? (Deafening applause from the audience)."

Bara briefly returned to the screen but with little success, unable to make the transition to a new era of sound in motion pictures. In 1925 she decided that she was through with vamping and that high comedy was to be her new medium. She took up a contract with Hal Roach and starred alongside Oliver Hardy in *Madame Mystery* (1926), directed and co-written by Stan Laurel, prior to the legendary comic duo's teaming up together. The film was badly received and signaled the end of her onscreen career. She also claimed at this time that she was writing a book about her life. It was to be an epilogue to her role of screen vamp, and was to be named *What Women Never Tell*. In an interview with *The Los Angeles Times* (17 November 1925), Bara stated, "It's not a full confessional, only a part of what women never tell." She also added that, "One of the chapter heads is 'Men, Animal, Vegetable and Mineral,' and another is 'Let Her Who is Without Sex Cast the First Stone.'" At the time of her death, in 1955, her book remained unpublished, although she had sold the rights to Columbia with the intention that it was to be made into a musical, titled, of course, "The Vamp." Rita Hayworth was even rumored to be in the running for the leading role, but the film failed to ever reach production. Perhaps more devastating is the fact that most of the movies that she did star in between 1914 and the mid–1920s were lost in a fire at Fox studios storage facility in Little Ferry, New Jersey, in 1937.

Thus, Bara's image today is a credit to the enduring power of what little remains of her screen career, the few films and the catalogue of exotic images, which continue to provoke and enthrall new audiences. Theda Bara's female vampire has proved a powerful marker for representations of female vampires and in her day she set the standard for the force of the vampire's kiss. In an era, as one newspaper journalist wrote, that was "nauseated with the baby-doll and bored with the flapper" (*The Atlanta Constitution*, 23 April 1922), Bara's vampire precipitated the rise of the vamp and the birth of noir's femme-fatale. Her successors include Valeska Suratt, Nita Naldi, Pola Negri, Hedy Lamarr, Mae West, Greta Garbo, Marlene Dietrich, Lauren Bacall and Lana Turner, and more recently, Glenn Close in the notorious *Fatal Attraction* (1987). In vampire cinema, notable successors to Bara's vamp are Ingrid Pitt, Barbara Shelley and Béatrice Dalle and her devastating cannibalistic kiss in *Trouble Everyday* (2001). Bara's portrayal of the Vampire in *A Fool There Was* and in her roles that followed tapped into a cultural sensibility which was still railing against the gains of first wave feminism. As Bram Dijkstra has noted, the film's emblematic force was in its ideological depiction of a test of manhood and Bara's "contemporaries knew that they were watching the social vampire of female sexuality depreciate civilized society" (*Evil Sisters*, 1996).

In an era that has witnessed a continuing backlash against feminism, as well as a supposed post-feminist liberation, such gendered ideology continues to persist in cinema's ongoing fascination with dangerous female sexuality. And, amidst all this, Theda Bara's powerful image remains as dangerously enigmatic as it did in 1915.

SUGGESTED FURTHER READING

Craig, Joan, and Beverly F. Stout. *Theda Bara, My Mentor: Under the Wing of Hollywood's First Femme Fatale.* Jefferson, N.C.: McFarland, 2016.

Flom, Eric L. *Silent Stars on the Stages of Seattle: A History of Performances by Hollywood Notables.* Jefferson, N.C.: McFarland, 2009.

Genini, Roland. *Theda Bara: A Biography of the Silent Screen Vamp, with a Filmography.* Jefferson, N.C.: McFarland, 1996.

Golden, Eve. *Vamp: The Rise and Fall of Theda Bara.* Lanham: Vesta Press, 1996.

Ralph Bates
(1940–1991)

PETER HUTCHINGS

There is a moment in the Hammer film *The Horror of Frankenstein* (1970) when someone describes Baron Frankenstein thus: "One moment you can be kind and charming, the next you can be as cold as the grave." For an audience who by the early 1970s would have been well versed in the nature of Frankenstein as a character, this might have seemed a rather obvious statement. Nevertheless, the association it makes between charismatic charm and outright villainy could also be used to characterize the short but lively horror career of Ralph Bates, the actor playing Frankenstein here, who would offer entertaining performances in half a dozen other British horror films and, despite some of the terrible things his characters got up to, emerged as an amiable genre presence. Despite this, Bates has never attracted the cult following associated with some other horror stars, possibly because his subsequent popularity on television has obscured his early association with horror, possibly because some of the horror films in which he featured were not very distinguished. This is a shame because his contribution to the British horror cycle is noteworthy, not just for its intrinsic value but also because of what it suggests about the nature of British horror production during the first half of the 1970s.

Bates was one of a number of young actors who came to brief prominence in British horror from the late 1960s onwards. Others included Ian Ogilvy (*The Sorcerers* in 1967, *Witchfinder General* in 1968), Shane Briant (*Demons of the Mind* in 1972, *Frankenstein and the Monster from Hell* in 1974) and Ingrid Pitt (*The Vampire Lovers* in 1970, *Countess Dracula* in 1971, *The House that Dripped Blood* in 1971). Together they—along with a wave of young directors that included Michael Reeves, Peter Sasdy and Peter Sykes—contributed to a re-energizing of the genre at a time when the horror conventions established principally by Hammer in the late 1950s were looking decidedly tired.

In the case of Bates, it was probably his eye-catching turn as evil Roman emperor Caligula in the television series *The Caesars* (1968) that earned him his big break in horror cinema. Bates's screen debut, *Taste the Blood of Dracula* (1970), was one of Hammer's first attempts to refocus its horror formula around younger characters, and Bates was key to this thematic change. Indeed, his impressive first appearance crystallized the film's impatience with the middle-aged authority figures that had been so important in earlier Hammer horrors. Three ostensibly respectable "gentlemen" are paying their monthly visit to a brothel. As played by Geoffrey Keen, John Carson and Peter Sallis, they are an unprepossessing bunch, whose hypocrisy has by this stage thoroughly alienated us from them. Enter Lord Courtley, who, in the form of Ralph Bates, is not just darkly handsome and self-assured but also possesses a perverse integrity—he knows he is bad and does not try to disguise it—entirely lacking in the wretched men whose orgy he interrupts.

Courtley could so easily have become just another of Hammer's evil aristocrats, and yet, for all his depravity, Bates invests him with a liveliness that renders him a winning figure. The actor certainly has the aristocratic demeanor required for the part but he also finds an unexpected boyishness in Courtley. Most notably, it is present in the character's obvious excitement at the possibility that he might finally have found financial backers for his satanic experiments. As Courtley leaves the brothel with the "gents" he has met there, he announces that they should all go to the Café Royal. "It's the only place," he exclaims, and just for a moment we are given a glimpse of an attractive *joie de vivre*.

Unfortunately, Courtley's attempt to resurrect Dracula does not go as planned, and he ends up beaten to death. In what is for Hammer a very self-conscious transition that assures the audience that the old horror is still present in this revisionary film, Courtley's body is before our eyes transformed into Christopher Lee's vampiric body, and Dracula lives again. In essence, this is a degeneration rather than a regeneration inasmuch as it shows the old replacing the new, and while Lee provides a gravitas lacking in the then relatively unknown Bates, his stately performance itself lacks the nuance and energy associated with Bates (with this no doubt reflecting Lee's increasing disinterest in the role of Dracula). While the remainder of *Taste the Blood of Dracula* is an intelligent treatment of its subject—it is easily the best of Hammer's later Dracula films—Bates's engaging presence is sorely missed.

Underlining the way in which Hammer seemed to be positioning Bates as a young replacement for Christopher Lee and Peter Cushing, his next role for the company was as Frankenstein in the aforementioned *The Horror of Frankenstein*, a part played by Cushing in Hammer's six other Frankenstein films. This was the first of three films that Bates made with writer-director Jimmy Sangster, who had written most of the classic Hammer horrors from the late 1950s and early 1960s. Film direction was not Sangster's forte, however, and *The Horror of Frankenstein*, along with the two other Sangster-Bates efforts, *Lust for a Vampire* (1971) and *Fear in the Night* (1972), were, to put it mildly, lesser Hammer productions. However, Bates gave spirited performances in all of them. Unlike the sardonic dandyesque figure essayed by Cushing, Bates's version of Frankenstein was a mixture of infectious enthusiasm, arrogance, ruthlessness and vulnerability; he was also much more sexualized than Cushing had been in the role. By contrast, Bates was made to look older than his actual age in the lesbian vampire film *Lust for a Vampire*, a lackluster sequel to *The Vampire Lovers*. In a role that was originally intended for Cushing, Bates turned out to be one of the film's few highlights, capturing perfectly the grotesquery of his schoolteacher character as he shifted from pompous pedantry to a willing masochistic surrender to the vampire. *Fear in the Night*, in which Bates finally appeared alongside Cushing rather than just replacing him, was the last in Hammer's series of psychological thrillers and offered less opportunities for the sort of melodramatic transformations found in the gothic horrors and at which Bates had proved so adept. Instead he was cast as an apparently dutiful husband who was eventually revealed to be a villain. Although the most restrained of all his Hammer roles, his portrayal of an ostensibly ordinary, domesticated male did, in retrospect at least, point the way to his later successful television career, which was founded in part on such domestic, if more benign, roles.

Much better as a film was Hammer's *Dr. Jekyll and Sister Hyde* (1972), a transsexual-themed treatment of the Jekyll and Hyde story in which the doctor was transformed into a woman (with Sister Hyde played by Martine Beswick) that also threw Burke and Hare and Jack the Ripper into the mix for good measure. The excitability of such a narrative could have resulted in a farcical tone, particularly in the scenes in which Bates, gradually changing into a woman, tries to get rid of guests before the embarrassing truth is revealed. However, Bates managed to ground the film with a nuanced performance that captured yet again transitions from charm to ruthless acts of murder with precision and considerable conviction and which treated the whole business with a seriousness that perhaps it did not fully merit.

Bates's horror career came to a rapid conclusion as British horror production wound down in the mid–1970s. There were two further horror credits, neither for Hammer and neither especially impressive. *Persecution* (1974) was an odd psychological thriller in which Bates, back in mundane domestic mode, played the downtrodden son of the domineering Lana Turner who eventually turns on her and, in an unforgettably embarrassing scene, drowns her in a bowl of milk. *I Don't Want to Be Born* (aka *Sharon's Baby*, 1975) reunited Bates with Peter Sasdy, who had earlier directed the impressive *Taste the Blood of Dracula*. Sadly this possession thriller was a labored attempt to cash in on the success of *The Exorcist* (1973) and for once Bates seemed ill at ease. That was the end of Bates as horror star, although he went on to find television fame as another villain, George Warleggan, in the popular historical melodrama series *Poldark* (1975–1977) and subsequently in the very different role of the cuckolded hero in the sitcom *Dear John* (1986–1987). In both cases, as he had done with his horror roles, he managed to make ostensibly unsympathetic or pathetic figures unexpectedly likeable.

Perhaps unavoidably, Bates's death at the age of 51 from pancreatic cancer has bestowed a retrospective poignancy on these early performances in his career. When watching them now, one can't help thinking that he would have been affable company among the dwindling band of Hammer artists as they reminisce in interviews or on DVD commentaries about the making of these films. However, the value of Bates's short-lived horror stardom is more tangible than this, for his horror performances offered a high level of unpretentious but thoroughly professional accomplishment, with a commitment and attention to detail often fashioned in unpromising circumstances. To a large extent, Bates's virtues as an actor are also the virtues of Hammer horror at its best, eschewing the abstract and the extravagant in favor of something more considered and more solid.

SUGGESTED FURTHER READING

Hutchings, Peter. *The A–Z of Horror Cinema*. Lanham, MD: Scarecrow, 2009.
Johnson, Tom, and Deborah Del Vecchio. *Hammer Films: An Exhaustive Filmography*. Jefferson, N.C.: McFarland, 1996.
Sangster, Jimmy. *Inside Hammer*. London: Reynolds and Hearn, 2001.
Smith, Gary A. *Uneasy Dreams: The Golden Age of British Horror Films*. Jefferson, N.C.: McFarland, 2006.

Charles Beaumont
(1929–1967)

Edward O'Hare

In a lifetime which was all too brief, Charles Beaumont made a distinguished contribution to horror and the fantastic in almost every medium. The author of some of the most dazzlingly original short-stories of the '50s and '60s, he was also an accomplished screenwriter who adapted a constellation of Gothic works for television and the cinema. Moreover, Beaumont's incandescent imagination was the pivotal force which brought together and shaped the talents of an exceptional generation of American writers, whose combined influence on the genres of horror, science fiction, and fantasy has been immeasurable. Although it was tragically and terribly cut short, at its height Beaumont's career was a multifarious extravaganza of overflowing creative energy.

Beaumont's biography is nearly as bizarre as one of his weird fictions. Born Charles Leroy Nutt on Chicago's North Side in January 1929, his peculiar surname was only one of many things that made his childhood miserable. Victimized by a psychologically troubled mother who dressed him as a girl and threatened to murder his pets, he ended up in the care of his five widowed aunts who ran a grim boarding house. It was during the months the youth spent bedridden battling spinal meningitis that he discovered literature, and developed a passion for the morbid and ghoulish. After dropping out of high school at 17, Beaumont served in the U.S. Army and flirted with a diverse range of professions (including acting, broadcasting, animating and illustrating) before devoting himself completely to writing.

The closing years of the 1940s were a time of desperate struggle for Beaumont, and as he worked on his early stories he took every kind of employment, including railroad clerk, theatre usher, dishwasher, and sign painter. By now he was not alone, having married his wife, Helen, and started a family.

It was while toiling away copying documents at Universal Studios that Beaumont sold his first tales to *Amazing Stories*. He had to wait until 1954 before he made his name, placing stories in *Playboy*, *Rogue*, and other high-profile magazines. In the meantime, the quantity and quality of Beaumont's tales dramatically increased, and he started producing some of his best work. Equally as important, he became the intellectual center of a band of West Coast writers known as "The Group," which included Richard Matheson, Harlan Ellison, William F. Nolan, and Jerry Sohl, who reinvented speculative-fiction for the second half of the Twentieth Century.

With his first collection, *The Hunger and Other Stories* (1957), Beaumont established himself as an innovative storyteller capable of producing hallucinations on paper, and he followed it with *Yonder* (1958), and *Night Ride and Other Journeys* (1960). The seventy tales he wrote encompass a multitude of styles, but all deal with otherworldly ideas and are full of wondrous imagery and horrific surprises. As with the finest modern Gothic fiction, Beaumont's stories are funhouse mirrors in which familiar reality is fabulously distorted, revealing just how grotesque our "normality" really is. Whether set in some sinister alternate world, a mysterious and dreamlike corner of the United States, or in some terrifying future age, Beaumont's brilliant control over his material meant that his works were never less than electrifying.

Charles Beaumont.

Beaumont may have excelled at delivering the unexpected, but his stories have a central theme. This is the monstrousness that lurks beneath ordinary appearances, and it found its clearest expression in two of his most celebrated tales. In "'The Howling Man" (1959), a young American touring '20s Europe discovers a prisoner being held captive beneath a hermitage. Thinking him a sympathetic victim of religious zealotry, the American releases the prisoner despite being warned that he is pure evil. No sooner has the "howling man" been freed than he is unmasked as the Devil, and sets about returning the world to chaos. Another of Beaumont's masterpieces, "The New People" (1960), sees an alienated family move into an apparently unremarkable town. Slowly they sense that the pleasant rhythms of suburban life are concealing something terrible. Along with cocktail parties and bridge evenings, their dehumanized new neighbors practice Satanism.

Having mastered the short tale, Beaumont pursued other ambitions. A lifelong fan of the cinema (he interviewed his hero Fritz Lang when Beaumont was only 16), he was eager to write for the screen. When Matheson was unable to take on an adaptation of Poe's *The Premature Burial* (1962) for Roger Corman he passed it to Beaumont, and eleven more of his scripts were eventually produced. The projects he chose reflected his connoisseur's knowledge of the field, and included *Night of the Eagle* (1962), based on Fritz Leiber, Jr.'s exquisitely cunning novel *Conjure Wife* (1943), adaptations of Charles G. Finney's *The Circus of Dr. Lao* (*7 Faces of Dr. Lao*, 1964) and *The Wonderful World of the Brothers Grimm* (1962), both for the legendary director George Pal, *The Haunted Palace* (1963), Corman's eerily atmospheric version of H.P. Lovecraft's *The Case of Charles Dexter Ward* (1941), and a final and stunning Poe movie, *The Masque of the Red Death* (1964).

Beaumont's own stories were also perfect material for television. At the very time when his literary star was in the ascendant a veteran television playwright was looking for contributors for a new anthology series. The playwright was Rod Serling, the series was *The Twilight Zone*, and this inventory of post-war American anxieties became the ideal showcase for Beaumont's hauntingly strange ideas. He ultimately penned twenty-two of the show's most highly acclaimed episodes, including "Shadow Play" (1961), "Printer's Devil" (1963), "Miniature" (1963), and "Long Live Walter Jameson" (1960), and it is for these that Beaumont is most often remembered.

None of the darkness of Beaumont's work showed itself in his personality. He was a devoted husband, and adored his three children. Apart from his creative genius (Ray Bradbury said he possessed a brain like a pomegranate, bursting with the seeds of incredible new stories), Beaumont's defining trait was his exuberant sense of humor. He was famed for instigating madcap escapades: he once gathered together a gang of his writing friends at three in the morning and they hopped on a plane to crash Princess Grace's inaugural ball; Harlan Ellison recalls being summoned at a similar hour to meet a writer (who turned out to be Ian Fleming), and the trio spent the remainder of the night competing for the affections of the same female bar-owner. When not writing, "Chuck" was a keen sports car racer who often travelled to Europe to compete. With his domed forehead, prematurely gray hair, and sharp suits, he cut a suave figure as one of Hollywood's most sought-after ideas men.

After years fighting for recognition, in the early 1960s Beaumont found himself inundated with work. He was known to juggle as many as twelve projects at one time and often enlisted the help of his friends to meet deadlines, giving many their first breaks. Then, as Beaumont seemed about to enter the first rank of American fabulists, the nightmare began. His speech started to slur and he found it increasingly impossible to write. He already looked twenty years older than he really was, but now he began to age dramatically. Struck down with what was suspected to be but never fully diagnosed as either Alzheimer's or Pick's disease, Beaumont was confined to a nursing home. He died in February 1967 aged only 38, but with the haggard appearance of a 95-year-old. It was as though he had been attacked by one of his worst fantasies.

Overshadowed by his more famous contemporaries for too long, Beaumont's work has only improved with the passing of time. Less didactic than Serling, free from Bradbury's whimsicality, not as icily intellectual as Matheson, his stories have transcended their age. His astute understanding of human nature and his concern for individual freedom, seen in such daring stories as "The Crooked Man" (1955) (in which a heterosexual couple engage in a forbidden love affair in a world where homosexuality is the norm) and "The Beautiful People" (1952) (about a young girl who rebels against a society where conformity has reached insane extremes), are only more relevant today. Beaumont remains one of literature's most unusual voices, and one which cries out for rediscovery.

SUGGESTED FURTHER READING

Beaumont, Charles. *The Hunger and Other Stories*. Kansas City, MO: Valancourt, 2013.
Beaumont, Charles. *A Touch of the Creature*. Richmond, VA: Valancourt, 2015.
Beaumont, Charles. *Perchance to Dream: Selected Stories*. London: Penguin Classics, 2016.
Prosser, Lee. *Running from the Hunter: The Life and Works of Charles Beaumont*. Rockville, MD: Wildside, 2010.

Ingrid Bergman
(1915–1982)

Mark Jancovich

Although Ingrid Bergman may seem an unlikely topic for a collection on horror and the gothic, this is due to changing understandings of these terms. During the 1940s, when she was at the height of her popularity, and one of the most revered stars in Hollywood, Bergman was strongly associated with horror and did most of her important work within the genre as it was then understood.

She was brought over to Hollywood from Europe largely on the basis of two films. *Intermezzo* (1936, remade by Selznick in 1939) was not associated with horror but featured Bergman as the kind of tormented melodramatic heroine that she played in numerous 1940s horror films; and the second, *A Woman's Face* (1938), was frequently referenced in profiles of Bergman as an international prize winner, although the *New York Times* described its Hollywood remake as "a macabre Gothic tale" with a heroine that has "fallen under the spell of a frustrated madman."

Two of Bergman's key Hollywood films are now acknowledged as horror classics, *Dr. Jekyll and Mr. Hyde* (1941) and *Gaslight* (1944). She even won her Oscar for the latter. These films are often presented as individual or isolated cases, but they were actually part of a larger pattern of film production that establishes a clear relationship to Bergman's other films, many of which were therefore explicitly understood as horror at the time. In early 1944, the *New York Times* identified *Gaslight* as one example of a larger horror cycle that featured "films bulging with screams in the night, supercharged criminal phenomena and esthetic murder." "This new horror cycle" also included another Bergman vehicle, *Spellbound* (1945), which the same article described as "Francis Beeding's 'The House of Dr. Edwardes,' which Alfred Hitchcock will direct for David O. Selznick."

The same article also noted that this cycle was not confined to low budget production but was "being launched on a far more ambitious scale" and featured "full Class 'A' paraphernalia, including million dollar budgets and big name casts." Nor was this cycle's ambition simply financial and its films were also described as "fresh psychological efforts." Indeed, during this period, the "psychological film" and the "horror film" were almost interchangeable terms, and the horror films of this period were seen as psychological in two ways. Their villains were often madmen and their method of attack was often psychological. As Siegfried Kracauer claimed in a 1946 article on these films, these madmen "no longer shoot, strangle or poison the females that they want to do away with, but systematically try to drive them insane" so that these horror films featured "the theme of psychological destruction."

It is therefore significant that in 1945, one year after the *New York Times* article on this new cycle, a *New York Times* profile of Bergman observed that she had "gone, cinematically, though a succession of schizophrenic and paranoid husbands and lovers" during her time in Hollywood. For example, *Rage in Heaven* (1941) was described by *Variety* as "one of those psychopathic 'studies' of a suicidal paranoiac" in which a "major portion of the film is devoted to scenes of cruelty which are devised by the mentally unbalanced" protagonist, cruelty that is largely directed at his wife (Bergman). *Dr. Jekyll and Mr. Hyde* was also "a psychological study," even if the *New York Times* thought that a "little Freudian theory is a dangerous thing" and that the film's account of Bergman's "tortured" barmaid ends ups as "an affront to good taste rather than a serious, and thereby acceptable, study in sadism." *Gaslight* (1944) was another psychological tale for the *New York Times* and one in which a madman who was trying "to drive his wife slowly mad" so Bergman's wife "goes to pieces in a most distressing way." *Spellbound* (1945) was also a psychological study but this time the *New York Times* claimed that Bergman was "a female psychiatrist who falls suddenly and desperately in love with a man upon whom dark suspicion of murder is relentlessly cast." In *Notorious*, *Variety* claimed that Bergman was trapped between two deadly males, a duplicitous secret agent who persuades her to infiltrate a Nazi conspiracy, and the "head of the Brazilian Nazi group" that she infiltrates. Furthermore, Bergman's character becomes another potential victim of another disturbed husband, when this head Nazi "discovers that [he and his confederates] have a spy under their roof." Finally, in his biography of Bergman, Donald Spoto claims that *Under Capricorn* (1949) was specifically chosen as "a subject that suited" Bergman, while the *New York Times* claimed that it cast her as another "wronged and wretched lady" who is married to a dark and troubled man and is being driven slowly mad by guilt, alcoholism and "an easily perceived villainess."

Even Bergman's non-horror films often put her in situations of psychological distress and/or breakdown, often due to her relationships with men. Both *Intermezzo* and *Adam Had Four Sons* (1941) were stories of "self sacrificial devotion" (as the *New York Times* claimed of the latter) and in which the heroine is virtually destroyed by and for her love. For *Variety*, Bergman's character was again tormented to the point of breakdown in *Casablanca* (1942), when she finds herself "torn between love and duty." *For Whom the Bell Tolls* (1943) cast her as another "abused" woman and *Arch of Triumph* (1948) was a story of doomed love, while *Joan of Arc* (1948) was another narrative of "torment" and "disillusion," although, here, her devotion is to God and the Dauphin rather than a husband or lover. Finally, and perhaps most interestingly, given that it was supposed to be her break from Hollywood, Bergman's collaboration with Roberto Rossellini also featured a narrative in which *Variety* claimed that she was trapped in a loveless marriage on "the bleak volcanic isle of Stromboli," a situations that turns out to be "a worse prison" than the internment camp from which her marriage had allowed her an escape. Furthermore, the film also features domestic violence against her and her gradual mental disintegration, and therefore operates as an "art cinema" version of the kinds of films in which Bergman had specialized in Hollywood throughout the 1940s. Ironically, this film, and Bergman's affair with Rossellini during the making of it, abruptly ended this stage of her Hollywood career, a career that she was only able to reconstruct slowly and even then on very different terms.

Consequently, David Thomson refers to Bergman in his *New Biographical Dictionary of Film* as an actress who often "played romance in a mood of torment, indecision and incipient suffering"; who offered a "searching study of deterioration" in films such as *Under Capricorn*; and whose "beauty seemed more vivid in masochistic situations." If this account seems at odds with her idealized image in the period, these two aspects were intimately related. From the first, critics and commentators repeatedly presented Bergman as both "unique" and "fresh" in contrast to the "glamour" of other female stars. Rather than artificial, Bergman was continually praised for being "natural" in her personality, beauty and acting. It was claimed that her look avoided cosmetics, and that her performances were "free from stylistic traits" or "mannerisms."

In other words, critics continually associated Bergman with health, warmth and radiance, but this was not at odds with the psychologically tormented women that she so often played. On one hand, the progressive disintegration of her idealized persona worked to dramatically emphasize the monstrousness of the threat within these films but, on the other, there was a connection between her public persona and the distraught screen characters that she played. Her naturalness was associated with emotional honesty, openness and transparency, a quality that reviewers often praised in her performances but was also a feature of many of her characters, qualities that also made them vulnerable to deception, manipulation and domination. In its review of *Rage in Heaven*, *Variety* even found this element to be overdone so that "not even a love as great as hers could blind her from the character of her husband's illness," although in *Casablanca* it is precisely the ways in which her nobility and honesty threaten to tear her apart that was praised by reviewers. Moreover, in numerous films such as *Gaslight*, *Spellbound* and *Notorious*, she throws herself into love with an unguarded abandon that verges on the self-destructive, and it is her capacity for performing this open, spontaneous and impulsive love that was seen as both her pre-eminent talent and a quality almost indistinguishable from masochism.

SUGGESTED FURTHER READING

Bergman, Ingrid and Alan Burgess. *Ingrid Bergman: My Story*. New York: Warner Books, 1995.
Björkman, Stig (dir). *Ingrid Bergman: In Her Own Words* (documentary, 2015).
Chandler, Charlotte. *Ingrid Bergman, A Private Biography*. New York: Simon and Schuster, 2007.
Smit, David. *Ingrid Bergman: The Life, Career and Public Image*. Jefferson, N.C.: McFarland, 2012.
Spoto, Donald, *Notorious: The Life of Ingrid Bergman*. London: Harper Collins, 1998.

Guy Boothby
(1867–1905)

Ailise Bulfin

Though he was an immensely popular author in his own period, Guy Newell Boothby's reputation did not survive much beyond his early death in 1905. This prolific writer produced a staggering fifty-three novels in the short decade of his writing career, all characterized by a breathless, lightweight, plot-driven style, with many elements of the gothic blended into this heady mixture. Following his arrival in London from what was then known as the British colony of South Australia in 1894, the rise of his literary career was meteoric. His first book, *On the Wallaby* (1894), was a travelogue recounting his peregrinations through South East Asia and Australia, after running out of funds on a prior attempt to reach London and having to work his way back to his hometown of Adelaide. According to colorful but questionable family legend, the dire poverty he faced on this journey led him to accept any kind of employment he could get. As described by his only biographer Paul Depasquale in *Guy Boothby: His Life and Work* (1982), "This meant working before the mast, stoking in ocean tramps, attending in a Chinese opium den in Singapore, digging in the Burmah Ruby fields, acting, prize fighting, cow punching." He finally ended up as a pearl diver off the north Queensland coast, before making an arduous overland trek home across the Australian continent. All of this formative experience provided Boothby with a stock of colonial anecdotes and assumptions that informed most of his writing.

By October 1895, just a year after his arrival in London, Boothby had completed three further novels. These included *A Bid for Fortune; or, Dr. Nikola's Vendetta*, which introduced Dr. Nikola, his most memorable character and the one which launched his career. Dr. Nikola captured the popular imagination from the publication of the first installment of the series, with his picture emblazoned on the advertising billboards, the novels on the bestseller lists, theatre productions on the London stage, and even a racehorse named Dr. Nikola running by the late 1890s. By the end of 1896 Boothby was comfortably established as a rising popular author as an interview in the *Windsor* magazine attests. Here Boothby made the startling revelation that after only two years as a professional writer, he was now working on his seventeenth novel and gave tips to aspiring young writers. A follow-up interview in 1901 is accompanied by photos of a stouter and more affluent Boothby engaged in country pursuits in his impressive, new, forty-acre Thames-side residence. As the con-

Guy Boothby, "The Creator of Dr. Nikola" (*The Windsor Magazine*, December 1896) (courtesy Board of Trinity College Dublin).

temporary literary press observed, "Boothby ... found story-writing not only easy and pleasant, but a rapid means of providing for the hobbies of a country gentleman." At the height of his career, Boothby was one of the most financially successful novelists of the time, earning an estimated £20,000 a year. It was not, however, enough to sustain the lavish lifestyle he had adopted. He was forced to keep writing at a tremendous rate to maintain it, dictating his novels onto a phonograph for transcription by a team of secretaries, while the quality of his output steadily declined. His career was cut short in February 1905 when, at the early age of 37, he died suddenly of pneumonia, quite possibly brought on as a result of overwork.

Despite its speedy production, Boothby's fiction was sufficiently engaging to satisfy the demands of much of the reading public. While he wrote across many of the genres that were emerging in the late nineteenth century, including detective fiction and the romance, dark themes abound in his fiction, pushing themselves into the detective and romance stories as well as into his horror tales. One characteristic of his work is its depiction of an array of intriguing and subversive villains whose larger than life personas eclipse those of the unremarkable English protagonists. These villains range from the classic supernatural fiends of the *fin-de-siècle* gothic, to deformed freaks (a particular penchant of Boothby's), to sophisticated international master criminals that anticipate the adversaries of Ian Fleming's Bond character. Dr. Nikola, the best known of these, is a distinctive combination of proto-typical Bond villain and Mephistophelean mad scientist, encapsulated in a refined, debonair and disconcertingly foreign exterior. He graced the pages of a series of five novels, each essentially turning upon the extraordinary machinations of the devilish doctor in pursuit of his arcane and nefarious schemes, with a hapless English dupe in tow, against a variety of international backdrops. Suave, striking, cosmopolitan and accompanied by his familiar, a fiendish black cat named Apollyon, Nikola's debut appearance was memorable, and ably reinforced by the illustrations of Stanley L. Wood, who emphasizes the brooding, arresting quality of Nikola's eyes, and habitually depicts him with the great black cat poised upon his shoulder, glaring at the reader with similar malevolent intensity. As well as commanding a global network of dedicated, ruthless agents, Nikola is revealed to be a devotee of the occult and master of an array of extraordinary mental talents, including mind-reading and mesmerism. The mid-point of the first novel, *A Bid for Fortune* (1895), also provides a glimpse of Nikola in his mad scientist guise at work in a secret laboratory in Port Said, Egypt. The remarkable contents of his lab include oriental weaponry, implements of black magic, a living collection of human freaks including what is referred to as a "Burmese monkey-boy," and a dissecting table where Nikola, after the fashion of H. G. Wells's Dr. Moreau, is busy dismembering "an animal strangely resembling a monkey."

Boothby's most gothic character is the eponymous, undead, ancient Egyptian high-priest of the 1899 bestseller *Pharos the Egyptian*, a novel which presents one of deadliest threats to white European civilization to be found in late-Victorian gothic fiction. After inheriting a collection of artifacts including a magnificent mummy-case from his Egyptologist father, mild-mannered English artist, Cyril Forrester, becomes enmeshed in the designs of a seemingly modern-day Egyptian, Pharos, who turns up on his doorstep intent on obtaining the mummy-case. Unsurprisingly Pharos turns out to be its original occupant, and his attempt to retrieve it only the personal part of a wider quest to exact vengeance on all Europe for its interference in Egypt. Pharos has been cursed with eternal life by the ancient Egyptian gods and designated the architect of their revenge against those guilty of plundering modern Egypt. Falling under the sway of Pharos's powerful mesmeric will, Forrester is lured to Egypt where Pharos infects him with a virulent plague.

On their return journey, under Pharos's direction, he spreads this plague westwards from Constantinople across Europe to London, leaving millions dead in his wake. In appearance this undead Egyptian villain is repulsive, a classic Boothbian combination of supernatural invader and misshapen monstrosity, whose "height was considerably below the average, his skull was as small as his shoulders were broad... his eyes, the shape of his face, the multitudinous wrinkles that lined it, and, above all, the extraordinary color of his skin ... rendered his appearance [like that] of a corpse ... after lying in an hermetically sealed tomb for many years." And this sensational description is once again reinforced by the atmospheric illustrations of Wood which show the freakish Pharos looming menacingly at Forrester from behind the mummy case, shadow blurring the division between his form and its, emphasizing the irruption of hostile ancient Egyptian forces in Forrester's London sitting room.

As in much contemporary *fin-de-siècle* gothic fiction, the revenge motif dominates Boothby's works. It is the unifying theme of the Nikola novels, in which a series of complex, vengeance-driven schemes are unleashed by Nikola against his adversaries, among whom colonial governors figure prominently—interesting given that several members of Boothby's family were senior Australian colonial officials. And it pervades *Pharos the Egyptian*, which contains one of the largest-scale and most successful revenge plots enacted against England in contemporary fiction. It is possible that despite his success, the Anglo-Australian Boothby may have suffered from feelings of colonial inferiority, of not being fully accepted in the imperial capital, and that these sentiments fueled such fantasies of revenge upon its citizens and its dominions. *Pharos* makes a landmark contribution to the vengeful mummy narrative which was emerging in this period partially in response to British colonial interference in Egypt. The vengeful mummy was such a compelling horror trope that it transcended the popular fiction of the *fin-de-siècle* period to become a recurrent icon of popular film in the twentieth century. Similarly, the international master criminal, of whom Boothby's Nikola is the prototype, became a stock figure of twentieth century film. Thus as well as acting as a veritable index to the social and cultural concerns of their own period through their transparent rehashing of current events, prevailing theories and popular themes, Boothby's novels were influential in establishing two key tropes of the cinematic age, which persist long after the novels themselves have faded into obscurity.

SUGGESTED FURTHER READING

Bulfin, Ailise. "Guy Boothby's 'Bid for Fortune.'" In *Changing the Victorian Subject*, ed. by Mandy Treagus, et al. Adelaide: University of Adelaide Press, 2014, online at https://www.adelaide.edu.au/press/titles/victorian-subject/.

Depasquale, Paul. *Guy Boothby: His Life and Work*. Seacombe Gardens, South Australia: Pioneer, 1982.
Dixon, Robert. *Writing the Colonial Adventure: Race, Gender and Nation in Anglo-Australian Popular Fiction, 1875–1914*. Melbourne: Cambridge University Press, 1995, chapter 9.

John Buchan
(1875–1940)

Anna Powell

John Buchan, best known for action-packed adventure yarns like *The Thirty-Nine Steps* (1915) and imperialist thrillers like *Prester John* (1910), was a deeply contradictory writer and thinker. The son of a minister in the Free Church of Scotland, Buchan became the First Baron Tweedsmuir and Governor General of Canada in 1935. His politics combined Whig and Tory, Unionism and Scottish nationalism. A staunch Presbyterian and elder of the Kirk of Scotland, some of his fiction surprises us by its pagan inclinations. With their fundamental ambivalence towards nature and the supernatural, several novels and tales reveal a darkly Gothic mix of desire and dread.

Buchan's autobiography, *Memory Hold-the-Door* (1940) reflects on his dualism towards "fallen" nature he so passionately loved. His childhood Calvinism led him to believe that "backsliding Judah built altars to Baal on some knoll under the pines" and "Sin, a horrid substance like black salt, was intimately connected with a certain thicket of brambles and spotted toadstools. This odd habit long remained with me." The narrator of "The Outgoing of the Tide" (1902) ponders "what must be the hellish joy of those lost beings who have forsworn God and trysted with the Prince of Darkness, it is not for a Christian to say. Certain it is that it must be great" and the Devil's allure is explored in several stories.

A prolific storyteller, Buchan's supernatural interests and sources are very diverse. They range from Scottish folk history ("The Rime of True Thomas" [1912], "Skule Skerry" [1928], the classical myth of his university days ("Basilissa" [1914], "The Wind in the Portico" [1928], fears of miscegenation (with bestial Pictish throwbacks in "The Watcher by the Threshold" [1901]), and more traditional haunted houses, magic and encounters with the devil ("The Keeper of Cademuir" [also known as "On Cademuir Hill" 1894],

"Fullcircle" [1920]). A self-reflective humor emerges, as when he when he evokes "the day of warlocks and apparitions, now happily driven out by the zeal of the General Assembly. Witches pursued their wanchancy calling, bairns were spirited away, young lassies selled their souls to the evil one, and the Accuser of the Brethren in the shape of a black tyke was seen about cottage doors in the gloaming."

In *Witch Wood* (1927), Buchan's own favorite historical novel set in the seventeenth century of the Covenanters and Montrose, a pagan desire for nature wars with the Christian dread of it. David Sempill is the newly ordained minister of Woodilee, where the wood "flowed in black waves to the village brink," its birches like "smoke from some unhallowed altar." The forest of Melanudrigill is an eerie place, "a moving thing, a flood which lapped and surged" and its nature is viewed as "eldritch" and potentially evil by Sempill, who wonders, "did the Devil use the place as a stronghold and seduce the foolish into its shadows?" Here, the minister discovers his parishioners, led by Elder Ephraim Caird, "takin the wud at the proper season" and secretly celebrating ancient pagan festivals. On Beltane Eve, in the clearing by an old Roman altar, Sempill witnesses a bestial dance of what appears to be "demons from the Pit," but these are, rather, his own congregation, "one with the snout of a pig, one with a goat's horns, and the piper a gaping black hound." The novel's tortured vision of fallen nature combines the romantic allure of paganism and the cruel repression of the Covenant doctrines that bring a sadistic witch-pricker to investigate and torture an elderly witch to death.

Nature and women are often elided as damnable temptations of the flesh. One hot afternoon, Sempill forgets decorum as his "mood became insensibly more pagan. He could not resist the joy of the young life that ran in his members." Deep in the wood, he meets Katrine, a lovely Cavalier, but he seeks to repress his desire for this "daughter of Heth," whose "beauty was of the flesh, her graces were not those of the redeemed. [...] will I too be unregenerate? He asked himself with terror." The coven's "infernal sacrament" is feminized, as Sempill is held by "the white tranced female faces, the obscene postures, above all, that witch-music as horrid as a moan of terror." At the same time, he blames the "neurotic supernaturalism" of the Covenanters for these pagan rites. Their condemnation of the "natural pleasures and affections" in "frolics and mummings and blithesome bridals [...] drove men and women to sinister and perverted outlets" (*Montrose: A History*, 1928). In "The Outgoing of the Tide," the powers of nature are themselves in league with the Kirk as well as the Devil when a witch's daughter with Christian leanings is tragically drowned to protect her virginity. The laird's son, her would-be seducer, ironically becomes a "pillar of Christ's Kirk, prompt to check abominations, notably the sin of witchcraft."

As well as his study of the classics, historical documents and oral folk narrative Buchan drew on James Frazer's *The Golden Bough* (1890) Margaret Murray's *The Witch-Cult in Western Europe* (1921) and other archaeological/anthropological studies for accounts of goddess worship. At the start of "The Grove of Ashtaroth" (1912) the "manly" Lawson is "wholesome in mind and body." He spends his fortune from gold-mining on building a mansion in a remote part of Africa. His chosen site abuts onto a grove sacred to Ashtaroth (Ishtar or Cybele), the fertility goddess who inveigled the Old Testament Israelites into "hankering after forbidden joys." Eventually, Lawson is himself seduced and his rituals are secretly watched by the narrator-friend. On the night of the full moon, Lawson, naked apart from his crescent headdress, emulates the goddess's transgender priests. He dances round a conical tower as he slashes his chest while "absorbed in some infernal ecstasy." To save Lawson, his friend hacks down the lovely grove and slaughters the green doves that live there. The contradictory account of the narrator's "strange passion" during this destruction is typical of Buchan's own ambiguity. He has a "repellent sense of acting against nature and violating a beautiful, female presence […] the heart of all sorrow and the soul of all loveliness." He draws on a strongly Gothic image mixing religion with eroticized cruelty "even so must a merciful inquisitor have suffered from the plea of some fair girl with the aureole of death on her hair […] as I felt dazed and heartsick, the whole loveliness of nature seemed to plead for its divinity." The closing return of the narrator's common sense and "the power of a sterner will" are typically undermined again by his knowledge that he "had driven something lovely and adorable from its last refuge on earth." Piety and paganism thus vye for precedence in Buchan's supernatural fantasies. Their unresolved struggle has much to offer readers of the Gothic. As well as having relevance to current debates on nature and supernature in the "ecoGothic," they offer a suggestive key to open up wider ambiguities at work in the Gothic.

SUGGESTED FURTHER READING

Buchan, John. *Supernatural Tales*. Edinburgh: Black and White, 1987.
Buchan, John. *The Watcher by the Threshold*. Looe, Cornwall: Stratus, 2008.
Buchan, John. *Witch Wood*. Edinburgh: Polygon, 2008.
Foxwell, Elizabeth, and Kate Macdonald. *John Buchan: A Guide to the Mystery Fiction*. Jefferson, N.C.: McFarland, 2008.
The John Buchan Society: A website for those interested in Buchan's Life and Work: http://www.johnbuchansociety.co.uk/
Lownie, Andrew. *John Buchan: The Presbyterian Cavalier*. London: Thistle, 2013.

Susan Cabot
(1927–1986)

Tom Weaver

Susan Cabot began her screen career as an extra in the 1947 drama *Kiss of Death*, in which she's only seen from the back (as a diner at a restaurant) but is instantly recognizable by her then-waist-length hair. Her exotic look made her a good choice for the role of an island girl in the low-budget *On the Isle of Samoa* (1950); at Universal in the early 1950s, she specialized in these types of parts (Middle Eastern gals in *Flame of Araby* (1951) and *Son of Ali Baba* (1952), American Indians in *Tomahawk* (1951) and *The Battle of Apache Pass* (1952), etc.). But it was away from the major studios, working with producer-director Roger Corman, that she made the movies that elevated her to cult status: the rock 'n' roller *Carnival Rock* (1957), the crime drama *Machine-Gun Kelly* (1958), the surreal *Viking Women and the Sea Serpent* (1957), the sci-fi *War of the Satellites* (1958) and, most notoriously, the title role in *The Wasp Woman* (1959).

It's been so many years since I met and got to know Susan Cabot, almost half-my-lifetime ago, and there was so much that was unusual (to say the least) about the experience, that it all sorta feels a bit like a dream now.

It was on my first-ever trip to California, around 1984, that I met Susan, who had been at or near the top of my find-and-interview list almost since Day One of my pursuing that hobby. I not only thought she was a knockout looks-wise in movies like *The Wasp Woman*, *Machine-Gun Kelly* and others, but acting-wise too, and it frustrated me that no one knew where she'd ended up. Roger Corman told me, wrongly, that she was living happily in Washington, D.C.; that bum steer was the closest thing to a "lead" that I had. So I was bowled over when, on that first California trip, Lori *Revenge of the Creature* Nelson mentioned casually that she'd seen Susan just the other day, at some sort of reunion of Universal Pictures veterans. She gave me the phone number of Jim Pratt, who was head of feature productions at Universal from 1946 to 1952 (and had, I believe, arranged the reunion), and he was able to put me in touch with Susan.

To make a long story short, my brother Jon and I were soon very friendly with Susan, the fun of knowing her only slightly spoiled by her aggressively oddball son, Tim. The kid was pleasant but ... strange. He struck me as looking like about 12 years old (facially and height-wise) but he was obviously much older, because he had his own car. Too often he did "little things" that would drive his mom nuts, like wearing sunglasses when we'd go out at night (and clamming-up and ignoring her requests to take them off), refusing to watch some of her movies with us even though she was practically begging him to, etc. Things that seemed to me to be designed to get her worked up. A Swift Kick in the Ass (a SKITA, as I call them) would have solved a lot of her problems with Tim, I always thought, but being a starstruck twenty something kid from upstate New York, getting to visit (on various trips) with one of my favorite B-movie stars, it certainly wasn't my place to say so. (Today, in a similar situation, there'd be no stopping me!)

Susan's house was.... ALSO strange. A mini-mansion, walled and gated, including a kennel full of vicious-sounding dogs—a lot fancier than you'd think a single mom whose long-ago credits were mostly on the *War of the Satellites* level could afford. There were rumors that, Back in the Day, she and King Hussein of Jordan were an item; when I'd bring that up, SHE was the one who did the clamming up. Eventually I began to think that was where the money was apparently still coming from.

Inside, it got weirder. The place was a wreck and apparently always had been. There was junk piled everywhere, to the point that finding a place where three or four people could sit down was a major project involving lots of moving of stacks of junk. The dust was piled almost as high as the junk; I

Susan Cabot (collection of Tom Weaver).

still remember picking up a chessman from a dust-covered chessboard practically in the middle of the room, uncovering a round, perfectly clean spot in the deep dust that indicated that the board had been set up many years before, there in the middle of the room, and then never once touched. I couldn't help but think of, say, *Thriller* episodes where unsuspecting folks ventured into creepy old mansions unoccupied for decades. I was once with Susan when she needed something out of the trunk of her car; she unlocked and lifted the trunk hatch but, looking at the car, it was as if nothing had been opened. Clothes were crammed so tightly into the trunk that they held the shape of the underside of the trunk hatch; the back of the car retained the trunk-closed look even when the trunk was open!

Despite all the weirdness (Susan was Norma Desmond and the Collyer Brothers rolled into one—and then there was Tim), she was almost always fun and funny and laughing. Yes, it was a "Somebody ELSE told the joke and took the spotlight off of me, so now I'll laugh TOO loud to get it back" kind of laugh but … hey, I was hangin' with Susan Cabot. Now and then we'd be out in public and somebody would tick her off, and I'd get a glimpse of the Cabot temper also.

Things went from strange to shocking one afternoon in 1986, after I'd known Susan for a couple years and been visiting/phoning her fairly often. I got a phone call from a friend in the Bronx who'd been half-listening to an all-news radio station and told me he could swear he'd just heard a news report that Susan Cabot had been murdered. I didn't think it could be true; even if she HAD been, her heyday was too long ago that a New York City radio station would make a big deal about her passing, even if it WAS murder. I turned on the radio and waited for that tidbit to come around again, and for an hour or so it did not. Finally, I phoned the radio station and found myself talking to some very friendly worker who didn't mind digging through some papers and discovering that, yes, the station WAS reporting Susan Cabot's murder. And I also found out what it was about her death that had made it unusual and newsworthy thousands of miles from Hollywood: It sounded like Timothy was a suspect.

It turns out he DID do it, in "self-defense"; of course; he'd had to "defend himself" against tiny Susan by bashing her to death with a weight-lifting bar. His earliest story involved a home invasion by ninjas (have I mentioned that my whole Cabot experience now seems dreamlike?) but once that myth was easily exploded and the kid was charged, the trial typically made the victim the accused, with Tim's lawyers charging that the "massive filth and decay" in the house constituted child abuse. ("Child" Tim was in his 20s.) There was also talk of experimental hormones that Susan had once given Tim to prevent him from becoming a dwarf (!), and reports of King Hussein or actor Christopher Jones being his out-of-wed-lock dad. (King Hussein?? The kid was whiter than a glass of milk!) Anyway, enough hot air was spewed that, after his being convicted of involuntary manslaughter in 1989, this characteristically Californian court slapped Tim on the wrist with a three-year suspended sentence. In other words, he got away with it.

The house became his; I later heard that it was sometimes used for filming, and that one group of moviemakers, without even knowing about the house's history of murder, became so creeped-out by the atmosphere of the place that at least one of them, a woman, wanted to flee (or DID flee). A few years ago I started getting occasional e-mails from a complete stranger, a Cabot family friend who said that Tim was hospitalized and suffering from some weird irreversible disease that was slowly making his brain disappear within his skull (!) After NOT getting an update from this Mysterious Stranger for a while, I tried to contact HER, but my e-mails bounced back. I telephoned the California company where her e-mails had originated, and the receptionist made it sound like she'd never heard of her. Another character come and gone from this weird scenario, again in a dreamlike fashion.

I don't know if Tim is still with us but of course Susan isn't, which is tragic for all the "big," obvious reasons, and also (as a trivial footnote) because she would have been a smash at the various horror and Western conventions with her fabulous personality and exuberance and she'd have had a blast herself. Now her movies, once favorites of mine, aren't as much fun to watch, because she can't be on-screen without my wandering mind reliving the strange-but-fun (but strange!) get-togethers I had with her, and the awful ending to her life, and all the other weirdness associated with the Susan Cabot Story. It might make an interesting TV movie someday, if it doesn't "play" too much like a bad dream.

SUGGESTED FURTHER READING

Raw, Lawrence, *Character Actors in Horror and Science Fiction Films, 1930–1960.* Jefferson, N.C.: McFarland, 2012. 37–39.

Rhodes, Gary Don. *Horror at the Drive-In: Essays in Popular Americana.* Jefferson, N.C.: McFarland, 2003.

Warren, Bill. *Keep Watching the Skies! American Science Fiction Films of the 1950s: The 21st Century Edition.* Jefferson, N.C.: McFarland, 2009.

Weaver, Tom. *Return of the B Science Fiction and Horror Heroes.* Jefferson, N.C.: McFarland, 2000. 65-74.

Oscar Cook
(1888–1952)

Darryl Jones

"I am afraid I must admit to a strain of insubordination running through my nature." Oscar Cook was a product of the British middle class—public-school educated, Home Counties—who, as he would recollect in his memoir *Borneo: The Stealer of Hearts* (1924), spent the 1910s as "a member of the Civil Service of North Borneo, a British Protectorate, a country the size of Ireland, owned and governed by a Chartered Company." From the experiences of this formative decade, Cook would produce a very slim but rather extraordinary *oeuvre* of horror stories—eleven in all—which would make him a minor staple of the British short-form horror anthology in the middle decades of the twentieth century.

Cook specialized in a particularly nasty variety of colonial horror. In his Borneo memoir, he writes:

> I cannot help wondering to-day whether there is in some districts an indefinable atmosphere or presence that is beyond our comprehension, which sets its seal upon the white men who have lived longest within their borders and claims from them a toll which must be paid. Strange and fanciful idea!

Cook's stories take two basic forms. Some are colonial clubman stories, in which the narrator and his friend Warwick, a ghoulish journalist, swap unpleasant tales of something nasty brought back from the colonies over whisky and soda in the smoking room of a London gentleman's club. Others, set in in Borneo itself, read like a kind of pulp Conrad, a lurid mix of ethnographic detail and a variety of *unspeakable rites*.

Returning to England after the Great War, Cook, still only in his early thirties, set about writing an account of his days as a District Officer, the book which was to become *Borneo: The Stealer of Hearts*. The title seems to have been suggested by Christine Campbell Thomson, his literary agent at

Curtis Brown, who soon became his wife. In the mid-1920s, Cook and Thomson both began publishing horror stories, first in *Hutchinson's Adventure-Story Magazine* and then in the influential American magazine *Weird Tales*, where Thomson published under the pseudonym Flavia Richardson. In 1925, Thomson edited *Not at Night*, the first in a series of anthologies published over the next decade. Eight of Cook's stories were published in this series. Cook died in 1952, just too early to witness a revival of interest in his work when in 1959 Herbert Van Thal published the first of the long-running *Pan Book of Horror Stories* series, a postwar publishing phenomenon which was to sell 5.6 million copies in total. Van Thal drew heavily on *Not at Night* for the earlier *Pans*—Thomson may have advised him on selection—and so the first volume included Cook's story "His Beautiful Hands" (first published in 1931), while *The Second Pan Book of Horror Stories* (1960) featured two Cook stories, "Piece-Meal" (1929) and "Boomerang'" (1931). Emboldened by the success of the *Pans*, Thomson reissued selections from the *Not at Night* series: *Not at Night* (1960) contained "When Glister Walked" (first published as "The Sacred Jars" in 1927); *More Not at Night* (1961) contained Cook's first-published story, "Golden Lilies" (1922); and *Still Not at Night* (1962) included "Si Urag of the Tail" (1923).

"His Beautiful Hands" is narrated from the gentleman's club, where Warwick, who smokes "beastly Philippine cigarettes," tells the story of Paulina, an expert manicurist who has "The touch of the East" owing to her "Javanese blood." Paulina tends to Mr. A, a famous violinist with hands which "weren't a man's hands, and they weren't a woman's. They were.... Ethereal." Paulina and Mr. A have an affair, and she becomes pregnant. Then his fingers begin to decompose: "It had just rotted off—and the stink as one touched it was enough to ... to –." Paulina, it transpires, is Mr. A's daughter, who is slowly poisoning him as part of an elaborate revenge because he has seduced and abandoned her mother. She dies giving birth to a stillborn baby without fingers or toes: "hardly hands and feet—just red, puffy lumps of flesh, not even webbed."

"His Beautiful Hands" is one of a number of Cook's stories dealing with sexual transgression leading to horrifying vengeance. The taboos of incest and cannibalism recur in his memoirs and his fiction. In *Borneo*, Cook recalls investigating an allegation of incest, and has to exhume the remains of an infant: "The child, reported to be the offspring of the supposed guilty parties [a father and daughter], was credited with having been born with head and face of a rat on a human body."

Grislier still is "Piece-Meal," another tale of sexual vengeance in which Gregory, a brilliant surgeon, goes on an expedition to Borneo in order to research an ethnographic monograph. While he is away, his wife Moyra leaves him for his friend Mendingham. On his return, Mendingham disappears, and Moyra starts getting severed body parts through the post. The narrator tracks Gregory down to his houseboat:

> I became conscious of a smell—a cooking, roasting smell. The fire was burning, a big, glowing mass now, and on a huge grid was what I took to be a side or half-side of beef. ... That joint, roasting over the fire, was Mendingham—all that was left of him—his trunk. Hanging from the roof, like a round ball of fly-catching paper, was his severed head.

Cannibalism, Gregory's ethnographic study concludes, is in Borneo "a solemn ritual. It was tribal punishment for adultery."

"Boomerang" is another tale of adulterous revenge, told again by Warwick from the smoking room, about "two planter fellows in the interior of Borneo—and, as usual, there's a woman." Macy is having an affair with Thring's wife, and so Thring plots his revenge, "an idea as devilish as man could devise." He inserts a terrifying Bornean earwig into Macy's ear, which burrows its way into his head and starts eating though his brain. By a million-to-one chance, the earwig eats clean through Macy's brain and out the other ear—but it is a female, and has laid eggs! In 1972 "Boomerang" was adapted by Rod Serling as "The Caterpillar" for his *Night Gallery* series. In an unforgettable scene, Laurence Harvey's Macy is tied to the bed (to prevent him, we are told, from tearing off his own face in agony), writhing and silently screaming as the earwig makes its inexorable way though his brain. Like all the best British colonial horror stories, this is all the more powerful for the veneer of polite manners and civilization overlaying the dreadfulness.

"When Glister Walked" is Cook's most Conradian tale, and also the one most closely rooted in the specifics of his own experience. Much of this tale of the restless spirit of a colonial administrator haunting his former home, and of outlandish religious rites, is lifted near-verbatim from his memoir. The tale reaches its climax at the ceremony of Mandikan Gusi (the Bathing of the Sacred Jars):

> From [two poles], like a gruesome necklace, hung two rows of ghastly human heads—blackened and dried from the smoke of years—save at each end. And there hung two heads with staring sightless eyes and bared lips exposing whitened teeth, and from them red blood dripped.

According to Cook, Mandikan Gusi was an authentic religious ceremony of the Bornean Dusai people, which he witnessed during his time in Borneo. "When Glister Walked" greatly exaggerates the gruesomeness of these rites: Cook records finding the actual ceremony "not exceedingly interesting to watch."

Like much colonial writing, Cook's stories can make for uncomfortably racist reading. Certainly, his account of his experiences as a colonial administrator betrays attitudes very similar to those which George Orwell criticized so powerfully in his own fictionalized colonial memoir, *Burmese Days* (1934).

Unquestionably, when Cook attempts to excuse the system of indentured labor as suitable for "laborers of Asiatic origin and of a low mentality," or of summary floggings ("There must be discipline"), he is simply defending the indefensible. But Cook also recognized that the success of the British Empire required acts of imagination similar to those which produced his stories:

> For it is in respecting beliefs and superstitions which, though possibly foolish and non-understandable in themselves, are yet not inimicable [sic] to administration or control that success lies in a country like British North Borneo.

SUGGESTED FURTHER READING

Cook, Oscar. "Boomerang." In *The Second Pan Book of Horror Stories.*
Cook, Oscar. *Borneo: The Stealer of Hearts.* London: Hurst and Blackett, 1924.
Cook, Oscar. "His Beautiful Hands." In *The Pan Book of Horror Stories*, ed. Herbert Van Thal, with a new Foreword by Johnny Mains. London: Pan, 2010; first published 1959.
Cook, Oscar. "Piece-Meal." In *The Second Pan Book of Horror Stories*, ed. Herbert Van Thal. London: Pan, 1960.
Cook, Oscar. "When Glister Walked." In *Not at Night*, ed. Christine Campbell Thompson. London: Arrow, 1960.
Mains, Johnny. *Lest You Should Suffer Nightmares: A Biography of Herbert Van Thal.* Bargoed: Screaming Dreams, 2011. Contains sales figures for the *Pan Book of Horror Stories* series.

Marie Corelli
(1855–1924)

CAITRIONA KIRBY

Marie Corelli (born Mary Mackay), the illegitimate child of the journalist Charles Mackay and his housekeeper Mary Elizabeth Mills, began her writing career in 1886 after a less than impressive stint as a piano improviser. Her first novel, *A Romance of Two Worlds* (1886), commenced an almost forty-year reign as a best-selling author that saw the publication of twenty-five novels, various non-fiction diatribes and didacticisms, and a barrage of press observations that earned her the nickname "the life-boat of journalism." Her great popularity with the general reading public, which included readers as illustrious as Queen Victoria herself, contrasted sharply with a very uneasy relationship with the critical establishment of the time that often descended into outright hostility on both sides. Her eighth novel, *The Sorrows of Satan* (1895), is often referred to as the first of the modern bestsellers, and its publication coincided with the end of the libraries' domination of the book trade. As library patronage waned, Corelli became the popular choice of an increasingly literate public, and it is this popularity that informed much of her own self-positioning within her contemporary literary milieu. Corelli made self-positioning an art: she peopled her novels with idealized cameos and variations of herself, she maintained an iron grip on her literary image, and she consistently denied the paparazzi of her day any opportunity to capture her appearance.

Riding high during the *fin-de-siècle* era, Corelli's literary reputation began to suffer from the effects of neglect almost immediately after her death in 1924, and her reign as "Queen of the Bestsellers" is now a mere footnote in the annals of literary and socio-historical criticism. Marie Corelli should therefore be considered a "Lost Soul," and resurrected accordingly, not only because of this intriguing contrast between her luminous life and her ignominious afterlife, but because her body of fiction—a heady blend of quasi-spiritualism, speculative science, gothic horror and passionate romance—warrants a closer look. Corelli's intense aversion to unauthorized images of herself can be attributed, at least in part, to the fear that these images would obstruct a "true" interpretation of herself and her work, and this fear is articulated through a variety of fictional characters across her oeuvre. "The Soul of Lilith"'s (1897) El-Râmi, for instance, when refusing to sit for a portrait, explains to the artist,

> If you can paint the imagined Soul of a man looking out of his eyes, you are a great artist,—but if you could paint the Soul itself, stripped of its mortal disguise, radiant, ethereal, brilliant as lightning, beautiful as dawn, you would be greater still. And *the soul is the Me*,—these features of mine, this Appearance, is mere covering,—we want a Portrait, not a Costume.

Much of Corelli's fiction is an attempt to offer a "portrait" of the "soul"; though the "covering" of many of her female protagonists point toward the art of the self-portrait. *A Romance of Two Worlds*, Corelli's debut novel, has as its narrator a beautiful piano improviser and artist who has been struck low by an illness that confounds mainstream medical practitioners. When she meets the charismatic Raffello Cellini, he inculcates her into the mysterious "Chaldean" religion, a form of pseudo-scientific spiritualism whose tenets are outlined (at some length) in his "The Electric Principle of Christianity." This "doctrine," coupled with the physical and artistic attributes of the first-person narrator of the novel prompted much autobiographical speculation, and

Unretouched photograph of Marie Corelli in fancy dress (© Shakespeare Birthplace Trust).

Corelli fanned those flames with a prologue that placed the novel within a very contemporary cultural context: "Recognizing, therefore, that in this cultivated age a wall of skepticism and cynicism is gradually being built by intellectual thinkers of every nation against all that threats of the Supernatural and Unseen, I am aware that my narrative of the events I have recently experienced will be read with incredulity." These narrative tactics, where Corelli deliberately plays on the boundaries between autobiography and fiction, where she oscillates between expressions of deference to readers and thinly concealed disdain for "intellectual thinkers," and where she re-frames fiction as philosophical and religious treatises, would become hallmarks of her style, and this novel, in particular, forms the basis for Corelli's late twentieth-century reputation as a spiritual thinker. Corelli, rather uniquely, grounded her fascination with the "Supernatural and the Unseen" in the rhetoric of the more prosaic preoccupations of literary reputation and the contemporary book industry, and this combination is the subject of her most enduring novel, Faustian bestseller *The Sorrows of Satan*.

Geoffrey Tempest, its protagonist, is a lackluster author attempting to make his mark on the overcrowded book industry of late nineteenth-century London. At the beginning of the novel, Tempest unexpectedly comes into a large inheritance, and almost simultaneously meets the mysterious Prince Lucio Rimânez. The wealthy Prince offers to assist Tempest both with an introduction to his new social surrounds, and with the promotion, or "booming," of Tempest's as-yet unpublished novel. The suggestively named "Lucio," possessed of a "finely shaped head [that] denoted both power and wisdom, [which] was nobly poised on such shoulders as might have befitted a Hercules" impresses Tempest with his savoir faire and his ability to negotiate societies' "upper ten," and he accepts the Prince's offer.

Mavis Claire, a reclusive best-selling author, is the only character in the novel to see beyond Lucio's "fleshly covering" to a deeper truth, "as if she saw something in his beauty that she disliked or distrusted." Clare's initials, her looks, her profession and her literary reputation all point toward her rather obvious function as a mouthpiece for, and idealized version of, her creator Marie Corelli. She is, as one bookseller in the novel points out to Tempest, "too popular to need reviews" and he dismisses those who write her down as "log-rollers" who "are mad against her for her success, and the public know it." These "log-rollers," reviewers and writers who are demonstrably unable to account for Clare's popularity, offer their support for Tempest's demonically "boomed" [sic] new novel.

Clare also serves as a foil for Sybil Elton, the aristocratic wife that Tempest acquires with Rimânez's "assistance." She, too, succumbs to Rimânez's supernatural allure, a seduction facilitated by her increasingly poor reading choices. Sybil is clear-eyed about the effects of her cultural conditioning: "I cannot feel. I am one of your modern women—I can only think and analyze." She blames her "contaminated" state on "the lax morals and prurient literature" of her day, an implicit reference to the scourge of the feminist-leaning "New Woman" literature, and she takes great pains to describe her "condition" to Tempest before their wedding takes place. She insists that while "the beauty of my body is quite genuine!" it is "not the outward expression of an equally beautiful soul."

Corelli's Faustian metaphor for the book industry is, while admittedly quite heavy-handed, a fascinating glimpse into the minutiae of the trade in a vein similar to George Gissing's *New Grub Street*, published four years earlier. Lucio, in true Miltonic fashion, offers a Gothic corrective to definitively Realist woes. He enacts his "temptations" with great reluctance, hoping all the while to encounter a soul capable of resisting his charms. In Mavis Clare, he finds a woman immune to the corruptive influence of the "New Woman" literature, a writer whose "genius" allows her to bypass the degradations of the literary industry, and a human who offers an embodied integrity that appears in stark contrast with Satan himself:

> I am a living lie, and knowing it I admit it, which gives me a certain claim to honesty above the ordinary run of men. This woman-wearer of laurels is a personified truth!—imagine it!—she has no occasion to pretend to be anything else than she is! No wonder she is famous!

No wonder, indeed. Marie Corelli, in the guise of Mavis Clare, lends her own popularity an air of divinity, takes a few well-aimed digs at her hostile critics, and excoriates the decadent society of late Victorian London, personified by a handsome Devil. Marie, through Mavis, offers hope, while the novel itself offers various portraits of irredeemably Lost Souls.

SUGGESTED FURTHER READING

Corelli, Marie. *The Romance of Two Worlds*. 1886.
Corelli, Marie. *The Sorrows of Satan*. 1895.
Federico, Annette R. *Idol of Suburbia: Marie Corelli and Late-Victorian Literary Culture*. Charlottesville: University Press of Virginia, 2000.
Galvan, Jill. "Christians, Infidels, and Women's Channeling in the Writings of Marie Corelli." *Victorian Literature and Culture* 31, no. 1 (2003): 83–97.
Ransom, Teresa. *The Mysterious Miss Marie Corelli : Queen of Victorian Bestsellers*. Thrupp: Sutton, 1999.

Aleister Crowley
(1875–1947)
Clive Bloom

Crowley was born to strict Plymouth Brethren parents against whose lifestyle and attitude his whole life was a continuous rebellion. Their stifling, evangelical and puritanical way of seeing the world ironically opened to Crowley the possibility of imagining the world otherwise. How to achieve that other vision of a world freed from his parents' privileged but suffocating conformity was a task which he would undertake by the emulation of writers he admired and lifestyles that his fortune (soon unfortunately squandered) allowed. His sense of self and mode of being were forged between the last ten years of Victoria's reign and the short Edwardian flowering of the first decade of the twentieth century. Specifically, the avant-garde's preoccupations in the 1890s became Crowley's determining raison d'etre. This was to culminate in 1904, in Cairo, with the "dictation" of *Liber legis* ("The Book of the Law"). By World War I he had found his calling and his style, something he clung to until his death and which would be endlessly reworked through his magic works, his refinement of occult ritual (renamed "magick") and his continuing dalliance with literature.

For Crowley, the "the universe [was] insane," godless and meaningless. Such forces that did inhabit the cosmic realms were violent and chaotic, embodied as gods by the ancients and still potent and problematic. Crowley slowly groped towards what force might balance such insanity. He finally resolved on the doctrine of the "will," part borrowed from Nietzsche and with its slogans of "Do what thou wilt shall be the whole of the law" borrowed from Rabelais.

Crowley lived life both so eccentrically and willfully theatrically. Crowley's whole demeanor was a lifelong dramatic masquerade, that even as he grew older seemed to lend a greater Satanic splendor to his personal façade.

Consequently a detailed and comprehensive understanding of Crowley's literary productions within any clear framework becomes a problem especially as his occult works borrow from the same sense of theatre as his fictional work and poetry. Crowley was a showman, albeit a very serious one.

Perversity seemed to inform Crowley's every move and every life decision, most of it forced on him by the destruction of relationships or the lack of money or the smell of corruption that seemed to accompany both. In the 1890s, Crowley posed as a decadent romantic who climbed mountains, played chess and dabbled in poetry. He was a self-confessed "reactionary conservative" with a perverse fancy for Jacobitism and a morbid dislike of "traitor" Gladstone and liberal radicals who were "Red fleas," politics which he had learned from his parents. Yet he was no straightforward conservative reactionary, being rather a new type of alienated and existential individualist who could rely on no moral certainty except his own sense of self.

Most of all Crowley was a restless and frustrated personality whose revolutionary sense of self seemed only to interest a small group of fractious followers and whose own refusal to be "confined to one life" meant his own ego was also fractured and intangible. He was never able either to fully understand himself or his situation (which was always one of precariousness) nor was he able to reconcile himself to the leading political ideologies of his time which led him on a lifetime quest to find a means of reconciling secular politics with a spiritual sense of destiny.

It was only in 1904 while in Cairo that his first wife (his first "Scarlet Woman") dictated *The Book of the Law* from which Crowley inferred that he had been specially chosen to be a great spiritual leader and the "messiah" of the new aeon of the twentieth century.

Crowley's ideas further developed when he joined the German Ordo Templi Orientis and began practicing their version of sex rituals. He was now convinced that the central thesis of his philosophy, that of "do what thou wilt" was being revealed in the various political upheavals of the 1920s and 1930s. This explains his continuing attempt to locate who ran the secret "high lodges" that controlled the world and to supersede them all by the founding of his own Abbey at Thelema in Sicily which he describes in great detail in *The Diary of a Drug Fiend* (1922) and *Moonchild* (originally *The Butterfly Net* [1917] republished 1929) in language which might suggest the reader was already knowledgeable regarding his communal farmhouse (no doubt because the readers, such as they were, already were followers).

Nevertheless, the rumors of what went on at the "abbey" brought him into conflict with the Italian authorities who expelled him, exacerbating his problems with a finding regular income and which forced him back to earning a living by writing fiction; a lifestyle to which he turned his hand whenever necessity called, just as it had done when he was down on his luck in America during 1914 to 1919. Then he had turned to short magazine fiction in the *International* (previously he had published with the *Equinox*) where he published tales of his alter ego, "Simon Iff, Psychoanalyst," and where he was to develop stories of neo-paganism based on J.G. Frazer's *The Golden Bough* (part one: 1914).

Although he rejected Mussolini as a false messiah and dallied with Stalinism, Crowley was convinced that Hitler was the new messiah to whom he might act as a secret priestly advisor. Thankfully Crowley's career as a novelist had already ended. Crowley found his own Thelemic creed in Hitler's words. Yet he was never a follower. Crowley believed too much in the individual; the racism, misogyny and anti–Semitism of his fiction were the unthinking prejudices of a man of his time and of a journalistic hack.

Crowley was a wanderer and it was this sense of internationalism which he explores in the hedonistic lifestyle of the hero and heroine of *Diary of a Drug Fiend*. The solution to Europe's loss of moral authority necessitated the rejection of Christianity and the embracing of neo-paganist practice. At the same time his hatred of the Victorian past led him to attack middle class conformism with a waspishness bordering between farce and pathological disgust. His reinvention of magical practice and his war with Samuel Lidell MacGregor Mathers and the Golden Dawn which he spends so much time rehearsing in *Moonchild* (where both W.B. Yeats and Mathers come to very sticky ends) was essentially a private fight turned into an apocalyptic struggle over the liberation a new European self.

For all this, Crowley remained a man of habit and a traditional Edwardian, always a lover of the mental symbolism of chess, the physical achievement of mountaineering and the importance of good living. His influences were, on the whole from the symbolist and decadent poets and writers of his youth. He combined a lifelong interest not only in Algernon Swinburne's symbolist poetry and erotic sadomasochism, but saw himself as the guardian of a type of wit, insouciance and bon viveurship epitomized by absinthe and the Café Royale that had apparently died with Oscar Wilde.

His poetic arabesques, which he first published privately as *White Stains* (1898), was an attempt to revive and outdo Baudelaire with greater emphasis on the taboo and the sexually perverse in a style that might suggest both Swinburne's interest in the more selective brothels with Frank Harris's sexual adventures. The book was willfully pornographic, intended to be self-selecting in its coterie of readers in a way absolutely in line with yellow book aestheticism and the cult of Aubrey Beardsley. Although Crowley modified his concerns as his writings progressed, he never abandoned the *Yellow Book* world of lilies and panthers when he wished to elevate by the tone of his ideas.

Meanwhile his fiction, divided between short journalistic pieces and longer novels sought not to invent but to "rewrite" Edgar Allan Poe and

Arthur Conan Doyle with the dream like musings of Thomas de Quincey. If this was not enough, Crowley was happy to incorporate the ideas of Madame Blavatsky and the Golden Dawn (who appear as the evil Black Lodge) with the intense interest in Pan, faerie and paganism that is so important in Arthur Machen, J. M. Barrie, and Kenneth Grahame's *Wind in the Willows* (1908). Into these writings Crowley would infuse Wildean satires on thinly disguised friends and enemies, amusing comments on gourmandizing and his own ideas regarding the "will" and the teachings of the "abbey" at Thelema. The end result is a curious mixture of social satire and occultism which takes as its central paradigm the decadent world of aristocratic excess and the nature of the true self which can only be found through contact with a master adept. Such a master is always Crowley disguised as a fictional character.

What emerges is fiction of little particular originality edited together quickly and for money. Passages are interrupted by long disquisitions on the Crowleyan magick system, on considerations of the value of various drugs, on how to fight Word War One by occult means, on the vacuous nature of spiritualism and on the significance of the pagan virtues. Poetry of inordinate length and dubious quality is interjected whenever Crowley feels the fiction flagging (he was always a poet manqué). The structures are weak and sometimes it is hard to follow the narratives which, by chance rather than intention, seen close to magic realism with their odd juxtapositions and strange character development and their often peculiar settings and situations that combine drug addiction with the mystical proceedings of occult ideas and ceremonies, all of which are never properly explained and which leave characters disbelieving the reality of their situation.

Crowley's most commonly used word is "madness." This produces a type of "extra" literary experience of a hallucinatory nature where what is written seems no longer directly attached to the nature of the subject. Ontological uncertainty makes the contents of his narratives more dreamlike and deranged as the books proceed. Indeed in *Moonchild*, Crowley willfully abandons the plot, which is centered on the occult production of a homunculus, to pursue a long and bizarre narrative regarding the secret history of World War I. Most of Crowley's fiction is a type of meta-fiction in which the reader needs a key to what is being actually discussed rather than what appears to be being discussed; no more so than in his detailed and "daring" descriptions of black masses and sexually nuanced obsessional relationships.

His works are dedicated to finding the self through an awareness of the true will. To do this one might liberate the will through drug taking, sexuality and paganism (Crowley always insisted he was not a hedonist). His works, including his two novels, did not find a wider audience until his own philosophy of life coincided with a new generation who had rejected the world of their parents. This was the counter cultural that Crowley was born to address.

Crowley, knowingly, crafted a persona for himself that combined various elements of the last decade of the nineteenth century into one new persona that would sustain his image in his lifetime and climax in his mythic reincarnation during the 1960s when *The Book of the Law* and *Moonchild* were on every countercultural reading list and Peter Blake and Jann Haworth included Crowley's staring face on the cover of The Beatles' *Sgt. Pepper's* album as one of the heroes of avant-gardism.

SUGGESTED FURTHER READING

Ashe, Geoffrey. *Do What Thou Will: A History of Anti-Morality*. London: W. H. Allen, 1974.

Bloom, Clive. *Victoria's Madmen: Revolution and Alienation*. Basingstoke: Palgrave, 2013.

Booth, Martin. *A Magick Life: A Biography of Aleister Crowley*. London: Hodder and Stoughton, 2000.

Newman, Paul. *Aleister Crowley and the Cult of Pan*. London: Greenwich Exchange, 2004.

Pasi, Marco. *Aleister Crowley and the Temptations of Politics*. Durham: Acumen, 2014.

Danielle Dax
(1958–)

Catherine Spooner

Danielle Dax is probably best known for her cameo in Neil Jordan's 1984 film *The Company of Wolves*, in which she plays a wolf-girl who rises naked from a well to be taken in by the village priest before returning to the dark regions from whence she came. Although she has no dialogue, it is a strikingly charismatic performance, simultaneously vulnerable, seductive, animalistic and otherworldly. However, Dax also had a musical career on the fringes of the 1980s British Goth scene, where she gained a cult following for her flamboyant stage performances, lavish style and experimental art-pop. With albums such as *Pop Eyes* (1983), *Jesus Egg that Wept* (1984), *Inky Bloaters* (1987) and *Blast the Human Flower* (1990), she carved out a distinctive niche that combined wildly inventive musical arrangements, big pop choruses, and psychedelic imagery. Darker and edgier than Kate Bush, more gutsy and feral than the Cocteau Twins' Liz Fraser, more ethereal than Siouxsie Sioux, Dax has yet to receive the reappraisal she deserves.

Dax was born Danielle Gardner in Southend-on-Sea in Essex on 23 September 1958. In 1979, she was recruited by Karl Blake to his avant-garde post-punk band the Lemon Kittens, playing keyboards, saxophone and flute, and later contributing vocals. Their first live appearance, under the pseudonym Amii Toytal and the Croixroads, was at the University of Reading, where Dax appeared onstage in a lab coat and a balaclava. She and Blake had little formal musical training (Dax had learned classical flute at school), but in the post-punk scene of the late 1970s that was incidental. Defining herself as an "all-round artist" from the outset (*Star Test* 1989), Dax designed subtly disturbing record covers for the Lemon Kittens as well as for Robert Fripp's *Let the Power Fall* and *The League of Gentlemen* (both 1981). By 1980, the Lemon Kittens had shed their other members and become a duo. Blake and Dax became notorious for their live performances in which they occasionally appeared naked except for body paint. They released two LPs, *We Buy a Hammer for Daddy* (1980) and *Those that Bite the Hand that Feeds them Sooner or Later Must Meet.... The Big Dentist* (1982), before the band split, Blake forming the Shock-Headed Peters and Dax pursuing a solo career.

Dax's early solo career was bound up with her participation in the nascent Goth scene circulating around seminal London nightclub the Batcave. She played her first gig there, and her style in the early 1980s—black rags, extreme face and body make-up and wildly disheveled hair—echoed that of Batcave house band Specimen. Memorably, at the club's second birthday party she "emerged from a giant cake and spat blood and Chinese food at everyone while cuddling an Indian Rock Python" (Mercer 1990: 44). Her music, however, did not fit comfortably into the early Goth mold and as a result she remained askew of the Goth scene.

Danielle Dax (courtesy Danielle Dax).

Dax's first solo release was the album *Pop Eyes* in 1983. She wrote, played and produced the entire album, later complaining that the predominantly male studio technicians of the time would be incredulous of her skills (O'Brien 2002: 158). This overt feminism was an important part of her persona from an early stage, evidenced by her track "The Shamemen," which pokes fun at hypermasculinity. The album as a whole was characterized by a sense of the grotesque, with lyrical preoccupations melding human and animal ("Everyone Squeaks Gently") and even imagining anthropomorphic loaves of bread ("Here Come the Harvest Buns"). This was reinforced by the cover artwork, a composite face created from medical photographs, which was deemed too disturbing for the packing company to handle. A subsequent reissue replaced the offending image with a more demure sleeve designed by Holly Warburton. The new cover maintained something of the flavor of the original by projecting vintage medical illustrations of flayed flesh over Dax's face and torso. Warburton designed eleven of Dax's record covers in total, characteristically projecting sumptuously colored photographs of animal and plant life over Dax's immaculately made-up face, evoking a metamorphic and even mythical body. Dax also appeared in Warburton's dream-like, occult-inspired film *Fragments Towards the Chimera* in 1986.

Musically, *Pop Eyes* mixed electronic beats with tribal rhythms, and displayed an eclectic array of musical sounds, with Dax performing on guitar, percussion, bass, flute, keyboards, banjo, tenor and soprano saxophones, trumpet, tapes, drone guitar, TR-808 drum machine, toys and of course vocals, ranging from a guttural rasp to an eerie falsetto. This musical experimentation continued into her second release, the 1984 mini-album *Jesus Egg that Wept*, which Goth journalist Mick Mercer described as "musky orchestral swamp blues" (Mercer 1990: 44), although its eclecticism also encompassed Eastern exotica. The seven tracks were more immediately melodic than those on *Pop Eyes*, and were steeped in Southern Gothic imagery: "Evil Honky Stomp" dealt with lynching; "Pariah" with voudou; "Hammerheads" with malignant neighborhood rivalry. The surrealism of her early work began to crystallize into narrative, a feature that would continue to develop in her later compositions. As the 1980s progressed Dax's look evolved into one of opulent psychedelia, featuring towering hair styles, exotic fabrics and elaborate jewelry, creatively reinterpreting Goth style by way of hippy and prog rock imagery.

The 1987 album *Inky Bloaters* demonstrated an enhanced pop sensibility, and spawned three single releases: "Big Hollow Man," "Where the Flies Are" and "Yummer-Yummer Man." These tracks, along with the title track "Inky Bloaters" and "Bad Miss M," showed an intriguing country and western influence, with Dax's creaky vibrato sometimes recalling cult folk blues singer Karen Dalton. Lyrically, Dax ranged from protesting against American TV evangelism ("Big Hollow Man") and prime minister Margaret Thatcher ("Bad Miss M") to disturbing evocations of psychic unease ("Inky Bloaters," "Sleep Has No Property," "Fizzing Human Bomb," "Yummer-Yummer Man").

Dax released a compilation album, *Dark Adapted Eye*, in the United States in 1988, incorporating most of *Inky Bloaters* as well as the sexed-up dance-rock singles "Cat House" (her first straightforward love song, although with such camp use of automotive metaphor that it was hard to interpret as anything other than tongue-in-cheek) and "White Knuckle Ride." At this time, she began to achieve more media exposure, appearing on the British Channel 4 interview program *Star Test* in 1989, where she revealed her left-wing politics (anti–Thatcher, anti-privatization, anti–Clause 28) and her somewhat unsurprising love of David Lynch, J. G. Ballard and Iain Banks's novel *The Wasp Factory* (1984). Signing to major record label Sire, in 1990 she released *Blast the Human Flower*, her bid for pop stardom. The album was produced by Stephen Street, at that time known for his work with The Smiths and Morrissey. An overly reverent cover of The Beatles' "Tomorrow Never Knows" influenced by the acid house movement of the late 1980s reached number 5 in the U.S. alternative charts, her biggest hit. As a whole, however, the album underperformed, being too mainstream for the alternative music scene but remaining too strange for the mainstream charts. While Street ironed out some of Dax's vocal idiosyncrasies and added big, shiny pop arrangements, Dax's lyrics were ever more politicized, addressing the economic exploitation driving war ("The Id Parade," "16 Candles"), organized religion ("Jehovah's Precious Stone"), and activist complacency ("The Living and Their Stillborn"). Dax was dropped by Sire and disappeared for much of the 1990s while she dealt with debilitating illness. A new EP, *Timber Tongue*, released on her own label Biter of Thorpe in 1995, saw her return to her experimental roots, while a further compilation, also released in 1995, was sarcastically named *Comatose Non-Reaction: The Thwarted Pop Career of Danielle Dax*.

Dax's pop career may have been over, but she had a curious afterlife as a designer. Appearing on the BBC interior design show *Home Front* several times, in 1997 she was awarded BBC Designer of the Year. In 2000 she graduated with a distinction in garden design at the English Gardening School at the Chelsea Physic Garden, and subsequently studied Fine Art at Chelsea College of Art, making sculptural work focused on feminism and abjection. She has largely disappeared from the public eye, with the exception of some low-key spoken-word performances in 2006. Nevertheless, her influence looms large. A blog by Dave Simpson on the *Guardian* website in 2009 compared her to Natasha Khan of Bat for Lashes and therefore, implicitly, to a new breed of female performers mixing art-pop, electronica and guitars that might also include Goldfrapp, St. Vincent and Florence and the Machine. Dax's experimentation with psychedelia had parallels in the work of other Goth musicians such as The Cure and Siouxsie and the Banshees, but it also anticipated shoegaze and the wider influence of dance music. As Lucy O'Brien indicates, she worked with "looping and mix tapes long before they became common currency" (2002: 157). She also was ahead of her time in her incorporation of blues, folk and country into the Goth musical repertoire. Dax is an unsung Goth feminist icon; her exhilaratingly strange music reminds us of how elastic the terms Gothic, and Goth, can be.

SUGGESTED FURTHER READING

Danielle Dax Official Website. http://www.danielledax.com/.
Mercer, Mick. *Gothic Rock*. Birmingham: Pegasus, 1991.
O'Brien, Lucy. *She-Bop II: The Definitive History of Women in Rock, Pop and Soul*. London: Continuum, 2002.
Simpson, Dave. "Danielle Dax, Catwoman in Hats." *Guardian* music blog, http://www.theguardian.com/music/musicblog/2009/may/07/danielle-dax-bat-for-lashes. Accessed 18 December 2015.
Star Test: Danielle Dax. UK: Alive Productions, 1989.

Dulcie Deamer
(1890-1972)

JIM ROCKHILL

Two photographs taken during the 1920s offer an illuminating contrast in the life and work of the Australian actress, journalist, poet, dramatist, novelist and *bon vivant* Dulcie Deamer.

The first, dated c. 1920s by Leighton Studios, shows an attractive woman seated, her short dark hair curling forward from her temples to accentuate the half-closed lids of dark eyes, which peer downward at the book in her lap. Her dark dress, the dark chair and dull colored background make the pages of the book, her white blouse and the flesh of her face, neck, and hands luminous. She is contained, demure, and studious; the highlights in her hair and the glow emanating from the paler features in the portrait lending her a hint of saintliness.

The second, bearing the date 1924, depicts her barefoot in a leopard skin with a garland of flowers on her brow, a necklace of teeth round her neck and a band round one arm. The leopard skin, ragged round the bottom, fully exposes both arms and barely reaches her thighs. She stands like some primal priestess in an attitude that mixes ecstasy and command, her hair falling freely about her shoulders, her wide eyes staring into the distance, lips parted, and arms flung upward with outspread fingers.

Mary Elizabeth Kathleen Dulcie Deamer was born 13 December 1890 in Christchurch, New Zealand, the child of a physician and former governess of genteel origins who, holding the era's "social round" and education system in contempt, cherished their daughters' talents, fostered their independence and taught them at home. Deamer recalls being raised in an atmosphere of "almost Rabelaisian candor" that left her incapable of being shocked by anything.

This openness to experience had a significant impact on the decades she spent as an adult in Kings Cross as the "Empress of the Holy Bohemian Empire," but its religious permutations were equally strong and had a major impact on her fiction. At the age of 7, she encountered a "Presence" in nature, which left her profoundly impressed. When she met it again after the family moved closer to the Bush a few years later, she repeatedly sought the experience during "secret 'religious' gully quests" both around her home and while touring abroad with a theatrical troupe. These encounters with a felt but unseen Pan-like presence did not induce the panic usually described in such encounters, but an awed, respectful reverence akin to that in much of Algernon Blackwood's work. She even admits that during one venture she "was irresistibly constrained" to remove all her clothes: "How heavenly was the sun and wind all over me!"

Nor were either of the houses in which she lived as a child free from supernatural influence. The Christchurch bungalow came to be haunted by the spirit of her father's brother following his premature death from alcoholism; but this benign haunting was followed by more aggressive activity in the home they occupied close to the Bush in Featherston. Here a poltergeist threw cups, rattled doorknobs, and flung open doors during the day, then crashed and shrieked during the night. Accompanying it were even more menacing "dark figures with sometimes audible tread" that moved around and within the house.

It should not be surprising that a significant portion of Deamer's work infuses the supernatural with an elemental, erotic force or that the omnivorous love for reading she inherited from both parents lent her inspiration that she would channel in her own distinctive direction. If H.G. Wells' tales of the Stone Age inspired "As it was in the Beginning" [sic] (*The Lone Hand*, January 1, 1908), the story that won her a short story award and fame throughout New Zealand at the age of 17, the wealth of sensual detail she deploys in relating this theme of sexual conquest is uniquely her own. Similarly, unlike Lew Wallace's *Ben-Hur: A Tale of the Christ* (1880) whose passive and chaste heroines are miraculously cured of leprosy following the crucifixion of Christ, Deamer's *Revelation* (1921) details the very active life of the adulteress saved by Jesus from stoning and her passionate love affair with the man who would become St. Stephen; resurrected by Jesus earlier in the book, she is mortally injured during the earthquake that signals his death.

Supernatural and mystical themes appear in several of her works, but are best represented by the short story "Hallowe'en" from *In the Beginning: Six Studies of the Stone Age and Other Stories; Including A Daughter of the Incas: A Short Novel of the Conquest of Peru* (1909) and the novel *The Devil's Saint* (1924), an excerpt from which was published separately as "The Devil's Ball" in 1923. Both works feature women who escape by supernatural agency from the strictures imposed upon them, one through lycanthropy and the other witchcraft. The uncanny events in these stories are described with a sensual power made all the more remarkable by its concision and precision. Once the heroine of "Hallowe'en" steps through her door and into the night, the natural world embraces her in a synaesthetic profusion of things seen, heard, smelt, tasted, and touched, all teeming with motion and life in all its manifold forms. It is a work that rivals the rich allusiveness and rare beauty of Arthur Machen's "The White People" (1904) and *Ornaments in Jade* written at the end of the nineteenth century. Sidonia's world in *The Devil's Saint* is equally full of color and even more full of incident; in a characteristic touch, the trend towards asceticism towards the end, following various intrigues and romances, a love philtre, a Witch's Sabbath, a Black Mass, and a burning at the stake, culminates in a final scene that concerns itself not with the activities inside a convent but a kiss between two lovers.

Deamer gained fame for her bohemian lifestyle as well as her writing when, after divorcing the man she had wed at 17 and entrusting their children to her mother's care, she experienced a "second birth" in Sydney's party capital in 1923 at the age of 32. Cavorting about in her "never-to-be-dead-and-buried leopard skin," she was crowned "Queen of Bohemia" at one party in 1925 and made Empress two years later. The 1964 Australian television documentary *The Glittering Mile* features a brief interview with her conducted in 1962 about the riotous lifestyle of the region during its prime. These activities did not prevent her from writing, and she was also involved in the formation of the Fellowship of Australian Writers as the Roaring '20s limped into the Great Depression. Until interest in her work waned with changes in taste following the Second World War, however, she saw ten plays staged and published five novels, two collections of short stories, and two volumes of verse. A quantity of verse published in various venues later in life remains uncollected, and the National Library of Australia houses the manuscripts of two novels and a novella she deemed among her best work, though none have yet appeared in print.

Deamer suffered a heart attack in 1963 and a stroke in 1970, the latter making it necessary for her to shift residence to the Little Sisters of the Poor in Randwick, where she died on 13 December 1972, in a room of her own amid her beloved mementoes and collection of books.

The serious, studious side of Deamer's personality revealed by her careful craftsmanship and the frequent melding—but never tempering—of carnality with spirituality in her work has been eclipsed for decades by the prevailing image she granted in her leopard skin of the Flapper as Earth Goddess. Thanks to the efforts of Peter Fitzpatrick in bringing her delightfully witty, candid autobiography to print and the efforts of scholars like James Doig in gradually returning her short fiction to print, it will be her bookish side that ultimately saves her from oblivion.

SUGGESTED FURTHER READING

Deamer, Dulcie. *The Golden Decade,* published as *The Queen of Bohemia: The Autobiography of Dulcie Deamer*, edited by Peter Fitzpatrick. St. Lucia: University of Queensland Press, 1998.

Doig, James. "Dulcie Deamer: Spiritual Awakenings." *Wormwood 23*, edited by Mark Valentine. Leyburn: Tartarus, October 2014, pp. 38–50.

Rutledge, Martha. "Deamer, Mary Elizabeth Kathleen Dulcie (1890–1972)." *Australian Dictionary of Biography*, vol. 8. Melbourne: Melbourne University Press, 1981.

Maya Deren
(1917–1961)

WENDY HASLEM

In 1961 Teiji Ito scattered the ashes of his late wife, Maya Deren, across the port side of Mount Fuji. Ito selected this location because it is a space both sacred and beautiful, where the soul could linger on in the tranquility of the mountain, at a distance from the activity around the port of Shimizu. Across her research and creative practice, Deren repeatedly returned to an exploration of the soul and its connection to the spirit, dreaming, mythology and ritual. Deren was the first female recipient of a Guggenheim Foundation Fellowship dedicated to researching Haitian Voodoun ritual. This resulted in her book *Divine Horsemen: The Living Gods of Haiti* (1953), two audio recordings of the sounds of the rituals and 18,000 feet of film footage, each a significant contribution to the anthropological examination of the living practice of Voodoun. Deren's personal participation in the rituals offered direct insight and resulted in her initiation into Haitian culture as a high priestess. In *Maya Deren: Incomplete Control* (2014) Sarah Keller writes about the resemblance between Voodoun and the rituals represented in her films. As Keller notes, "Capturing the signs of an elusive state such as possession becomes Deren's objective. In this endeavour, she attempts to render what is invisible somehow visible (142)." Deren's experiments with cinematography and narrative form also render the visible invisible. A fascination with invisible forces, otherworldly visions and transformation are compelling influences in Deren's research and creative practice.

Traditionally, the Gothic has been defined by a similar fascination with invisible presences, spectral and spiritual forces. In *The Gothic Vision: Three Centuries of Horror, Terror and Fear* (2002), Dani Cavallaro explores the expansion of the word spectral to incorporate apparition and spectacle, absence and presence (75). Ann Radcliffe distinguishes terror from horror writing that, "Terror and horror are so far opposite, that the first expands the soul, and awakens the faculties to a high degree of life; the other contracts, freezes, and nearly annihilates them" (qtd. in Cavallaro 3). This awakening of the senses emerges from the depiction of spectral visions where characters appear and disappear, where dreams blend with reality. The multiplication of identity, transformation and disappearance of characters within Deren's films, results in instability of vision, a characteristic effect of the Gothic mode of storytelling. Invisible forces are alive in Deren's cinema. Her films focus on an exploration of the edges of rational vision. Deren's films highlight the potential for the invisible as a powerful, illusory force within her films.

Maya Deren in *Meshes of the Afternoon* (1943) (courtesy Anthology Film Archives).

In 1943 Maya Deren and Alexander Hammid made their landmark avant-garde trance film *Meshes of the Afternoon*. This film is an experiment with dislocation, a theme that is supported by non-linear, circuitous temporal patterns that often feature in Deren's narratives. For films like *Meshes of the Afternoon* this translates as narrative cycles, spiraling into the realm of the dream. Dream and reality are difficult to distinguish in this film. *Meshes of the Afternoon* undermines the certainty and presence of people and objects in the world of the film. The key falls and bounces down the front steps of the house. It appears, disappears and reappears in unlikely places. Deren highlights this play of concealment and revelation as she presents her hand in the gesture of the magician, turning her palm up to show the disappearance of the key. Another character, Deren again, reveals the key between her lips.

It is in the space between what is seen but not heard that the Gothic asserts its presence in Deren's cinema. *Meshes of the Afternoon* refuses to offer diegetic sound, sound that we expect to hear in synchronicity with the image track that shows a record rotating as it is played and later a knife dropped falling in slow motion onto a table. This silence is augmented by Teji Ito's soundtrack, a supra-diegetic chorus of rhythmic drumbeats that was retrospectively layered over the silent film. While the rhythm of the drums was created in response to the movement on screen as well as the editing patterns, it also seems to impact and accentuate the movement of characters, objects and the film itself. Deren's character is subjected to a range of invisible forces. She seems to be pushed left and right as she tries to climbs the stairs. She finds it difficult to maintain her footing as the camera jolts and rocks to emphasize the invisible forces that impede the momentum of her ascension. The drum beats measure out the pace of her steps.

Similar invisible forces impact the narrative of Deren's subsequent film, *Ritual in Transfigured Time* (1946). This short experimental film begins with Deren involved in a ritual of unfurling and winding a loom of wool with Rita Christiani. Sequences showing the repetition of gesture as Deren's hands move up and down to support the unfurling wool establish a continuous pattern of movement. It is just at the point that the rhythm of the ritual is established, that it is undermined. Within the film we notice the impact of an increasingly strong wind, inside the apartment. The exterior invades the interior in this film as the wind strengthens and finally Deren vanishes, seemingly carried away by the wind. Like *Meshes of the Afternoon*, *Ritual in Transfigured Time* unfolds in a manipulated time frame as slight pauses in the narrative emphasize the ethereal movement of characters and objects appearing and disappearing in space. Deren uses editing to allow her characters to slip away between shots. She also manipulates the flow of time to highlight the rhythms of rituals.

Deren's collaboration with the Metropolitan Opera Ballet School, *The Very Eye of Night* (1952–59) is a film created to reflect the power of the invisible forces of the universe. The opening credit sequence presents a series of still images acknowledging the cast against a graphic background image of an eye with an iris shaded with grey lines that propel out from the yin yang symbol within the pupil. Etched into the pupil is the bodily form of Leonardo da Vinci's *Vitruvian Man* (1490). This immediate reference to Renaissance art links science and nature with the body as a microcosmic element of the universe. The film begins in starlit darkness, but here the stars seem to be moving, travelling slowly (and later disarmingly rapidly) across the deep black of the nocturnal sky. Mobile dancing bodies are introduced, all inverted projections of stark, white negative humans set against the cosmic background. Deren names these bodies after angels and astrological constellations. Bright Ariel, dark Ambriel, the weighty Oberon, the light Titania, Uranus and Urania pivot, twist and spiral across the background in various directions unencumbered by gravitational forces. Bodies sail across the universe, satellites glide within a constellation of physical and heavenly bodies. Deren understands movement here as similar to sleepwalkers setting their course by celestial navigation, as she writes: "in three directions at once: down into the abyss, up into the heavens, and inwards into the self" (1959). In Deren's final film the human form revels in its spectral form as it floats weightlessly across the night sky.

Ephemeral visions, dreams, hallucination and trance are pivotal within Deren's film work and similar Gothic forces extend into her anthropological research. Deren describes the Haitian Voodoun religion by identifying the immaterial, animating spirit or soul having the power to displace a living person, temporarily possessing the body and becoming its animating force (1953, 15–16). Similar invisible elemental, cosmological or spiritual forces coalesce in Deren's experiments with the potential for cinema to present uncanny visions of transfigured identities in doubled, tripled, quadrupled characters, or unstable presences that seem to vanish between shots, even in the stark white bodies that float against the forces of gravity. It is also in the dissociation of image and sound that Deren is able to present an illusion of movement driven by music layered over the silence of film, retrospectively adding rhythm to rituals. Maya Deren's *oeuvre* shows a clear desire to apprehend and explore the immaterial using images, sounds and words that combine to produce a similar "high degree of life" and "expansion of the soul" that in 1826 Radcliffe described as the effect of the terror of anticipation and instability that is characteristic of the Gothic.

SUGGESTED FURTHER READING

Cavallaro, Dani. *The Gothic Vision: Three Centuries of Horror, Terror and Fear.* London: Continuum, 2002.
Deren, Maya. *Divine Horsemen: The Living Gods of Haiti.* New York: Documentext, 1953.
Deren, Maya. *Experimental Films.* New York: Mystic Fire Video, 2002.
Keller, Sarah. *Maya Deren: Incomplete Control.* New York: Columbia University Press, 2015.

The *Erkenwald* Poet

Brendan O'Connell

Though the literature of the Middle Ages often betrays a strong fascination with the macabre, ghostly and grotesque, these impulses are typically subordinated to an ethical or didactic impulse that makes it difficult (if not impossible) to classify such works as Gothic and Horror fiction. Nonetheless, medieval writers often manipulate gothic and horror elements to elicit a particular affective response, and the emotion of fear plays an important and underappreciated role in medieval moral fiction. Moreover, while the aim is ultimately to increase the audience's devotion to God or a particular saint, devotional and hagiographical works often feature distressing and uncanny violations of the natural order. In light of this, I would like to draw attention to a neglected medieval poet, the anonymous author of *Saint Erkenwald*, an alliterative poem in the Cheshire dialect of the late-fourteenth century.

The titular hero was a seventh-century Saxon bishop of London, whose shrine at Old St. Paul's (destroyed in the Great Fire of 1666) was the focus of an important cult throughout the Middle Ages. The Latin *Vita* and *Miraculae* of the saint recount an exceptional number of violent and vengeful miracles in which those who refuse to pay due homage to Erkenwald are brutally punished. In one vivid scene from the *Miraculae*, a disrespectful artisan labors on the saint's feast day and mocks the priesthood; as he strides across the churchyard he trips on a half-buried skull and brains himself on a tombstone. In another, the saint himself rises from his tomb and inflicts a merciless beating—with his bishop's staff—on a man who failed to observe his feast day. In reimagining the saint's life, the author of *Saint Erkenwald* capitalizes on this association with the macabre, while offering a more humane representation of the titular saint.

Saint Erkenwald opens with a compelling summary of the history of the English church and people: the pagan Saxons drive out the Christian Britons, only to be converted in turn by Saint Augustine, who hurls the idols from the temples and converts them to churches. The greatest temple of all belongs to a mighty devil, but it falls to a later bishop, Erkenwald, to demolish this and rebuild it as St. Paul's. While the workmen dig to secure the foundations, they discover a marvelous tomb, obviously of great age, but described in strikingly contemporary gothic terms, and decorated with gargoyles of grey marble. There are bright gold characters carved around the edges, but the letters are "roynyshe," mysterious, and no one can translate them. The marvelous discovery causes quite a stir, and the poem brilliantly captures the hordes of people converging on the cathedral, leading the mayor and sexton to seal off the site of this "toumbe wonder."

The mystery only deepens, however, when the mayor orders the workmen to lift the enormous lid from the sarcophagus, and they discover an ancient, but perfectly preserved corpse, magnificently attired and bearing the symbols of kingship (crown and scepter). To a medieval audience, the marvelously preserved body would have immediately suggested the discovery of the sanctified remains of a holy man, and the poet describes the wonder in striking detail:

> And als freshe hym the face and the fleshe nakyde
> Bi his eres and by his hondes that openly shewid
> Wyt ronke rode, as the rose, and two rede lippes
> As he in sounde sodanly were slippide opon slepe.
>
> [And fresh were the face and the naked flesh,
> by his ears and his hands, which were openly exposed
> with vivid red, like the rose, and two red lips,
> as though he had suddenly slipped into a sound sleep.]

Thus described, the body occupies a disconcerting space between life and death: though buried for centuries, it seems to be merely sleeping. The description of the flesh as "ronke rode" ("vivid red") is powerfully suggestive, since "ronke" might also signify "proud," "ripe" or even "loathsome" (later, we are reminded that the incorrupt corpse has been spared from the "ronke wormes"). The body's flushed appearance is deliberately disconcerting. The poet has borrowed from romance descriptions of youthful beauty in painting the corpse's soft skin and red lips: this transference of the language of erotic description to the centuries-old cadaver unsettles the reader by blurring the boundaries between the living and the dead, and neatly encapsulates the ambiguous response elicited by the marvelous body, poised between powerful attraction and visceral repulsion. For a modern reader, the description of the body as flush with blood might evoke an almost vampiric quality; to a medieval audience, however, this would have suggested a different set of associations, centered on the incorruption of the sanctified body. Indeed, the visible presence of blood becomes tangible evidence that the corpse's incorruption is the product of divine grace, and not due to embalming, as even the bishop himself wrongly suspects.

When an extensive search through the records yields no clues as to the identity of the corpse, the people turn to Erkenwald for a spiritual answer to the mystery. The bishop prays for divine guidance, and is directed to undertake the simplest but most extraordinary course of action: he turns to the corpse and asks it to reveal its secrets. On being addressed in the name of Christ, the corpse stirs:

> The bryght body in the burynes brayed a litelle
> And wyt a drery dreme he dryves owte wordes,
> Thurghe sum Goste lant lyfe of hym that al redes.
> [The bright body in the tomb stirred a little,
> and with a mournful voice he forces out words,
> through some Spirit-lent life from him who rules all.]

The corpse explains that he was not a king, but a pagan judge renowned for his perfect and fair judgments. When he died, the people declared him a "king of justices," and buried him in regal splendor, but it was God, who loves righteousness, who kept his body incorrupt. At this point, the reader may suspect that the judge is one of a specially privileged group of pre-Christians (such as the Trojan Ripheus) who were miraculously granted foreknowledge of Christ's sacrifice, and were consequently saved through faith. But when Erkenwald asks the corpse if his soul is in heaven, the body groans and reveals that his is a lost soul, damned to that "dark death" in which no day ever dawns. The bishop is shocked and weeps, wishing the corpse could regain life long enough to baptize him in the name of the Father, Son and Holy Ghost. As he utters the words of the baptismal formula, a tear falls on the body, and the judge lets out a sigh: the bishop's words and tears have baptized him, causing a light to flash out in the darkness of hell and his soul to spring to heaven, where she is nobly welcomed to the heavenly banquet.

In this way, the poem masterfully reworks a well-known legend, in which Pope Gregory prayed for, and obtained, the salvation of the pagan emperor Trajan. Nonetheless, the poet makes clear that the pagan body, which exerts such fascination on those who view it, is also a source of fear and disquiet. Once the judge is saved, the corpse, and the pagan past it represents, must be banished from the text in order to make way for the final triumph of the Christian faith represented by the construction of the cathedral of St. Paul on the site of the pagan temple:

> Bot sodenly his swete chere swyndid and faylide
> And alle the blee of his body wos blakke as the moldes,
> As roten as the rottok that rises in powdere.
> For as sone as the soule was sesyd in blisse
> Corrupt was that othir crafte that couert the bones,
> For the ay-lastande life that lethe shalle never
> Devoydes vche a vayne-glorie that vayles so litelle.

> [But suddenly his pleasing face vanished and wasted away,
> and all the color of his body became black as the soil,
> as rotten as the musty decay that rises like powder.
> For as soon as the soul was taken into bliss,
> the other craft that covered the bones was corrupt,
> because the everlasting life, which will never cease,
> expels all vainglory, which avails so little.]

The sudden decomposition of the corpse is startling and unexpected, but finally inevitable. The scene perfectly encapsulates the *Erkenwald* poet's exploitation of gothic and horror elements: the decomposition of the corpse is a vividly physical manifestation of supernatural power, but the reader's shock is ultimately revealed to be no more than man's uncomfortable confrontation with the inevitability of death and decay, a confrontation implicit throughout this poem, whose action centers, after all, on a conversation between the living and the dead. The shock of this confrontation, indeed, may be less than perfectly subsumed into the poet's devout insistence on the transcendent bliss of everlasting life. At the poem's close, as the bells of the city ring out and the Londoners return to their everyday lives, their songs of praise are tinged with grief, as "mournynge and myrthe" are mingled together.

SUGGESTED FURTHER READING

Grady, Frank. "*Piers Plowman*, *St. Erkenwald* and the Rule of Exceptional Salvations." *The Yearbook of Langland Studies* 6 (1992): 61–86.

Peterson, Clifford, ed. *Saint Erkenwald*. Philadelphia: University of Pennsylvania Press, 1977.

Smith, D. Vance. "Crypt and Decryption: *Erkenwald* Terminable and Interminable." *New Medieval Literatures* 5 (2002): 59–85.

John Farris
(1936–)

XAVIER ALDANA REYES

Despite having had a career that spans nearly six decades, John Farris is mostly remembered today for his 1976 supernatural terror novel *The Fury*, which was made into a very successful film directed by Brian De Palma, and starring Kirk Douglas, in 1978. Farris is primarily a mystery and horror writer whose work in the latter genre is, at times, a direct heir to the Southern Gothic tradition. His oeuvre is, however, very varied and stretches to the melodrama and teenage fiction of his bestselling *Harrison High* series (1959–74), which features the adventures, sexual and otherwise, of a group of teachers and teenagers at the eponymous American high school. Under the penname Steve Brackeen, Farris also produced a series of crime novels and thrillers, the most popular of which, *Baby Moll* (1958), was reprinted by Hard Case Crime in 2008. This interest in the psychological thriller with strong horror elements is also evident in a significant part of his literary output. His serial killer novels, which sometimes include supernatural events, include, among others, *Shatter* (1980), *Minotaur* (1985), *Nightfall* (1987), *The Axeman Cometh* (1989), *Dragonfly* (1995), *Soon She Will Be Gone* (1997) and *Solar Eclipse* (1999).

Farris is the author of forty-three books: thirty-nine novels and two collections of horror stories, *Scare Tactics* (1988) and *Elvisland* (2004). Although he delved in and out of the genre in the 1960s and early 1970s, his horror writing started in earnest after 1976 and the success of *The Fury*. Thematically, his work has, on occasion, adhered to more general trends in horror, such as the psychological thriller after Hitchcock's *Psycho* (1960), the Ira Levin-influenced supernatural mystery in the 1960s, the post–*Exorcist* demonic craze of the 1970s in his later *Son of the Endless Night* (1984), and the contemporary interest in paranormal mysteries in his hardboiled, lycanthropic *High Bloods* (2009). His best horror fiction, however, has explored less well-trodden paths and delved in the mythical. The complex and multi-layered narrative of *All Heads Turn When the Hunt Goes By* (1977) travels from American plantations to the dark heart of Africa in what is possibly one of the most accomplished treatments of the lamia and voodoo of the late twentieth century. Similarly, the "huldufólk," the unwashed children of Eve, are the fascinating protagonists of *Fiends* (1990). A curious mixture of Icelandic legend and the traditional vampire, the huldufólk covet the skin of humans, for they can fashion wings out of them, and have power over moths and nocturnal butterflies. *Sacrifice* (1994) turns to Mayan lore for the story of Greg Walker, who manages to avoid aging by rendering the heart of a virgin daughter to the Gods during a lunar eclipse every nineteen years. In *Wildwood* (1986), ancient Assyrian magic is responsible for the half-man, half-animal creatures that haunt a parcel of wooded land near the Smoky Mountains in 1958. As it turns out, the beasts are not ordinary monsters, but the ostentatiously dressed attendees of a masquerade ball that took place forty-two years earlier in the ill-fated Langford chateau and who have been locked in a time-warp since. Other notable works in this vein include *Catacombs* (1981) and *The Uninvited* (1982).

Farris is also connected to horror and supernatural cinema. He has worked on adaptations of his own work (*The Fury*), those of other writers (he adapted Alfred Bester's 1953 science fiction novel *The Demolished Man*, which was optioned by Brian De Palma but remains unfilmed) and written original screenplays (*Good Intentions*, *Good Behavior*). Unfortunately, most of these projects have remained in developmental limbo. In 1972, Farris also directed his own film, *Dear Dead Delilah* (1972), which boasted the tagline "gory, grisly, and gruesomely good!" But his most important work in this area is, undoubtedly, *The Fury*, which was a box office hit and marked his official "switch" to horror writing. A straightforward psychic horror film that draws from *The Exorcist* (1973), Stephen King's *Carrie* (1974) and *The Omen* (1976), it features psychic teenagers being hunted down by a secret intelligence organization and turned into governmental weapons. Interestingly, unlike Cronenberg's *Scanners* (1981), the "exploding head" of which has garnered attention and recognition, *The Fury*'s closing eighteen seconds, a bravura piece which records villain Ben Childress's (John Cassavetes) telepathically induced body explosion from every possible angle, has not. Beyond *Harrison High* and *The Fury*, Farris's fiction has also been adapted for television. The novel *When Michael Calls* (1967), premised on the possibility of a murdered teenager taking revenge from beyond the grave, was turned into a TV film in 1972 by 20th Century Fox, and his 1989 short story "I Scream. You Scream. We All Scream for Ice Cream" was adapted for the Showtime anthology series *Masters of Horror* in 2007.

Given his consistently good work in horror, that his novels have received praise by newspapers and magazines, from *The New York Times* to *Fangoria*, and that his name has been hailed by well-known authors such as Stephen King, Richard Matheson and Peter Straub, it is surprising that Farris is not more of a literary celebrity. His lack of mainstream and academic popularity might be a result of the very American nature of some of some of his writing (its Southern Gothic aspects), or the fact that, as he himself acknowledged in 1995, he has not gone out of his way to become famous. It might be that his delving in various genres, appealing to potentially very different audiences, has not contributed to building him a loyal following. Or maybe his relatively low profile is simply a consequence of the fact that, although Farris's most interesting work is starkly original and stylistically unique, some of his themes can sometimes appear derivational. In any case, lack of mainstream fame has not stalled Farris, who has continued to write into the twenty-first century and produced two further sequels to *The Fury*, the Southern drama with ghostly touches *Phantom Nights* (2005) and the supernatural chase from (and into) the Netherworld of *You Don't Scare Me* (2007). His appearance alongside Stephen King in the second volume of the *Transgressions* anthology in 2006, which included his novelette *The Ransome Women*, as well as the reprint of six of his best novels by Centipede Press in limited deluxe editions, might hopefully pave the way for a larger reclaiming of this lost soul's oeuvre.

SUGGESTED FURTHER READING

Farris, John. *All Heads Turn When the Hunt Goes By* (aka *Bad Blood*). New York: Popular Library, 1977.
Farris, John. *Fiends*. New York: Tor, 1990.
Farris, John. *The Fury*. London and Sydney: Futura, 1976.
Farris, John. *Sacrifice*. New York: Tor, 1994.
Farris, John. *Wildwood*. New York: Tor, 1986.

Nicholas Fisk
(1923–2016)

Katherine Farrimond

Described as the "Huxley-Wyndham-Golding of children's literature," Nicholas Fisk was the author of twenty-eight novels and over thirty short stories of science fiction and horror for children. These works unsettle the familiar, and ask "what if?" What if the strange old lady that moved into your house was not really an old lady at all? What if we could communicate with our pets, and they told us about something terrifying that we could not see? Much of Fisk's finest and most chilling work is reliant on the cozy ordinariness of middle-class middle England. Suburban children go to school, fight with their siblings, and roll their eyes at their parents' lack of technological know-how. Sherry, electronics catalogues, and squabbles over marmalade at the breakfast table all provide the backdrop to disturbing tales of quiet invasion and domination. Writing in 1975, Fisk explained that "The basis of successful fantasy is believable realism. The White Rabbit in *Alice* comes alive when he takes out his pocket watch and cries 'I'm late!' […] The plot can be allowed one thumping lie (say, the invasion of Earth), but only one. Everything arising from the thumping lie must make sense." Within these realistic settings lurk *On the Flip Side*'s Blobs (1983), invaders from another dimension, initially only visible to domestic animals and gaining power by the minute; *Grinny*'s Great Aunt Emma (1973), a terrifying alien invader in the skin of a frail elderly relative; and the sinister *Trillions* (1971) that fall to Earth as beautiful crystals, but begin to form elaborate structures of their own accord. These "thumping lies," situated firmly in the everyday and the ordinary, offer disconcerting narratives about the gothic potential of suburban England. Fisk's fiction is filled with technological horrors. In the short story collection *Sweets from a Stranger and Other Science Fiction Stories* (1982), a faulty domestic robot named Oddiputs begins to ruminate on the inefficiency of his human owners and their bullying daughter. These thoughts build at night, and "Each time he thinks them, the thoughts leave a tiny deposit on his hair-fine tapes. It is like a coral reef: the ages pass, the dead husks cement themselves together, the reef grows." He begins to see the humans as "dirty and incorrect." The robot concludes that "I am Oddiputs ... and they are only *They* ...!" with the consequence that he pushes the child out of an open window. In "Teddies Rule, OK?," a scientist's experiments turn his daughter's beloved teddy bear into a violent, razorblade-wielding monster, while in "Swap-Shop," a boy discovers that the hole in his bedroom wall yields an impressive array of alien technologies. When his greed and curiosity get the better of him, he flings himself into the hole, and his sister discovers, in his place, a perfect, unnaturally white doppelganger peppered with "crystal buttons in which turned little golden worms, in his neck, his brow, his belly, his chest. His eyelids fluttered again. They opened: then she saw the spiraling gold worms in his eyes." His sister, overcome with disgust, throws this uncanny creature back into the hole.

The media also functions as a forum for gothic nightmares throughout Fisk's novels. Most notably, the sequel to *Grinny, You Remember Me!* (1984), sees the return of the alien threat, this time in the form of Lisa Treadgold, a beautiful, charismatic television personality. Treadgold uses the powers of hypnosis and the cult of personality to convert England to her particular brand of violent puritanism, turning independent citizens into malleable slaves in advance of the alien invasion of Earth. Mary Whitehouse's attacks on the "permissive society" and calls for censorship of British media during the 1970s and 1980s loom large in this novel, and even its author is not immune. Fisk himself makes an appearance, and his letters to the protagonist increasingly demonstrate an enthusiasm for Treadgold's philosophy of Decency, Discipline and Dedication, characterized by the return of corporal punishment and of reporting on the activities of one's neighbors. Ideological brain-washing, the novel suggests, can affect everyone. Resistance is quashed through the hypnotic blurring of the adults' critical faculties and by terrifyingly calculated acts of violence. In one particularly disturbing instance, a group of smiling celebrities bludgeon a man to death on television when he dares to question their new doctrine: "the way the speakers move in, so slowly, so polite—and the way they hit him and hit him and hit him. If they had been in a rage I suppose it might have been bearable—but they're not, they're just machines, they smile and smile and hit and hit, taking their time, making sure they don't get in each other's way." However, despite the exploration of media and technology's potential for evil, there is also a delight in technical wizardry in Fisk's work. In *Monster Maker* (1979), Matt begins work with an eccentric visual effects creator, and marvels at the uncanny realism of the tiny monster models and giant robotic head of the Ultragorgon. The book is far removed from the dystopian science fiction of much of Fisk's other work, and demonstrates an affection for the work of Ray Harryhausen and other visual effects creators, an appreciation which came full circle when the book was adapted for *The Jim Henson Hour* in 1989.

Fisk's experiences in World War II, described in his teenage memoir, *Pig Ignorant* (1992) inform many of his gothic tales. In stories about futuristic dystopias, the war becomes a time of relative safety, comfort and ordinariness. In *Time Trap* (1976), the protagonist goes back in time to a farm and poses as an evacuee. This rural idyll soon offers an alternative to the air-conditioned horrors of the future as physical labor, the English countryside, and a sense of rural community replace media saturation, mass-produced meals and marauding gangs of teenagers. The authenticity of an honest day's work outdoors meets its gothic other in the climate-controlled sterility of the Ecoshield in 2079. This contrast is revisited in *A Rag, a Bone and a Hank of Hair* (1980), as humans become incapable of reproduction, necessitating the cloning of fertile bodies from the twentieth century. These bodies must be kept in a secure environment, a replica of the era of their origins, to be monitored. It is decided that the DNA for these "Reborns" should be taken from the 1940s, as blackouts and the closure of transport and leisure facilities during the war meant that "people led restricted lives. Like being in prison, almost. You were stuck in your home, once darkness fell, because there was no point going out [...] There was no point in *wanting* to go out." The wartime home constructed for the Reborns becomes both an artificial haven—again, the child of the future learns to enjoy the pleasures of home-cooked food and board games—and a place of incarceration and exploitation. Wartime Britain is an ambivalent space in Fisk's work, symbolizing nostalgic simplicity as well as the dangers of totalitarianism. The perilous erosion of democracy reverberates throughout Fisk's work, most notably in the dystopias of these two novels and in the domination of Earth threatened by Great Aunt Emma and Lisa Treadgold. That people might view fascism as a fair exchange for convenience and the smooth running of things lurks behind many of these narratives in which humanity becomes complicit in its own enslavement.

Fisk's work encompasses futuristic universes and twentieth century domestic fictions, but what underscores all of them is a creeping sense of invasion, corruption, and creeping darkness. The calm quiet threats that run throughout his writing have kept countless children awake at night over the years, and with the recent release of a new double edition of *Grinny* and *You Remember Me!*, will continue to terrify many more.

SUGGESTED FURTHER READING

Fisk, Nicholas. *Grinny: A Novel of Science Fiction*. London: Heinemann, 1973.
Fisk, Nicholas. *Pig Ignorant*. London: Walker, 1992.
Fisk, Nicholas. "One Thumping Lie Only." In *The Thorny Paradise: Writers on Writing for Children*, edited by Edward Blishen. Harmondsworth: Kestrel, 1975. 117–122.
Fisk, Nicholas. *Sweets from a Stranger: And Other Science Fiction Stories*. Harmondsworth: Kestrel, 1982.

Charles Fort
(1874-1932)

Tania Scott

Charles Fort was a mysterious figure, a man fascinated by the esoteric and unexplained, an eccentric and a master wit who loved to mock authority. He wrote fiction, most of which was never published, and a series of books that were part records of paranormal research and part disjointed musings on the failings of rationalism and scientific positivism. Fort's current fame however rests largely on the Fortean Society which bears his name, but the books themselves are little remembered and barely read outside the ranks of occultists and aficionados of the unexplained. Yet there is a strong case for their relevance to literary history—particularly the horror and supernatural genre—and it may be time for them to be reconsidered as more than mere curiosities.

Fort's first published work was a novel called *The Outcast Manufacturers* (1909), but he never gained the reputation he desired for fiction. The novel contains hints of what is to come in his later works. It combines a realist narrative of the gritty lives of poor Americans with typical Fortean taste for the bizarre: the novel opens with some street urchins using a dead horse as a makeshift trampoline; "boys jumping on it, enjoying the elasticity of its ribs." This work anticipates many of the eccentricities of content and style that characterize Fort's later works, especially the author's macabre sense of humor.

Although Fort continued to write novels and stories, it was *The Book of the Damned* (1919) that brought him public recognition. By "damned" Fort does not refer to religious judgment; instead he is denoting paranormal phenomena and anything excluded from the remit of modern science. Indeed, for Fort the ultimate authority that he wishes to question is always contemporary science and rationalism. The opening to the book sets out Fort's manifesto:

> A procession of the damned.
> By the damned, I mean the excluded.
> We shall have a procession of data that Science has excluded.
> Battalions of the accursed, captained by pallid data that I have exhumed, will march. You'll read them—or they'll march. Some of them livid and some of them fiery and some of them rotten.
> Some of them are corpses, skeletons, mummies, twitching, tottering, animated by companions that have been damned alive. There are giants that will walk by, though sound asleep. There are things that are theorems and things that are rags: they'll go by like Euclid arm in arm with the spirit of anarchy. Here and there will flit little harlots. Many are clowns. But many are of the highest respectability. Some are assassins. There are pale stenches and gaunt superstitions and mere shadows and lively malices: whims and amiabilities. The naïve and the pedantic and the bizarre and the grotesque and the sincere and the insincere, the profound and the puerile. [...]
> The power that has said to all these things that they are damned, is Dogmatic Science. But they'll march.

Even in these early lines we can see the literary pretentions of Fort's work, where he embraces the horror images of twitching corpses and animated skeletons as metaphors for his literary approach. *The Book of the Damned* and its successors deliver on the promise of this statement. Fort presents to the reader his research on impossible possibilities, a cacophony of alien stories presented in a wandering literary style that gives no certainties, only eternal doubt. The works themselves are fragmentary—disparate collections of studies and anecdotes collected from a range of sources. These books are charming nonetheless and there is a narrative throughout, one that demands skepticism of scientific reasoning.

The Book of the Damned and *New Lands* (1923) deal in the main with strange geographical and meteorological phenomena such as lost continents and weird rains (a lifelong obsession for the author). Fort's later books are more relevant to the horror genre. There is hardly a horror trope that Fort does not consider in *Lo!* (1931) and *Wild Talents* (1932). The earlier volume considers unexplained disappearances, werewolves and other strange creatures, ghosts and even human combustion. He is credited with inventing the term teleportation, and suggests that there may be unknown beings or even individuals who are responsible for the disappearances and appearances of anomalous objects. In *Wild Talents* Fort turns his attention to possible abnormal traits within human beings. This book reads like a guide on how to make a superhero film, featuring, as it does, telekinesis, poltergeists, witches, vampires, werewolves and even talking dogs.

Fort spends a considerable amount of *Wild Talents* on accounts of vampirism, always with his characteristic dark wit and macabre sense of humor:

> The fun of everything, in our existence of comedy-tragedy [...] mania without the smile. Every fiendish occurrence that gnashes its circumstances, and sinks its particulars into a victim, wags a joke. In June, 1899, there was, in many parts of the U. S. A., much amusement. Something, in New York City, Washington, and Chicago, was sending people to hos-

pitals. I don't recommend the beating of a gong to drive away a hellish thing: but I think that that treatment is as enlightened as is giving to it a funny name. [...]
"The kissing bug," it was called.

The kissing bug was a theory used to explain the appearance of several victims of unidentified bite wounds that were found across America in 1899. The irony of the name appeals to Fort's mischievous side, along with the stubbornness of scientists that are determined to find a rational explanation for everything. Fort teases the reader, never once positing that there are true vampires, but giving tantalizing hints at the possibility. All the while his personality leeches into the text, continually self-conscious and self-questioning: "I don't know whether I am of a cruel and bloodthirsty disposition, or not. Most likely I am, but not more so than any other historian. Or, conforming to the conditions of our existence, I am amiable-bloodthirsty. In my desire for vampires, which is not in the least a queer desire, inasmuch as I have a theory that there are vampires, I was not satisfied with the 'kissing bug.'" Fort may be unsatisfied with the kissing bug, but he refuses the temptation to give any other definite explanation. For explanations are not Fort's style: he wishes merely to give us multiple possibilities so that we might embrace doubt itself.

In these works Fort's questioning of science anticipates a form of scientific postmodernism. *The Book of the Damned* appeared eight years before Heisenberg's work on the uncertainty principle was published and just two years before Einstein won the Nobel Prize. Fort is ahead of the curve, demanding that uncertainty needs to be a part of science, rather than systematically excluded from it. Like the quantum physicists, Fort's works challenge scientific positivism, refusing to accept the tenets of authority and tradition. He puts this neatly in *Wild Talents*, stating that: "Conservatism is our opposition. But I am in considerable sympathy with conservatives. I am often lazy, myself." The laziness of those in authority who are happy to accept the status quo is challenged by the frenetic radicalism of Fort's oeuvre.

The strangeness and changeability of his literary works was reflected in his own life. He suffered from depression, was possibly bipolar, and prone to burning all his notes when in one of his depressed periods. The nature of his work understandably leads critics to question his sanity, something Fort acknowledges wryly in *Wild Talents* when he states: "my madness has been over-emphasized." Late in his life he became subject to something of a cult following, and the Fortean society was set up by fans who wanted to continue his work. According to his biographer, Damon Knight, Fort was highly amused by this turn of events, and steadfastly refused to join the society that bore his name. The notion of an organized, hierarchical society must have seemed a complete anathema to the author who refused to accept any authority, even his own.

One of the issues that Fort would have had with the members of the Fortean Society was their commitment to believing in the paranormal phenomena that he researched. Fort never categorically confirms whether he believes in any of these supernatural creatures and events, indeed in *Lo!* he firmly states, "I believe nothing." He refuses to draw a line between fact and fiction:

> I am so obviously offering everything in this book as fiction. That is, if there is fiction. But this book is fiction in the sense that *Pickwick Papers*, and *The Adventures of Sherlock Holmes*, and *Uncle Tom's Cabin*; Newton's *Principia*, Darwin's *Origin of Species*, *Genesis*, *Gulliver's Travels*, and mathematical theorems, and every history of the United States, and all other histories, are fictions. A library-myth that irritates me most is the classification of books under "fiction" and "non-fiction." (*Wild Talents*)

Fort declines to distinguish between fact and fiction as they are one and the same. It is notable that he mentions *Gulliver's Travels* in this list as Fort often described himself as a humorist and satirist in the style of Swift. The modern day reader may wonder if perhaps the issue that he had with the Forteans was that they failed to get the joke.

There is a legacy of Fort's work beyond the Forteans and their peers. His extensive research on supernatural and paranormal subjects has left an enduring legacy across different media. Television shows like *The Twilight Zone* and *The X-Files* owed more than a little to Fort's cataloguing of the unexplained and unexplainable. In fact, Fox Mulder bears more than a passing resemblance to Fort himself, with his office full of newspaper clippings and exile from the establishment. Superhero narratives, whether in film or comics, would be very different without Fort's work; see for example *X-Men*, which features humans with abnormal—or wild—talents. Parts of his work read like a plot for an epic movie, as in *Wild Talents* when he considers the possibility of supernatural beings being used for warfare: "I conceive of powers and the uses of human powers that will some day transcend the stunts of music halls and séances and sideshows [...] military demonstrations of the overwhelming effects of trained hates—scientific uses of destructive bolts of a million hate-power—the blasting of enemies by disciplined ferocities." Fort's armies of telekinetic super-humans are pure science fiction, another genre that has been influenced by his writings.

Once we accept the lasting influence of Fort's work it becomes imperative that we rediscover the books themselves. What we find there is a delight. Fort's writings are engaging and thought provoking, and imbued with a mischievous strain of irreverence. He repeatedly states that he is both humorist and scientist, and that is perhaps how the modern reader should approach his works: in a spirit of scientific investigation and with a keen sense of humor.

SUGGESTED FURTHER READING

Fort, Charles. *The Complete Books of Charles Fort*. Dover, New York: 1974.
Kripal, Jeffrey. *Mutants and Mystics: Science Fiction, Superhero Comics, and the Paranormal*. University of Chicago Press, 2011.
Steinmeyer, Jim. *Charles Fort: The Man Who Invented the Supernatural*. London: Heinemann, 2008.

Dion Fortune
(1890-1946)

KRISTINE LARSEN

Violet Mary Firth, better known as Dion Fortune, was born in Llandudno, Wales, in 1890 and died of leukemia in 1946. The complex journey of her life was, in itself, a Hollywood screenwriter's dream, and afforded her a valuable reservoir of unique experiences upon which to draw for her own inimitable writings. An imaginative child, she was considered a free thinker as an adult. This trait often put her into direct conflict with the leaders of the various occult organizations she was a part of (including the Golden Dawn and the Theosophical Society), as the dogmatic rites and rituals were not to be questioned by mere initiates. Dissatisfied with these occult organizations, she founded her own esoteric society, the Community of the Inner Light, which later became The Fraternity of the Inner Light and today exists as the Society of the Inner Light.

As a young woman she was a psychotherapeutic counselor at the Medico-Psychological Clinic in London, but became disillusioned with traditional psychological practices. After seeing the success Dr. Theodore Moriarty, an Irish Freemason who was known in occult circles for his system of Universal Theosophy, had with one patient, she began to study under him. Following Moriarty's death she married Dr. Thomas Penry Evans and continued her studies into the occult and its connections to the psyche, but never realized her dreams of setting up a clinic that would successfully combine esoteric and traditional medicine. Fortune believed herself to have psychic abilities, including a talent for trance mediumship or "channeling." In World War II she utilized these skills by recruiting likeminded individuals to contribute to the war effort in a rather unique way, namely through meditations that they trusted would spread hope to the British collective psyche and invoke the protection of positive esoteric forces. The effort (documented through letters) was later described in the book *The Magical Battle of Britain* (1993).

Fortune's works span both occult fiction and occult non-fiction/parapsychology, first under her birth name and later under her nom de plume. This she derived from "Deo Non Fortuna" ("By God not luck"), her motto in the Alpha et Omega (A.O.) temple of the Golden Dawn. Her writing career began in 1920s when she published as series of non-fiction works under her birth name, including *The Esoteric Philosophy of Love and Marriage* (1924). Most of her nonfiction works were psychic studies books, often published long after the material was originally written. The most notable include with *The Cosmic Doctrine* (1949), *Sane Occultism* (1938), and *Psychic Self Defense* (1930). The second of these caused quite a stir in the occult community, as this collection of journal articles from the 1920s pulled no punches when it came to discussing her harsh feelings towards some of her fellow occultists and what she deemed to be their sometimes horrifically unethical practices. *Psychic Self Defense*, one of her most popular works, was a largely autobiographic survey of her experiences with the occult, especially practices that she felt could be risky to a person's psyche or general welfare. *The Cosmic Doctrine* was an initially secret work on spiritualist psychology supposedly channeled to Fortune in the early 1920s at Glastonbury and used by initiates of the Society of the Inner Light. Another famous work was *The Mystical Qabalah* (1935), based on a series of articles written for *The Inner Light Magazine*. Fortune's inspiration for this work was her frustration at what she considered to be the limited interpretations of the Qabalah system that had been available to her.

In addition to a number of other book-length surveys of occult practices and doctrines (some of which were posthumously compiled and edited by Gareth Knight, a member of her Society of the Inner Light), Fortune published a collection of tales of esoteric short stories and five occult-based novels, many of which had a prominent element of horror, especially in the potential of occult practices and powers to be misused to harm individuals. Her first book-length work of fiction, *The Secrets of Doctor Taverner* (1926), is a collection of short stories that centers on a physician and magician who uses his esoteric powers to heal his patients. The title character is said to be based on Fortune's mentor in the A.O. and friend, Theodore Moriarty. *The Demon Lover* (1927) is a classic horror tale in which a black magician engages in a psychic war with his Lodge. His plans change when he falls in love with the young woman he initially plans to exploit in his war. This first novel has a decidedly psychological flavor to it, reflecting Fortune's early work in the field, with the plotline itself based in part on her experiences in the Golden Dawn.

The title of *The Winged Bull* (1935) derives from a Babylonian sphinx statue on display in the British Museum. The main character is troubled by his experience viewing the statue and afterwards invokes Pan, a decision that, through fate or fortune, leads him to join ranks with an older magician in the magical healing of the psychic damage done to the magician's niece by an unethical occult group. An invocation to Pan leads the young cuckolded widower of *The Goat Foot God* (1936) onto the path of magical healing, only to discover that his seemingly karmic troubles began in a prior incarnation, as a medieval monk who had been persecuted and eventually walled up for his pagan beliefs. In this work Fortune's deep-rooted belief in reincarnation take center stage.

Reincarnation is also a central theme in *The Sea Priestess* (1938) as the central character, Vivien Le Fay Morgan, is the reincarnation of a powerful priestess from Atlantis. Morgan vanishes before the end of the novel, but not before helping a meek town estate agent to realize his inner strength through a series of magical ceremonies. Morgan returns in *Moon Magic*, published posthumously in 1956. The unfinished manuscript was found among Fortune's papers, with the ending said to have been channeled to her followers after her death. In this novel Morgan has reappeared in London under the name Lilith, where she sets up a magical temple in a desecrated church. She finds an unlikely partner in a repressed physician, who uses his nascent psychic powers to aid her in her magical work while she, in turn, leads him to become a more emotionally healthy individual. In addition to these novels, Fortune also penned three romantic thrillers under the name V.M. Steele, *The Scarred Wrists* (1935), *Hunters of Humans* (1936), and *Beloved of Ishmael* (1937).

According to Alex Sumner in the article "The Occult Novels of Dion Fortune," her fictional work is a syncretism of her unique brand of occult thinking, drawing upon Jungian and Freudian psychology as well as the teachings of the various occult groups she had been a member of, especially the Qabalah. Her work also clearly espouses a feminist viewpoint, one which sees sexuality as central to spiritual as well as physical well-being. This is reflected in the prominent use of sexual magic in her novels. She clearly draws upon her personal experiences in which ordinary individuals successfully use magic outside of the hierarchical structures of official lodges and organizations. Even after her death in 1946 Fortune continued to initiate the curious into occult practices, through the rituals and rites she left behind that have been carried forth by her Society of the Inner Light.

But perhaps Fortune's most enduring legacy is her influence on fantasy writer Marion Zimmer Bradley and her famous Arthurian novel *The Mists of Avalon* (1982). As explained by Bradley's sister-in-law, Diana Paxson, Bradley encountered Fortune's work while in college, and she and her second husband (Paxson's brother) founded their own lodge, the Aquarian Order of the Restoration (A.O.R.), based on Fortune's teachings. Paxson notes that not only were *The Sea Priestess* and *Moon Magic* powerful influences on Bradley's novel (with their portrayal of Morgan Le Fay), but also the "syncretic theology" of the Golden Dawn and other occult organizations with which Fortune was associated.

SUGGESTED FURTHER READING

Chapman, Janine. *Quest for Dion Fortune.* York Beach: Samuel Weiser, 1993.
Fielding, Charles, and Carr Collins. *The Story of Dion Fortune.* Dallas: Star and Cross, 1985.
Knight, Gareth. *Dion Fortune and the Inner Light.* Loughborough: Thoth, 2000.
Paxson, Diana L. "Marion Zimmer Bradley and *The Mists of Avalon.*" *Arthuriana* 9.1 (1999): 110–26.
Sumner, Alex. "The Occult Novels of Dion Fortune." *Journal of the Western Mystery Tradition* 0 (2001).

Charles Gemora
(1903–1961)

Mark Cofell

From the untamed wilds of Hollywood cinema, a unique breed of man emerged to portray the mightiest of simians, the Gorilla, in the evolving medium of film. Menacing maidens, tromping through verdant jungle and lurking in the shadows of dark houses became the domain of a handful of performers who labored in uncomfortable conditions and often unaccredited. A tiny, impish Filipino would establish himself as the King of the Gorilla Men through his finely crafted suits and his ability to elicit both frightful cries and easy laughter.

Born in 1903 into the turbulent period of American occupation of the Philippines, Carlos Cruz Gemora was the last of 18 children. Charles lost his father at a young age, and his eldest brother proved to be a selfish and cruel steward. A substantial parcel of land had been left in equal lots to the surviving children but the greedy firstborn campaigned to have all of the land signed over to him. Charles fled from his brother to Manila but was soon discovered and detained at a monastery, where he would remain until he was of legal age to sign the necessary documentation to hand over his birthright. At the young age of fifteen, Charles once again ran off to the capitol, this time determined to travel beyond his sibling's grasp and make his way to the United States of America.

Manila was the center of American activity in 1920s Philippines and ships hustled personnel and goods from Californian ports. A teenage Charles managed to convince a few Yankee sailors to sneak him aboard their vessel and smuggle him into their home country. During the voyage, Charles was called upon to assist in some repairs that required a diminutive fellow, thus he entered the Port of Long Beach on the deck of the ship rather than huddled in the hold.

The future gorilla man and effects wizard began his stay in America washing bottles for a dairy and frequenting the gates of Universal Studios, hoping to earn some money as an extra in the burgeoning film industry. As he had once impressed American nationals and earned a few pennies back in his homeland, Charles would often sketch people as he waited for an oppor-

Charles Gemora and Valmere Barman in *Perils of Pauline* (collection of Mark Cofell).

tunity to become a face in the silver screen crowds. It was not long before his innate talent was recognized by a passerby who worked in a studio, and Charles Gemora found himself in the employ of Hollywood's dream factory.

Landing a position of sculptor, Charles worked on set pieces for grand Universal epics, eventually playing a major role in the creation of gargoyles prominent on the grand cathedral of *The Hunchback of Notre Dame* (1923). His craftsmanship on that film lead to his position as set designer for Lon Chaney's other opus, *The Phantom of the Opera* (1925). The Opera House set remains intact to this day and is apparently haunted by the Spirit of a Thousand Faces; high flattery from one industry marvel to another. Gemora's hand can also be found in numerous Douglas Fairbanks, Sr., films.

In 1927 Charles Gemora set upon the task of sculpting and creating a gorilla suit for a film adaptation of the popular play *The Gorilla*. Apparently fascinated by the problem of making a man a jungle monster, Charles built himself a suit and appeared in *The Leopard Lady* (1928), setting down a curious career path few men have trod, and fewer still have excelled in. Gorillas were a common feature in pictures of the period and were typically portrayed by extras or stuntmen in an ill-fitting suit cobbled together for the individual production. Charles frequented the San Diego Zoo scrutinizing ape movement and form, dedicating many hours and dollars towards perfecting his gorilla alter-ego. One attribute that aided in his believable portrayal of our evolutionary cousins was his size. At only 5'4" and 130 pounds, Charles' gorilla appeared entirely realistic beside larger human actors.

The ability to craft and alter his gorilla suit enabled Gemora to outclass his contemporaries. While Charles was the head of the make-up department at Paramount in his later years, a youthful Bob Burns sat down with his idol and had the rare opportunity to hear the gorilla man's trade secrets first hand. Bob himself portrayed gorillas throughout the '60s and '70s and also assembled a collection of genre memorabilia rescued from studio Dumpsters, preserving artifacts of beloved sci-fi and horror films. Charles explained his suits were constructed from scratch, including the head, torso and limbs (the articulated metal armature that served as the framework for the mask, was created by parties unknown). Two types of arms were used, an ordinary pair used for close ups and a set of "walking arms" that were critical to simulating ape-like locomotion. The performer reached down a sleeve to the "elbow" of the suit where he could grip the stilt-like solid forearm which ended in a closed fist. This enabled Charles to lope about in a truly animal-like fashion. The simple notion of creating the beasts head from a cast of the inhabitants' face and the use of eye black, resulted in a visually seamless mask that would solidify the illusion of a real ape menacing the screen and allowed for lingering tight camera shots. As noted, Charles was a slim fellow and therefore required a great deal of padding to flesh out his gorilla suits. Unfortunately, kapok was employed; a material that was often used in mattresses and sleeping bags and had substantial insulating properties. Suits would eventually utilize water filled pouches that gave the belly a realistic sway. The thick and lustrous coat gracing his suits consisted of yak hair, and in later years, his daughter and assistant, Diana, was responsible for crocheting them onto the suit and keeping the hair maintained. All of these separate elements contributed to gorilla suits that were unparalleled in excellence for many decades. Yet a suit alone is not enough to make an audience laugh or scream. Where Charles truly excelled was in his ability to take an awkward and uncomfortable costume and communicate with simple body language and his expressive eyes. Although all gorilla men have taken that journey to the local monkey house to seek the essence of ape-ness, Charles identified the subtle commonalities in emotion and gestures between man and simian that make our evolutionary cousins so fascinating.

Over his years portraying apes, there were several distinct incarnations (Bob Burns tallies at least six, perhaps more)—as Gemora's artistic skills improved and evolved, so did his simian counterpart. Suits that appeared in his early films were a reflection of the common man's subconscious impressions of this mysterious brute from the jungle. There was a harsh crudeness in their visage that oozed a weird terror that was as at home in the pages of pulp fiction as it was on film.

In 1930 Charles appeared in the now-forgotten exploitation blockbuster *Ingagi*. The despicable essence of the film is simple; although it purported to be a documentary picture depicting an expedition into Africa, Congo Pictures manufactured a degrading tale about a tribe that worshipped gorillas and who offered up their women to mate with them. The very name of the film *Ingagi* was claimed to be a native term for gorilla, but this was also a fallacy. It was not long before the exotic tale of Dark Continent bestiality was exposed as a fake. African American women in the picture were recognized by members of Californian audiences. One of the white explorers was also identified as a L.A. theatre actor. With the whiff of doubt in the air, savvy viewers also began to raise the possibility that the amorous ape of the picture was none other than Hollywood's new simian thespian, Charles Gemora. According to an article in *Motion Picture*, Charles denied any involvement until called in for questioning by the Hays Office. Whether or not the film was authentic was the last thing on the minds of enthusiastic moviegoers. Ticket sales reached record heights despite the eventual withdrawal of the picture from theatre chains (the unofficial second highest grossing film of 1931 at 2 million). Roadshow viewings swelled and the gorilla-gets-girl premise that pre-dated *King Kong* drew crowds for years and inspired other similar exotic exploitation films like *Angkor* and *Love Life of a Gorilla*.

Murders in the Rue Morgue (1932) saw Gemora paired with Bela Lugosi in what should have been a perfect vehicle to showcase the grotesque gorilla suit of his early career. Unfortunately for Charles, although he had proven that his suits and performing skills were more than adequate in previous films, jarring shots of an actual chimpanzee were substituted in for all of his close-ups. Gemora related to Bob Burns that he had no idea there was any problem with his performance until he viewed the finished project.

Besides the obligatory adventure and horror films, Charles Gemora would make several pictures over his career with a host of comedic greats like the Marx Brothers, Abbott and Costello and many others. In *The Chimp* (1932) Charles ably demonstrated his crack comic timing and mischievous wit in the company of comedy giants Laurel and Hardy. The short features the duo trying to discreetly enter their boarding house with a circus ape in tow and attempting to keep the creature's presence a secret from their landlord. Bob Burns recalled that both Charles and Stan had adoring praise for one another's talent and character. Gemora would appear again in their feature *Swiss Miss* (1938).

In 1941, *The Monster and the Girl* featured Charles as the titular monster in one of his finest gorilla suits and delivering a nuanced and affecting performance that would outshine all others. This odd entry into the '40s Universal horror revival provided the gorilla impresario with the added challenge of portraying a creature who possessed the transplanted brain of an executed prisoner bent on vengeance. The brain donor has a sister who had fallen into the clutches of a white slavery ring and his attempts to aid her result in a frame up for murder. This bizarre role taxed all of Gemora's emoting abilities as he struggled to relate the inner workings of a man agonized by his siblings fall from grace and his desire to utterly destroy those that precipitated it. *The Monster and the Girl* remains one of the great gorilla suit performances and is acknowledged by modern effects master and former gorilla man Rick Baker as Gemora's finest hour.

All gorilla men agree on one fine point of suit work; it's an uncomfortable and often brutal task. Enacting laborious scenes in hot, cramped suits that could weigh 60 pounds or more, took a heavy toll on even the fittest of men. Charles Gemora had a distinct reminder of the physical cost of gorilla suit work in 1943 when he suffered his first heart attack. Despite the obvious impact of his profession, Charles continued to appear onscreen in other ape roles, though less and less frequently.

Throughout his years of aping about on film, Gemora continued to work in the Paramount make-up department, a job which led to his most widely recognized contribution to cinema history. As recounted to author Tom Weaver by Gemora's daughter Diana, Charles collected his 12-year-old protégé around suppertime one night in 1952 and hustled her off to his studio lab for an emergency work session. The producer of *War of the Worlds* had just informed Gemora that the Martian created for the film would not work in the cramped farmhouse set and he had one evening to create a replacement. Father and child labored into the dawn hours and ferried a still soggy creature to the stage for shooting. The Martian upper torso was placed on a dolly with Charles half inside on his knees as he manipulated the arms. Prop men would pull the dolly through the scene as Diana worked the air pumps to create the realistic "throb" of veins. According to Diana, the fragile alien came very close to teetering over and blowing apart. Luckily, Gemora's talent and ingenuity carried off one of sci-fi's iconic moments (with no small assist from his girl Friday).

Poor health finally got the better of cinema's greatest gorilla man in 1961 when he passed away after another heart attack. One of his final gorilla appearances in *Phantom of the Rue Morgue* (1954) had found Charles weak and unable to do anything other than close-ups. All strenuous actions were performed by a stunt double.

When Bob Burns visited Charles around 1958 it was apparent that Gemora was excited about Bob's interest in him. "He said a few people had talked to him about making the *War of the Worlds* Martian suit ... but nobody had ever talked to him about doing the gorillas."

Gemora was a humble yet brilliantly creative mind whose talents were by no means limited to his gorilla suit mastery. He had an inventive streak that lead to numerous makeup and effects innovations that, according to Diana, were never properly accredited to him. Reflecting upon her father, Diana had this to say, "He lit the world for a brief starry period. He was blessed to be part of the Industry when raw talent was your only resume."

SUGGESTED FURTHER READING

Balducci, Anthony. *The Funny Parts: A History of Film Comedy Routines and Gags.* Jefferson, N.C.: McFarland, 2011.
Gott, Ted and Kathryn Weir. *Gorilla.* London: Reaktion Books, 2013.
Johnson, John. *Cheap Tricks and Class Acts: Special Effects, Makeup, and Stunts from the Films of the Fantastic Fifties.* Jefferson, N.C.: McFarland, 1996.
Klaw, Richard. *The Apes of Wrath.* San Francisco: Tachyon, 2013.
Soister, John T. *American Silent Horror, Science Fiction and Fantasy Feature Films.* Jefferson, N.C.: McFarland, 2012.

Gregory of Tours
(538–594)

Peter Dendle

At first glance it may seem out of place to include Gregory of Tours in a collection devoted to luminaries of Gothic and Horror fiction. The concept of "fiction" in any modern sense formed no part of the early medieval literary aesthetic, and what we now think of as Gothic and Horror would not see their earliest self-conscious inklings for well over a millennium. Gregory himself would no doubt be horrified to learn that in future ages his pious works might be read in a secular age, by an audience fascinated with the macabre. And yet, this is no less violence to Gregory's intentions, than that with which he himself read Virgil or the Old Testament: the evolution of readership and narrative expectations is an inescapable by-product of literary immortality.

Furthermore, even contextualized within his own period, I think a case can be made that Gregory was well aware of the artistic potential of what we now think of as "Gothic" and "Horror" elements in crafting a story to produce emotional impact and to invoke primordial questions of the human condition. In *Supernatural Horror in Literature* (1927), H.P. Lovecraft argued something similar with reference to ancient texts such as the Book of Enoch: "the horror-tale is as old as human thought and speech themselves."

At the opening of Horace Walpole's *The Castle of Otranto* (1764), a giant helmet has fallen out of nowhere and crushed the prince; at its conclusion, the colossus himself smashes into the castle to ensure a just and righteous conclusion to events. Not all contemporaries found these subtleties to their taste, but such injections of awesome power for the sake of supernatural retribution and public spectacle had long roots in medieval narratives of history and hagiography ("saints' lives"). To be sure, Gregory of Tours' mindset and literary strategies were not different in kind from other writers of his era.

Athanasius' *Life of St. Anthony*, Jerome's *Life of St. Hilarion*, and John Cassian's *Conferences* all deliver quirky, fantastic, cabalistic, and demonic passages that suggest a world of wonder and violence, a broken world swirling with dark forces and yet punctuated by the miraculous. Too many modern readers, however, have mistaken their carefully contrived narratives for descriptions of reality when visualizing life in Late Antiquity, or the early "Dark Ages."

The tableau that Gregory of Tours paints for his narrative backdrop is one of merciless treachery and misfortune. Swarms of locusts ravage crops, and the plague (or "plague of the groin," as Gregory usually refers to it) is a constant guest: "The blisters were white and firm without any softness, although they did produce a sharp pain. Once these blisters became ripe, if they popped and began to discharge, then [people's] clothes stuck to their bodies and the pain increased more severely," *VM* 272—for citations, see note on sources). The town of Vienne, according to Gregory, is shaken by earthquakes, and savage wolves overrun the city in packs, roaming through the streets (*HF* 149–50). Life is harsh and austere, and the cruelty of nature and of nobles are alike primal forces to be endured. A certain nobleman named Rauching, while taking his meals, regularly forces the serf attending him to hold a lighted candle pressed between his bare shins, "until the serf's legs were completely scorched." When one candle burned out, a new one would be lit. Gregory explains that Rauching "would be convulsed with merriment to watch the man weep" (*HF* 256). The embittered widow of Bishop Badegisil of Le Mans is given to having men's penises cut off (Gregory does not cite any particular reason, but simply says "on more than one occasion"), and "she burned the more secret parts of women's bodies with metal plates which she had made white-hot" (*HF* 471). Such Suetonian scenes of perverted aristocrats in their common recreations are, in the end, hard to distinguish from scenes of punitive torture: one man is placed on his back on the ground, "a block of wood was wedged behind his neck and then they beat him on the throat with another piece of wood until he died" (*HF* 363); on another occasion, an early Christian martyr Gregory describes is forced to suffer rebaptism under the heretical Arian sect: as she is immersed in the font against her will, the water turns blood red because her menstrual flow begins, and then she is made to suffer "the rack, the flames, and the pincers" (*HF* 107–8). The use of blood as a symbol, combined with its disarmingly intimate and physiological context as menstrual blood, is characteristic of Gregory's raw and compelling style.

Indeed, the human body in early medieval hagiography is often a wounded, diseased, or deformed locus of activity and attention. It is visceral and grossly biological. Demons and illness are essentially one, and the body is the site of cosmic battles between the divine and the demonic: one man bleeds a fever out through his nose (*LF* 14), a boy bleeds out his blindness itself through his eyes (*LF* 97), and another vomits forth his indwelling demon in a bloody soup (*VJ* 191). A deaf and mute man named Theodomund, who prays daily to St. Martin, finds himself cured one day most suddenly and most messily: "a stream of blood and filth flowed from his mouth. He spit it on the ground and then began to moan loudly and to cough up some unfamiliar bloody globs; as a result it was thought that someone was cutting his throat with a sword. The putrefaction hung from his mouth like bloody strings" (*VM* 209). Miraculous cures are not necessarily any more glamorous or sublime than the illness itself.

Compared with modern sentiments concerning religion and spirituality, early medieval Christianity may seem strikingly cold and comfortless, and—even within that context—Gregory's particular brand of Christian comfort is especially grim. This is a Christianity in which the saints can be as violent as the oppressive nobles, and both of them come across as capricious as the gods of Greece and Rome. Employing a fairly circuitous means of communication, Saint Nicetius appears in a dream to a certain man, telling him to warn the bishop Priscus that the bishop must mend his erring ways. The man passes the message on to a deacon, asking him to deliver the message instead. When that careless deacon neglects to fulfill this promise, Nicetius appears to him directly that night in a dream, and "began to hit him in the throat with clenched fists" (*HF* 232). Note that we are not yet in a time when dreams are considered expressions of the subconscious mind: Gregory and his readers would have taken this dream appearance as an actual visit by the saint.

The Earth, for Gregory, is alive with portents and spiritual forces. Some are simple parables: a merchant who refuses to give alms to a poor man finds his entire cargo of food turned to stone (Gregory himself claims to have seen the stone dates and olives from the miser's inventory). Another man—a sinner of some sort, Gregory is certain, though no particular crimes are mentioned—prays with feigned piety at a saint's shrine, and there takes such a fever that smoke eventually pours from his body, his limbs turn black, and he dies with an intolerable stench (*VJ* 175). A treacherous priest goes to the lavatory, and "while he was occupied in emptying his bowels he lost his soul instead" (*HF* 135). A lamp, having broken off from the cord suspending it in front of the tomb of innocent and wrongly slain Queen Galswintha, penetrates into the stone floor, and remains there, embedded to its midpoint (*HF* 222).

Other wonders are harder to interpret morally. Two islands are consumed entirely by fire falling from the sky, and a large pond full of fish on another island, off the coast of Brittany, is turned to blood and lapped at by dogs and birds (*HF* 455). Blood pours forth from a loaf of bread broken in two (*HF* 296). Sometimes, in Gregory's cosmos, these portents signify divine pleasure (or displeasure), injustice, or ominous things to come; much of the time they do not seem to signify anything in particular at all. In 587, Gregory records, a number of people discover in their homes vessels "inscribed with unknown characters which could not be erased or scraped off however hard they tried," though nothing further is ever really made of this (*HF* 483).

Students of the early Middle Ages will not find these anecdotes and narrative strategies unfamiliar. They are the stock in trade of an entire era of Western literary history, centuries before the playful romances of the High Middle Ages or other (ostensibly) more readerly genres. Romantic writers of the eighteenth and nineteenth centuries loved to hearken back to the Middle Ages as a brooding, gloomy time, and we are perhaps still too inclined to take Gregory and other early medieval writers' portrayal of a hostile and chaotic world at face value.

We are, in any event, clearly in the presence of a writer deliberately selecting facts, and describing them with calculated craftsmanship, for inclusion in his monumental *History of the Franks* and in his hagiography. His portrayal creates an energized emotional atmosphere pitched such that the humble miracles of local saints shine forth most brilliantly, and such that the misery of the human condition makes individual sufferers most obligingly beholden to their divine intercessors for the occasional cure or release from prison. Gregory surely believed much of what he put down was true, just as modern urban legends proliferate in a dynamic and cohesive society in which the incidents always happened to a friend, or a friend of a friend, and in which the social bonding itself is probably more important to most people than the historical accuracy of the original events. The fact that so much of what Gregory weaves into his sober and ascetic landscape—almost Beckett-like in its minimalism—draws from elements we readily recognize as the building blocks of Gothic and Horror fiction, I believe, warrants his inclusion in this august rogues' gallery of Lost Souls.

Note on the sources: Gregory's *History of the Franks* (*HF*) here refers to the translation of Lewis Thorpe (Penguin, 1974). References to the *Miracles of Julian* (*VJ*) and to the *Miracles of Martin* (*VM*) both cite translations in Raymond Van Dam, *Saints and Their Miracles in Late Antique Gaul* (Princeton University Press, 1993). *GM* refers to Raymond Van Dam's translation of the *Glory of the Martyrs* (Liverpool University Press, 1988), and *LF* refers to Edward James' translation of *Life of the Fathers* (Liverpool, 1985).]

SUGGESTED FURTHER READING

Murray, Alexander C. *A Companion to Gregory of Tours*. Leiden: Brill, 2015.
Murray, Alexander C. *Gregory of Tours: The Merovingians*. Plymouth: Broadview, 2006.
van Dam, Raymond (trans). *Glory of the Martyrs*. Liverpool University Press, 1985.
van Dam, Raymond (trans). *Saints and Their Miracles in Late Medieval Gaul*. Princeton University Press, 1993.

Victor Halperin
(1895–1983)

Murray Leeder

Just before the Halloween of 2014, the website The Dissolve published a list of "The 30 Best American Independent Horror Films," featuring contributions from established online film journalists like Nathan Rabin, Keith Phipps and Matt Singer. The list contained many great films, but nothing earlier than *Carnival of Souls* (1962). The implicit temporalization of the list speaks to the persistent idea of the 1960s as the cradle of American independent filmmaking, horror films included, which excludes and ignores earlier American independent horror directors. Chief among these is Victor Halperin.

Born in Chicago in 1895, Victor Hugo Halperin directed seventeen movies, including a slate of apparently lost silent features. The film that established Halperin's place in the history of horror was *White Zombie* (1932). Few subgenres are so neatly traceable back to a single originating work, but *White Zombie* is almost indisputably the first zombie film. Short years earlier, "zombie" was not a word in the American vernacular. Journalist/explorer/occultist William Buehler Seabrook's sensationalistic travelogue of Haiti, *The Magic Island*, told of "zombies," soulless reanimated corpses who operated as servants and slaves. That was in 1929, and in 1932, Halperin and his co-producer brother Edward saw an opportunity. Telling the story of a cruel voodoo-wielding sugar mill owner and his unholy plans for a beautiful young white woman, *White Zombie* is an impressive-looking independent film since the Halperins leased space at Universal Studios and were able to reuse props from horror classics like *The Hunchback of Notre Dame* (1923), *The Cat and the Canary* (1927), *Frankenstein* (1931) and *Dracula* (1931). For a pittance, they also hired *Dracula*'s star, the great Bela Lugosi, cast as the memorably named Murder Legendre—*White Zombie* makes even stronger use of Lugosi's piercing stare than *Dracula* did. Despite lukewarm reviews, *White Zombie* was profitable and has gone on to be considered a horror classic. Its eerie, still ambience comparing positively even to Val Lewton's *I Walked with a Zombie* (1943), a film which, it is fair to say, would not exist without *White Zombie*. Replete with gorgeous matte work, interesting dissolves, wipes, superimpositions, split screens and instances of rack focusing, as well as the clever interplay of sound and silence, *White Zombie* rivals *Dr. Jekyll and Mr. Hyde* (1931) as the most formally inventive horror film of its period. It also provides, if not quite a coherent critique of colonialism and American foreign policy in the Caribbean, at least a narrative intriguingly aware of greed and exploitation and empire. Having long since fallen out of copyright, *White Zombie* exists in a wide array of DVD releases, mostly low quality; viewers are commended to check out the remastered 2013 release from Kino.

White Zombie's success led the Halperin brothers to a contract at Paramount, where they made a film that far fewer remember today, titled *Supernatural* (1933). *Supernatural* is an odd beast, part fake spiritualist melodrama, part ghost possession-themed horror film, with a dash of a mad scientist movie. It also sports an improbable cast including Carole Lombard and Randolph Scott. Lombard plays Roma Courtney, an heiress who becomes the target of shady medium Paul Bavian (Allan Dinehart) after the death of her twin brother; meanwhile, Bavian's ex-partner, multiple murderess Ruth Rogen (Vivienne Osborne), agrees to donate her body to science after her execution but the strange electrical experiments performed on the corpse frees her spirit to possess Roma. Films debunking spiritualism were numerous in the '20s and '30s, from *Spiritualism Exposed* (1926) to *Palmy Days* (1931) to *Mystic Circle Murder* (1938), but *Supernatural*'s mix of Bavian fakery and Roma's genuine possession by Ruth Rogen makes for a very strange lesson. Nevertheless, the film is full of compelling sequences, including several intricate séance sequences that anticipate *Night of the Demon* (1957) and the unnerving scene where Bavian poisons his nosy landlady. The most compelling scene of all may be the pre-séance sequence of Bavian rigging the environment with his trickery—like some of the best scenes in *White Zombie*, it plays out almost silently. In contrast with the cultish appeal of *White Zombie*, *Supernatural* is all but forgotten and has barely warranted a DVD release; it has also received little scholarship, in part because it fits so uncertainly into the ghost-light "Golden Age of Horror" of the early 1930s. Nevertheless, it will reward those who seek it out.

The third (and third least interesting) Victor Halperin-directed horror film, *Revolt of the Zombies* (1936), saw the Halperin brothers returning to the zombie theme that gave them such success a half-decade earlier. It even resorted to reusing footage from *White Zombie* (the persistent superimpositions of Lugosi's eyes to signify hypnotic control). It was conceived of as a sequel to *White Zombie* but legal problems prevented it being marketed as such. In many ways, *Revolt of the Zombies* seems like a disguised remake, swapping Haiti for Cambodia as the requisite colonial setting, and Armand Loque (Dean Jagger) replacing Murder Legendre as the white villain who learns the secrets of zombification. It is a dreary film, its low budget seams showing everywhere, and without the sense of mood and experimentation to overcome these limitations the way *White Zombie* did. The use of nearly silent sequences, so transfixing in *White Zombie*, is perplexing and trying in *Revolt of the Zombies*. Nonetheless, it is not without interest, at least because it is the first film to tether zombies and war together (including the strange notion of Cambodian zombies fighting on the eastern front in World War I) and the first to conceive of zombies as a mass scale, potentially apocalyptic force (including paranoia that they might "wipe out the white race"). Perhaps more than any early zombie film, it anticipates that other mode of zombie film inaugurated by George A. Romero's *Night of the Living Dead* (1968). *Revolt of the Zombies*, out of copyright, is a mainstay of inexpensive horror film collections such as those from Treeline Films; perhaps a proper restored version would prove revelatory.

The Halperin brothers' production partnership ended with *Revolt of the Zombies,* and Victor Halperin, subsequently, directed a number of other programmers, ranging from the antiracist KKK drama *Nation Aflame* (1937) to the mad scientist movie *Torture Ship* (1939). He made his last film, *Girls' Town* in 1942, though he lived another forty years. Later interviews show that Halperin may not only have been the progenitor of the American independent horror director, but also the first horror film apostate. In 1978, he told an interviewer, "I don't believe in fear, violence, and horror, so why traffic in them [?] [...] The time arrived in my experience when I refused to supply the inordinate desire for that kind of entertainment." His wife later told Gary D. Rhodes, researching his exhaustive 2001 book about *White Zombie*, that Victor had stated, "If I had known then what I do now, I wouldn't have made a single [horror film.]" It is a hard thing to comprehend: having made a classic film like *White Zombie* and being *ashamed* of it. However little he might have liked it, though, his place in the history of horror is secure.

SUGGESTED FURTHER READING

Bishop, Kyle William. "The Sub-Subaltern Monster: Imperialist Hegemony and the Cinematic Voodoo Zombie." *The Journal of American Culture* 32.2 (June 2008): 141–52.

Mahoney, Phillip. "Mass Psychology and the Analysis of the Zombie: From Suggestion to Contagion." In *Generation Zombie: Essays on the Living Dead in Modern Culture.* Eds. Stephanie Boluk and Wylie Lenz. Jefferson, NC: McFarland, 2011. 113–129.

Rhodes, Gary D. *White Zombie: Anatomy of a Horror Film.* Jefferson, NC: McFarland, 2001.

Williams, Tony. "*White Zombie*: Haitian Horror." *Jump Cut* 28 (April 1983): 18–20.

Edward Jerningham
(1737-1812)

PETER N. LINDFIELD *and*
DALE TOWNSHEND

Edward Jerningham, the minor but extraordinarily prolific eighteenth-century poet, playwright, architect, translator, biographer, and polemical theologian, was born at Costessey (or "Cossey") Hall, Norfolk, to a wealthy, landed Catholic family with numerous connections to both the English and French Royal courts. Moving as a boy with his parents to Cambrai in the North of France, the young Jerningham was schooled in theology and the humanities at the English College, a Catholic seminary in Douai, subsequently finishing off his education at St. Gregory's College in Paris. For all his family's august political and religious affiliations, Jerningham became enamored of the Enlightenment philosophy of Voltaire and the Revolutionary principles of Rousseau; as his biographer Jules Smith in the *Oxford Dictionary of National Biography* (2004-15) notes, Jerningham converted to Anglicanism in the 1790s, and remained an ardent defender of Protestantism until his death. Returning to England in 1761, the now London-based Jerningham became extremely well connected with the literary, political, and cultural luminaries of his day, regularly interacting and corresponding with such seminal eighteenth-century figures as the Earl of Chesterfield, William Mason, James Boswell, Joseph Sheridan, David Garrick, Joseph Warton, the Countess of Ailesbury, Frances Burney, Elizabeth Montagu, Helen Maria Williams, Edmund Burke, and even the Prince of Wales. Having met him in Paris in 1765, Jerningham seems to have perceived in Horace Walpole, the major "architect" of the Gothic aesthetic in eighteenth-century Britain, a life-long friend, mentor, and even literary patron. Several letters passed between the two, Jerningham dedicated both *The Swedish Curate, A Poem* (1773) and a 1786 edition of *The Rise and Progress of Scandinavian Poetry: A Poem in Two*

Parts (1784) to Walpole, and Walpole himself, who kept several of Jerningham's literary works in his library at Strawberry Hill and attended his play *The Siege of Berwick: A Tragedy* in Covent Garden in 1793, seems to have regarded him as "a charming man."

Jerningham's literary endeavors were nothing if not ambitious, and in addition to the poems and play listed, his other published works include the individually published poems *The Magdalens* (1763), *The Nun* (1764), *An Elegy Written Among the Ruins of an Abbey* (1765), *Il Latte* (1767), *The Deserter* (1770), *The Funeral of Arabert, Monk of La Trappe* (1771), *Honoria, or, The Day of All Souls* (1782), *Lines Written in the Album, at Cossey-Hall, Norfolk* (1786), *Enthusiasm* (1789), *The Shakespeare Gallery* (1791), *Stone Henge* (1792), *Abelard to Eloisa* (1792) and *The Old Bard's Farewell* (1811); the plays *The Welch Heiress* (1795) and *The Peckham Frolic; or, Nell Gwyn* (1799); theological studies such as *Select Sermons Translated from the French of Bossuet* (1800) and *The Mild Tenour [sic] of Christianity* (1803); biographies such as *Biographical Sketches of Henrietta Duchess of Orleans and Louis of Bourbon Prince Condé* (1799); and such miscellaneous pieces of cultural commentary as *Lines on a Late Resignation [that of Sir Joshua Reynolds] at the Royal Academy* (1790). Together with a number of shorter pieces, Jerningham self-anthologized and republished some of his longer poems in such collections as *Poems on Various Subjects* (1767), *Poems* (1774), and *Fugitive Poetical Pieces* (1778), and contributed two shorter pieces to *The British Album*, the important anthology of Della Cruscan poetry that was published in 1790. Though seldom if ever in receipt of critical recognition and approval, Edward Jerningham was, by all accounts, a well-known and frequently read and cited poet in eighteenth-century England: his collected *Poems*, for instance, ran to at least eight editions, and he was certainly known to such later Romantic poets such as Lord Byron, who recalled fond memories of him in his Postscript to his otherwise deeply excoriating *English Bards and Scotch Reviewers* in 1809.

While Jerningham appears officially to have cast off the Catholic faith of his family in favor of the reformed Protestant religion only later in life, much of his literary work that pre-dates the 1790s indicates that his reservations with Catholicism had much older roots. Indeed, together with his Gothic-architectural pursuits at Costessey Hall and Stafford Castle, it is Jerningham's often startling poetic recourse to what we now take to be the conventions of "Gothic" writing in order to express his grave disaffection with Catholic faith and practice that renders him a crucial but hitherto overlooked figure in the history of the eighteenth-century Gothic Revival. In *The Magdalens* of 1763, for instance, Jerningham continued to explore the theme of the stifling effects of conventual life upon young women that he had first treated in his poem *The Nunnery* (1762) through a direct reworking of Alexander Pope's "Eloisa to Abelard" (1717), the influential verse epistle in which the Catholic Pope, albeit more subtly, had treated similar concerns. In *The Magdalens*, Jerningham figures the nuns' devotion to their faith as what he describes as a "prostituted Love," with the persona's particularly blighted impressions of monastic existence focusing upon the ways in which the Catholic demand for celibacy condemns its devotees to a death-like existence of life-long yearning and thwarted desire. In *The Nun* of the following year, Jerningham returned to the same theme, amplifying the already Gothic undertones to his depictions of the veritable "live burial" of Catholic nuns and monks in convents, nunneries, and monasteries through the inclusion of a tyrannical Abbess who "rules the Cloister with an Iron Rod," a figure not unlike that of the cruel and hypocritical Prioress of St. Clare in Matthew Lewis's *The Monk* (1796), or, indeed, the eponymous character of W. H. Ireland's vehemently anti–Catholic Gothic romance, *The Abbess* (1799). As an older nun who seeks to warn the young novice who has recently entered the convent of the horrors and terrors that await her there, the persona of *The Nun* makes strategic use of Gothic diction and convention throughout the poem, variously describing the nunnery as "this Dome of Misery," "a dreadful Void," a "chearless [*sic*] Cell," and a "gloomy Grotto," one in which a "Terror-shedding Grate" stands between the novice's future happiness and "This cloyster'd Scene in all its Horror drest." As Anna Seward observed of the poem in 1782, "Mr. Jerningham, though a Roman Catholic, has ably combated monastic enthusiasm, in his ingenious Poem, The Nun." In *An Elegy Written Among the Ruins of An Abbey* (1765), Jerningham's anti–Catholic stance would assume even greater Gothic inflection. Reworking Thomas Gray's *Elegy Written in a Country Churchyard* (1751), a poem that, like Pope's "Eloisa to Abelard," Jerningham would cite, appropriate, and even plagiarize throughout the remainder of his literary career, the persona describes a visit to the ruins of an abbey, a once-thriving community of Catholics destroyed by Henry VIII's Dissolution of the Monasteries of the sixteenth century. Regarding, like many eighteenth-century poems written about, in, and to ruined abbeys, the process of Reformation as the felicitous vanquishing of the powers of darkness and superstition with the reason and Enlightenment of Protestantism, Jerningham's *An Elegy Written Among the Ruins of An Abbey* assumes a significantly darker tone as the persona relates "A Terror-breathing Tale" of a pack of wolves that rushes into the ruin so as to devour the corpse of the abbey's founder, one Rufus, that lies buried within:

> From where yon Mountain shades the dreary Plain,
> Attracted by the Scent of human Blood,
> A Troop of Wolves voracious scour'd amain,
> And at this Charnel Vault required their Food:

When, horrid to relate! they burst the Tomb,
And swift descending to the deepest Shade,
Up-tore the shrouded Tenant from its Womb,
And o'er the mangled Corse relentless prey'd.

Interior of St. Augustine's Chapel, Costessey Hall, before 1920 (courtesy Brian Gage).

We see here, in a poem published in the same year in which Walpole subtitled the second edition of *The Castle of Otranto* as "*A Gothic Story,*" a full-blown sense of horror, one that, as the received literary-historical narrative goes, only really came into its own in the "horrid" novels of the 1790s. Although there is nothing inherently "Gothic" about the expression of anti–Catholic sentiment, the language in which Jerningham frames his distaste is continuously couched in the paraphernalia of horror, terror, spectrality, and Catholic excess, to the extent that several of his works stand as poignant examples of what Diane Long Hoeveler in *The Gothic Ideology: Religious Hysteria and Anti-Catholicism in British Popular Fiction, 1780-1880* (2014) has recently

John Chessell Buckler, *Detail of Costessey Hall, Norfolk, showing the exterior of Edward Jerningham's Catholic Chapel, St. Augustine's* (1831), pen and brown ink with watercolor over graphite on slightly textured, thick, beige wove paper, B1975.2.363 (Yale Center for British Art, Paul Mellon Collection).

outlined as "The Gothic Ideology" of her study's title: the anti–Catholic discourse that is inseparable from the established conventions of much eighteenth and nineteenth-century Gothic writing.

Like Walpole, the figure on whom he clearly based much of his own work, Jerningham's interest in the "Gothic" was more than simply a literary one. Seemingly inspired by Walpole's work at Strawberry Hill, Jerningham also turned his hand to Gothic architecture. His architectural endeavors in the Gothic style most noticeably manifested themselves at his family home, Costessey Hall, where he created a Perpendicular-style Catholic chapel for his brother, George William Stafford Jerningham (1771–1851), seventh Baronet, from 1824 eighth Baron Stafford, in 1809. Concentrating upon the window tracery, reredos paneling, and quadripartite vaulting, the chapel is a mixture of elaborate carving and plain wall space, and it is cast as a freestanding structure off of the fifteenth-century house. Composed of eight bays, it is often compared with King's College Chapel, Cambridge; however, the structure and vaulting are less ostentatious, and show, instead, an awareness of less extraordinary Gothic rib-vaulted medieval churches. Continuing his clear preference for Gothic design, Jerningham remodeled the Catholic Chapel at Stafford in the same mode, and from 1810 to 1815 he began to rebuild Stafford Castle. Despite being outshone in form and scale by the Bucklers' subsequent redevelopment of Costessey in 1826, who converted the Jerninghams' seat into a sprawling Gothic-Elizabethan pile with details modeled in part upon King's College Chapel, Edward Jerningham's interest in, and clear understanding of, the Gothic past was, like Walpole's, manifest in multiple fields. The subject of at least one of Jerningham's own poems, Costessey Hall's literary associations would be intensified when, after the death of Edward Jerningham, John Polidori, physician to Lord Byron and the future author of *The Vampyre: A Tale* (1819), ingratiated himself with Sir George Jerningham and his family upon his return to England from the Continent in 1817. Serving at Costessey as tutor of Italian to the Jerninghams' eldest daughter, Charlotte, Polidori seems to have fallen in love with his student.

To be sure, Edward Jerningham was not critically admired in his day. William Gifford referred to his as "sniveling Jerningham" in *The Baviad* (1791), T. J. Mathias dismissed poetry of Jerningham and his ilk as little more than witless rambling in *The Pursuits of Literature* (1798), while, in 1812, Henry Crabb Robinson opined that Jerningham and his literary works were "already forgotten." While this was almost certainly the case, it is worth returning to Jerningham as a crucial but overlooked figure, a veritable "lost soul" of the literary and architectural Gothic Revival in eighteenth-century Britain. If, as is so frequently argued, the Gothic literary mode did, indeed, grow out of the Graveyard verse of the 1740s, it is Edward Jerningham who was a key mediating factor in this process. Tirelessly rewriting versions of

Gray's famous "Elegy," and fusing with it the theme of thwarted Catholic desire figured in Pope's "Eloisa to Abelard," Jerningham's verse, like his architectural pursuits, indicates his forgotten role in, and engagement with, the multi-faceted Gothic mode in Georgian Britain.

SUGGESTED FURTHER READING

Bettany, Lewis, ed. *Edward Jerningham and His Friends: A Series of Eighteenth-Century Letters*. London: Chatto & Windus, 1919.

Eastlake, Charles Locke. *A History of the Gothic Revival*. London: Longmans, Green & Co., 1872.

Hoeveler, Diane Long. *The Gothic Ideology: Religious Hysteria and Anti-Catholicism in British Popular Fiction, 1780–1880*. Cardiff, UK: University of Wales Press, 2014.

Shepard, Mary B. "'Our Fine Gothic Magnificence': The Nineteenth-Century Chapel at Costessey Hall (Norfolk) and Its Medieval Glazing." *Journal of the Society of Architectural Historians* 54.2 (1995): 186–207.

Thomas, Sophie. "Ruin Nation: Ruins and Fragments in Eighteenth-Century England." *Eighteenth-Century Life* 38.3 (2014): 130–136.

Jerome K. Jerome
(1859-1927)

WILLIAM HUGHES

Jerome Klapka (originally Clapp) Jerome was something of a dilettante enthusiast for the Gothic, his contribution to the genre resting primarily upon one slim volume, *Told After Supper* (1891). His life was as colorful and varied as his writings—he was, successively, an actor, a journalist, a teacher and editor: in this latter incarnation, as the co-editor and later sole editor of *The Idler* he was to publish several authors with undoubted Gothic leanings, including Robert Louis Stevenson, Marie Corelli, Arthur Conan Doyle, Rudyard Kipling and W. W. Jacobs. As a humorist in his own right, Jerome made his reputation with the essay collection *The Idle Thoughts of an Idle Fellow* (1886), followed three years later by the highly successful *Three Men in a Boat, to Say Nothing of the Dog* (1889). The sequel to the latter, *Three Men on the Bummel* (1900), which featured the same listless cast of three human characters but not the dog, was less successful, though his *Second Thoughts of an Idle Fellow* (1898) was well received and maintained Jerome's reputation as a writer of satire and witty dialogue. Despite its origins in London literary culture, his work was highly regarded in the United States, a country which he toured in 1908.

Told After Supper, though, is a neglected work worthy of notice and one which, had it been written by a Victorian author with a credible supernatural reputation—a writer of the status of Charles Dickens or Sheridan Le Fanu, for example—might well have achieved a canonical status both within and beyond academic appreciation of the genre. Jerome's Gothic is somewhat literary and allusive. Despite his strong evangelical background—his parents were non-Episcopalian Protestants from the English midlands, his father at one time serving the office of a lay preacher—the origins of his ghost stories do not draw on the religious tension of the time, nor the crisis of faith, nor even the contemporary and fashionable interest in psychical investigation that influenced the works of his near contemporaries Algernon Blackwood and E. F. Benson. Rather, the whole project that is *Told After Supper* mocks not merely the paradigm of short supernatural fiction but also the almost ritualized telling of such tales at a certain time of year and within the curtilage of certain significant interior spaces.

The framing of the volume is both elaborate and wittily droll, and the irony begins with a title page that depicts a pipe-smoking skull wearing an eye patch within a hatchment-like diamond of bones. Beyond this, there is a perceptible Dickensian edge—a writer's, rather than a reader's, knowingness—to the introductory words of Jerome's little volume. Beneath a shrouded ghost whose garments bear the words "Our Ghost Party," the introduction proclaims, teasingly:

> It was Christmas Eve.
> I begin this way, because it is the proper, orthodox, respectable way to begin, and I have been brought up in a proper, orthodox, respectable way, and taught to always do the proper, orthodox, respectable thing; and the habit clings to me [1].

Indeed, so orthodox is Jerome's narrative that almost every cliché of the British ghost story is progressively exposed as the as the narrator explicitly parades a cast derived from a hypothetical "Ghostland" within the customary arenas of haunted bedrooms, country houses and deserted abbeys. These tales are framed, as the introductory gesture suggests, by the cultural ritual of *telling* ghost stories on Christmas Eve, for "Whenever five or six English-speaking people meet round a fire on Christmas Eve, they start telling each other ghost stories" (15–16). The unquiet spirits of the dead, it might be added, have a fondness for that particular night, for "the average orthodox ghost does his one turn a year, on Christmas Eve, and is satisfied" (14). The living and the dead, however, coincide not in the spiritual significance of the night in question but rather in its convivial associations. The night before Christmas, as the narrator reminds us, is conventionally distinguished by the consumption of considerable quantities of whiskey punch as well as the recollection of supernatural incidents which apparently happened to a relative, a friend or some other person not present.

Though he appears to promise those classic historic and histrionic ghost stories which feature "the murdered Barons, the crime-stained Countesses, and the Earls who came over with the conqueror, and assassinated their relatives, and died raving mad," Jerome's narrator actually regales the readers with a range of somewhat more domestic narratives, specifically those of a weeping, faithful ghost (who became rather boring to the family he troubled); the ghost of a miser who returned (but who *didn't* trouble to lead the householder to the hoard of gold reputedly secreted in the building; and the ghost of music-hating man who apparently once killed a Yuletide carol singer with a lump of coal. Interspersed with these well-crafted but heavily ironic stories, told by the increasingly inebriated members of a jovial male gathering on Christmas Eve, are a number of interludes, where apparently compelling ghost stories are told by a doctor and a curate, the specific details of which are forgotten by the progressively drunken narrator.

He, himself, attempts to crown the volume by spending the night in a haunted chamber which is the subject of one of the tales in the collection. In the so-called "Blue Chamber" he apparently meets the ghost of the music-hating ghost, whom he befriends, and whom he attempts to accompany home after the crowing of the cockerel signals the conventional end of the Christmas Eve vigil. In the latter action, unfortunately, he is detected by the local policeman, who comments gruffly upon the narrator's lack of trousers and escorts him back to his uncle's house. The reader, needless to say, is left to make up his or her own mind regarding the credibility of this narrative, which is styled as the only true ghost story in the collection.

Jerome's contribution to the ghost-story genre is a small one, but it is by no means insignificant. His literary perceptiveness is in many respects comparable to that of Jane Austen or Thomas Love Peacock, and his ironic observations on the telling and content of ghost stories has the added benefit of brevity. *Told After Supper* is a volume whose contents may provide a lighter counterpart to the enjoyable but still solemn rituals of Christmas-Eve Ghost Storytelling in the tradition of M. R. James.

SUGGESTED FURTHER READING

Briggs, Julia. *Night Visitors: The Rise and Fall of the English Ghost Story*. London: Faber, 1977.

Freeman, Nick. "Ghost Stories." In *The Encyclopedia of the Gothic*, vol. 2, eds. William Hughes, David Punter and Andrew Smith. Chichester: Blackwell, 2013, pp. 277–281.

Jerome, Jerome Klapka. *Told After Supper*, retitled *After Supper Ghost Stories*. Stroud: Alan Sutton, 1985.

McQuilland, Louis J. "Jerome Klapka Jerome." *The Bookman* (September 1926), pp. 282–284.

Smith, Andrew. *The Ghost Story, 1840–1920: A Cultural History*. Manchester: Manchester University Press, 2010.

Skelton Knaggs
(1911–1955)

JOHN EXSHAW

Had Skelton Knaggs been born fifty years later, it seems fair to suggest that not only would Peter Jackson, director of *The Lord of the Rings* trilogy (2001-2003), have made a substantial saving on his special-effects budget, but that Andy Serkis, the actor who played Gollum in Jackson's *magnum opus*, would still be shuffling round the casting suites of Wardour Street, waiting for his big break. A few hair extensions and a bucket of slime would have been more than sufficient to transform the stunted, pock-marked, and spectacularly ugly British character actor into Gollum, a character whose dual nature—good Sméagol, bad Gollum—pretty much covered the emotional extremes required of Knaggs during his largely overlooked Hollywood career.

Unfortunately, no such career-defining role was ever offered to Knaggs, nor does his 33-film résumé contain the sort of undisputed classic which might provide at least a flicker of recognition among mainstream viewers—if not of the man himself, then at least of the film in question. Instead, as even a cursory internet search will demonstrate, he remains a shiversome delight known to only the most committed movie hounds and incurable insomniacs, as well as the very definition of a "lost soul," both in the sense intended in the title of this collection of essays and in what little can be gleaned, or inferred, from his real life. Thomas Hobbes could not have had Skelton Knaggs in mind when he coined the phrase, "nasty, brutish, and short," but it does, nonetheless, provide a largely accurate description not only of Knaggs' screen persona but also the seemingly grim circumstances of his life—plagued by ill-health from childhood, typecast throughout a career that can hardly be described as successful, and dead of cirrhosis of the liver at the age of 43.

Cursed and blessed with a face only a Hogarth or Goya could have loved, Skelton Barnaby Knaggs tended to be cast in two types of parts. The first may

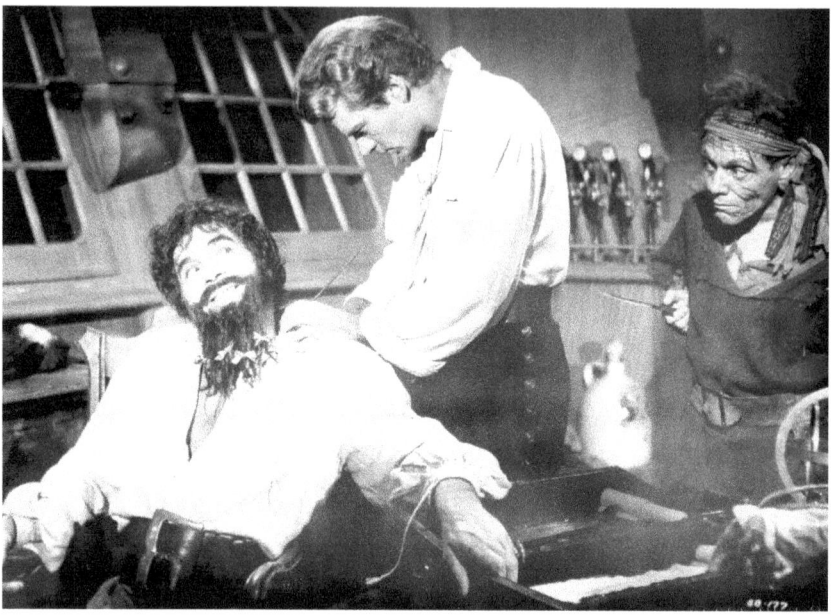

Skelton Knaggs, right, Robert Newton, left, and Keith Andes, center, in *Blackbeard, the Pirate* (1952) (collection of John Exshaw).

be referred to as his flat cap roles, in which he would usually be glimpsed as working-class characters: newsagent, costermonger, taxi driver, waiter, tinware salesman, fish-and-chips vendor, etc. So frequently did Knaggs appear in a flat cap, and so strongly is that particular item of headgear associated with the north of England, that it is legitimate to wonder if the actor chose to wear one at every available opportunity as a nod to his own Yorkshire background. Roles in this vein included such films as *South Riding* (1938, the only occasion he played a Yorkshireman), *The Lodger, The Invisible Man's Revenge, None but the Lonely Heart* (all 1944), *The Picture of Dorian Gray* (1945), and *Night and Day* (1946). The second type of part may be termed his wig roles. Set in either the 17th or 18th centuries, these were the period pieces for which he was particularly well-suited and which allowed him to play more colorful characters: an effeminate manservant in *Bedlam* (1946, a film inspired by, and dedicated to, William Hogarth), a denizen of a den of thieves in *Forever Amber* (1947), a conniving sea-dog in *Blackbeard, the Pirate* (1952), a condemned prisoner in *Botany Bay* (1952), an Italian creditor in *Casanova's Big Night* (1954), and a smuggler in *Moonfleet* (1955).

Knaggs' appearances tended to be brief, often amounting to no more than a few lines in one scene. *Botany Bay*, for example, opens with an uncredited Knaggs chalking an impressionistic skull on the wall of a cell in Newgate

Prison (a most appropriate image, given the actor's own death's head countenance). After aiming a few sarcastic remarks at an officer who enters to post a proclamation, Knaggs reads out the names of those prisoners whose sentences have been commuted to transportation. Knaggs' character is not on the list, and so he will be hanged. The film moves blithely on.... Considering that *Botany Bay* was made two years before Knaggs' death, it is sobering to consider how little things had changed in the 14 years since his similarly striking (and also uncredited) appearance in the opening sequence of Michael Powell's *The Spy in Black* (1939), in which his German naval orderly doggedly persists in delivering an order to U–boat commander, Captain Hardt (Conrad Veidt). His task achieved, the film continues; needless to add, without Knaggs.

The films for which Knaggs has posthumously received his small measure of retrospective renown include *House of Dracula* (1945), *Terror by Night* (1946), and two low-budget Dick Tracy features, *Dick Tracy vs. Cueball* and *Dick Tracy Meets Gruesome* (1946 and 1947, respectively). In the first of these, Knaggs is seen at his most physically repulsive, sporting a sickly sheen and lank hair as Steinmuhl, a whining malcontent constantly challenging the authority of Lionel Atwill's Inspector Holtz, before leading the traditional villagers' march on the domain of the mad scientist. In the second, Knaggs is a flat cap-wearing assassin who tries to kick Basil Rathbone's Sherlock Holmes off the London-to-Edinburgh train. "The guard in the van—dead. I had to kill him," he later informs his employer with a disturbingly off-hand, supercilious relish. Knaggs' exaggerated features and broad manner of acting ensured he fitted naturally into the cartoon-based Dick Tracy films, in both of which his sinister appearance was further enhanced by the addition of coke-bottle specs similar to those worn in his American début feature, *Torture Ship* (1939). He would later continue his connection with Chester Gould's characters by playing a henchman called the Creep in one of two episodes of the *Dick Tracy* TV series in which he appeared between 1951 and 1952.

Distinctive and memorable though he was in the afore-mentioned films, the roles themselves amounted to little more than notable bit parts, and it remains a mildly astonishing fact that only once in his entire career did Knaggs play a proper supporting role in which his character is integrated into the film from the beginning, remains relevant throughout, and is still there at the end. This was *Blackbeard, the Pirate*, directed by Raoul Walsh and starring Robert Newton at his eye-rolling, scenery-chewing, barnstorming best. Summoned by Blackbeard, Knaggs' Gilly, kitted out in a red headband, culottes, and a tatty red tunic, enters his cabin at a servile dog-trot, before surreptitiously trying to encourage the hero, a doctor forced to operate on Blackbeard, to twist his scalpel into the pirate's jugular. "Trust me!" he says later, "I hate his black heart!" After several setbacks, Gilly finally gets his wish when Blackbeard is overpowered by his men and, at Gilly's instruction, buried to his neck on a beach to be slowly drowned by the rising tide. In addition to the not-inconsiderable feat of standing his ground in the face of a full-throttle Newton, in *Blackbeard, the Pirate* Knaggs also demonstrated that he could make even an essentially grotesque character both likeable and sympathetic when the opportunity presented itself.

The high seas were also the setting for the most unusual film of Knaggs' career, *The Ghost Ship* (1943), the first of a three-film association with producer Val Lewton, whose unit at RKO studios was responsible for such classics as *Cat People* (1942), *I Walked with a Zombie* (1943), and *The Body Snatcher* (1945). Knaggs was cast as Paulo Lindstrom, a mute and illiterate sailor known as Finn, who acts as a Greek chorus to events unfolding on the S.S. Altair, as the new Third Officer discovers that the captain (played by Richard Dix), is gradually, and dangerously, losing his mind. Finn's thoughts, spoken in voice-over in a melancholy, almost other-worldly monotone, create a strange dissonance in what would otherwise be little more than a sub-*Sea Wolf* melodrama. In this film too, Knaggs' character stays the course, though only seen and heard infrequently, until the end when he plays a pivotal role in the dénouement. The sight of Skelton Knaggs (and his rather obvious stunt double) springing into action like a jungle cat is surprising enough in itself, but the abiding memory is of the unutterable sadness conveyed by the actor through facial expression alone, and to an almost uncomfortable degree.

How much of that sadness was Knaggs' own is impossible to know. How much, and to what extent, his alcoholism affected his career is also beyond knowing, but an average of less than two films a year over a nineteen-year period suggests its own answer. Studio records show that, at the time of *The Ghost Ship*, Knaggs was earning $400 for a six-day week, but it is hard to envisage many of his parts requiring more than two days' work, at most. Even allowing for the possibility of extra income from radio and theatre, it becomes difficult to see how he could have survived on acting alone. Considered in this light, the gaps in his personal history, together with the paucity of his professional employment, begin to fill with dark shadows—to the point where one cannot help wondering if the face Knaggs allowed us to see in *The Ghost Ship* was merely that of an actor inhabiting a role, or a glimpse into the depths of a truly lost soul?

SUGGESTED FURTHER READING

Bansak, Edmund G. *Fearing the Dark: The Val Lewton Career.* Jefferson, N.C.: McFarland, 2003.
Nemerov, Alexander. *Icons of Grief: Val Lewton's Home Front Pictures.* Berkeley: University of California Press, 2005.
Pitts, Michael R. *RKO Radio Pictures Horror, Science Fiction and Fantasy Films, 1929–1956.* Jefferson, N.C.: McFarland, 2015.
Senn, Bryan. *Golden Horrors: An Illustrated Critical Filmography of Terror Cinema, 1931–1939.* Jefferson, N.C.: McFarland, 2003.

Alfred Kubin
(1877–1959)

TRACY FAHEY

In the "oddest artist of all time" category, there are no shortage of entries. However, out of any possible line-up Alfred Kubin would definitely merit an honorable mention. An Austrian printmaker and draughtsman, Kubin produced a prolific stream of images that offer a vivid and nightmarish evocation of the feverish atmosphere of the *fin-de-siècle* and the dark sexuality of the unconscious explored by his contemporary Sigmund Freud. His highly emotive art falls somewhere between Symbolism and Expressionism. His 1926 autobiography, appropriately titled *Dämonen und Nachtgesichte* (*Demons and Night Visions*) offers an intimate view of an art riddled with personal symbolism: his strange and troubled life yielded an equally strange and troubled body of work.

Kubin's early life was beset with trauma that would have significant echoes in his later work. His mother died when he was ten, his father (whom he met for the first time at the age of two, and who he would later refer to in his autobiography as an "unwelcome character") married again, this time to his deceased wife's sister, who died in childbirth a year later. At the age of eleven, Kubin began a sexual relationship with an older, pregnant woman. His early drawings are a thinly veiled evocation of these intensely oedipal dramas, populated as they are by beatific mothers, pregnant seducers and hateful men; themes that were to occur repeatedly in his art. Sent away from home to pursue an apprenticeship, the unhappy nineteen-year-old Kubin resolved to commit suicide on his mother's grave, travelling home to Zell am See to do so. But his pistol misfired and, as he later put it in his autobiography; "I lacked the moral strength to try again. I became wretchedly sick." His apprenticeship was succeeded by an equally unhappy three-month period in the Austrian army in 1897, which led to a nervous breakdown. The panacea for this emotional distress was art. In 1898 Kubin finally began to study art in Munich, which was home to emerging Expressionist artists such as Kandinsky, Klee and Klinger who were exploring new and innovative ways to articulate emotional and spiritual ideas. Kubin was enthralled by this exciting work. In his autobiography, he describes his intense reaction to an exhibition of Max Klinger's etchings in Munich in 1883:

> I grew moody.... And now I was suddenly inundated with visions of pictures in black and white—it is impossible to describe what a thousand-fold treasure my imagination poured out before me. Quickly I left the theater, for the music and the mass of lights now disturbed me, and I wandered aimlessly in the dark streets, overcome and literally ravished by a dark power that conjured up before my mind strange creatures, houses, landscapes, grotesque and frightful situations [88].

These "strange creatures, houses, landscapes, grotesque and frightful situations" re-emerged in Kubin's drawings, a darker, more aggressive version of the creatures evoked in Klinger's prints. His first solo show in Munich in the winter of 1900–01 aroused shock due to the nature of his prints which featured scenes of copulation, decapitation and evisceration, and were populated by skeletons, impaled pregnant women, gigantic genitals and malformed humans and animals.

Kubin was interested in visualizing his own demons; however, literary monsters also fascinated him. An early engraving, *Das Grausen* (*The Horror*) of 1900–1901 is based on Poe's short story "A Descent Into the Maelstrom" (1841) but interpreted through Kubin's fantastical vision. *Das Grausen* presents the viewer with the spectacle of a helpless ship, whipped with waves, above which towers Kubin's original addition to the scene, a massive skull which fixes the shipwreck with one bulging, terrible eyeball. This interest in literature probably stemmed from his writing. Kubin's novel, *Die andere Seite* (*The Other Side*) which was published in 1908 offers another semi-autobiographical insights into his ideas about art and dreams. It describes the journey of an Austrian draughtsman through a kingdom of dreams where nightmares become reality. Kafka, who read it, was a fan, and elements of *The Other Side* can be discerned in his subsequent *The Castle* (1926). Several critics have related this fixation with fantasy literary worlds with the strange landscapes of his prints. As Assman puts it: "Alfred Kubin's art always suggests the 'other' side, an additional perspective. It is never one-dimensional, but always draws on various sources, masterfully combined by the artist in different layers of reality."

Kubin, despite the frenetic drama of his work, lived for most of his life in quiet seclusion in a castle in Zwickledt, where he was known colloquially by neighbors as "The Wizard of Zwickledt." This withdrawal from the world helped inure him from the diktats of the Nazi Party following the *Anschluss* in 1938, when his work, along with that of his compatriots Kirchner, Klee and Beckmann was officially declared to be "entartete Kunst" (degenerate art).

Kubin's art gripped the imagination of his contemporaries, and it continues to intrigue spectators. His work has been the subject of several large retrospective exhibitions, including a major show curated at the Neue Galerie New York in 2008 by Annegret Hoberg. Kubin's work forms an important bridge between Symbolist and Expressionist art. His mainly monochromatic prints are fiercely individualistic in character, but Kubin was interested in their potential to stimulate a sense of self-reflection in his audiences. As he put it in an interview of 1927: "Proper viewers, of the sort I would like to have, would not only look at my sheets with pleasure or critique but, as if moved at some secret level, would have to turn their attention to the rich images in the dark room of their own dreamy consciousness." His drawings and etchings also offer interesting visualizations of contemporary psychological ideas, especially in relation to the Oedipal dramas and infantile fears. Even today, Kubin's weird, fetishistic world of tortured and metamorphosed bodies, lascivious apes, pregnant monsters, and nightmarish crevasses remain as unforgettable and provocative as they are disturbing.

SUGGESTED FURTHER READING

Benfrey, Christopher. "The Shadow World of Alfred Kubin," *The New York Review of Books Daily*, November 18, 2014. http://www.nybooks.com/daily/2014/11/18/shadow-world-alfred-kubin/

Hoberg, Annegret, and Audrey Walen. *Alfred Kubin: Drawings 1897–1909*. New York: Prestel, 2008.

Horodisch, Abraham. *Alfred Kubin: Book Illustrator*. New York: Aldus, 1950.

Kubin, Alfred. *The Other Side*. Cambridge: Dedalus, 2014.

Francis Lathom
(1774–1832)

David Punter

Francis Lathom wrote a succession of Gothic novels in the years between 1795 and 1830, including *The Castle of Ollada* (1795), *The Midnight Bell* (1798), *Mystery* (1800), *The Mysterious Freebooter* (1806), *Italian Mysteries* (1820) and *Mystic Events* (1830). Until recently, the only one of these which had remained in the public consciousness was *The Midnight Bell*, which is one of the "horrid novels" named for their corrupting power by Jane Austen in *Northanger Abbey* (1817) in the past few years, however, a number of the others have been reprinted in new editions, and considerable effort has been made to uncover the facts of a strange life.

Before briefly looking at that life, however, it is worth noting that Lathom's literary career is typical of an often neglected fact about the work of many of the minor Gothicists of the period: namely, that they were not only, or even necessarily first and foremost, writers of Gothic. Lathom, for example, first made his name as a formidably precocious writer for the theatre, with plays like *All in a Bustle* (1795) and *Orlando and Seraphina* (1800); he also interspersed his Gothic fiction with novels which we might now call "comedies of manners," like *Men and Manners* (1799) and *Human Beings* (1807). We might now think of Lathom as something of a hack; he picked up on what were then fashionable genres and tried his hand at them, with predictably varying results.

It has recently been established that he was born in Rotterdam, the son of a highly successful merchant in the East India trade (which probably accounts for the independent means which he appeared to enjoy throughout his life), but his family returned to their native city of Norwich when he was still a child. It was in Norwich, at the Theatre Royal, that he had his first dramatic successes, and, according to James D. Jenkins, "by the age of twenty-one, [he] had become something of a minor local celebrity … the author of a Gothic romance and at least one popular comedy, Lathom was off to a brilliant start in his life and career." Quite what happened to this early promise remains uncertain; what we do know is that despite marriage and having four children, at some point in 1802 or 1803 he left Norwich to spend the remainder of his life peripatetically, mainly in the Highlands of Scotland, but with at least one attested visit to America.

The principal reason which has been advanced for this peculiar development is that Lathom was homosexual, and there appears to be plenty of evidence for this in his novel *Live and Learn* (1823), which has been referred to as the first gay novel written in English, concerning as it does an explicitly described friendship between two "beautiful youths." In fact, a number of myths have been woven around Lathom; while it seems probable that he was gay, and that this was the reason, for example, he was viciously cut out of his father's will, it was also asserted for many years that he was in fact the illegitimate child of an English nobleman, a claim which now seems without foundation.

Although, of course, such a foundation could well be in the way in which writings, Lathom's included, are so frequently "read back" into biography. In his Gothic vein, Lathom's writings, as we might expect, are all about the "mysteries" of paternity; about illegitimacy and uncertainties of birth, including such fantastically complicated unravellings as we find in *The Castle of Ollada*; and about the multiple sins and crimes of an unhinged aristocracy. Whether Lathom, like Matthew Lewis, wove Gothic fantasies around his own life, or whether these fantasies were imposed by his contemporary and later readership, remains undecidable.

What is certain is that Lathom's Gothic novels are characterized by a certain vivacity, and a sense of rush and urgency which places them firmly in the school of Lewis rather than Ann Radcliffe. The words, for the most part, tumble over each other; even in the later work, there is the sense of a youthful (some might say "immature") imagination at work, with the advantages and faults thus suggested. There is also a certain salaciousness typical of the minor Gothic: not as overt as in Lewis, but nonetheless showing pleasure in temporary torment and adversity.

Yet—and perhaps this is the bridge between Lathom's Gothic mode and his other writings—he clearly sees himself as ameliorating this darker imagination through his engagement with the comedic aspects of life, and especially of the lives of servants and underlings. Like Radcliffe and many others, his chapter epigraphs often hint at the presumption that he is following Shakespeare in this regard; without, it goes without saying, Shakespeare's skill, but with something of the master's regard for the absurdities of pomposity and how this can be deflated by providing different perspectives on the same apparently supernatural phenomena. For there is no evidence whatever in the texts that Lathom believed in, or was at all interested in, the supernatural; everything is explained—but not necessarily by stark reason, more by the excesses of passion which may cloud the intellect. The stock characters of Gothic fiction are all here—the frenzied nobleman, the equivocal priest, the deluded heroine—but occasionally, as in *The Midnight Bell*, there are hints at the structures of social prejudice which may engender such stereotypes.

One is thus returned to the notion of Lathom as a kind of "outlaw": not, of course, as a member of a romantic banditti, but as a writer who has a certain sense of what the price might be for one who has defeated, or evaded, expectation and has had to come to terms with what exile—even what was apparently a well-funded and prosperous exile—might entail. To conclude with his own words, which are addressed in *The Midnight Bell* by the young gaoler Jacques to his prisoner Byroff, but which might as well be addressed, and in similarly ambiguous and seductive terms, by Lathom to his reader:

> Some how, monsieur, I had taken a liking to you above any of the prisoners I had attended; and all I kept wishing for, was some means of setting you at liberty, that we might run away together; I knew, if I could contrive it, you would not dislike it, and there was something in your countenance that told me you would be kind to me afterwards.

Suggestive, of course; boyish, perhaps; but with a certain irony about what a reader might fairly find in texts, and about the subterranean designs an author might have, and which, indeed, the Gothic in general might have as it plays with notions of innocence and forbidden knowledge and interrogates the willingness with which we are able to engage with the exiled and the secret.

SUGGESTED FURTHER READING

Lathom, Francis. *The Impenetrable Secret, Find It Out!* Richmond: Valancourt, 2007.
Lathom, Francis, *The Midnight Bell: A German Story Founded on Incidents in Real Life*. Richmond: Valancourt, 2007.
Potter, Franz. "The Business of Morality: Francis Lathom" (in) *The History of Gothic Publishing, 1800–1835: Exhuming the Trade*. Basingstoke: Palgrave Macmillan, 2005. 131–144.
Punter, David, with Alan Bissett. "Francis Lathom in the Eighteenth Century." *Gothic Studies* (Summer 2003).

Ira Levin
(1929–2007)

BERNICE M. MURPHY

It may seem strange to devote an entry in a book dedicated to resurrecting "lost and neglected" personages to a writer whose work frequently topped the bestseller lists and whose death in 2007 occasioned warm tributes in many major newspapers. And yet, while Ira Levin could hardly be called obscure, his immense contribution to horror and gothic fiction has yet to be fully appreciated, the breadth of his fertile imagination perhaps inevitably overshadowed by the lasting resonance of his two most famous novels—*Rosemary's Baby* (1967) and *The Stepford Wives* (1972). Among other things, Levin could, with considerable justification, be called the father of the modern popular thriller. His oeuvre also encompassed works of science fiction (*This Perfect Day*, 1970), supernatural horror, and suspense, and he often combined elements from all of these genres (as in *The Boys from Brazil* [1976]). Levin was particularly good at coming up with resonant "high-concept" premises for his novels, most of which can be summarized in a single intriguing sentence (indeed, it is no wonder that all four novels cited below were rapidly adapted for the screen):

A college student decides to murder his wealthy girlfriend when her unplanned pregnancy jeopardizes his future plans (*A Kiss Before Dying*, 1953).

A young mother-to-be suspects that the "nice" old couple next door may have sinister plans for her unborn child (*Rosemary's Baby*).

A holocaust survivor realizes that neo–Nazis have successfully (and repeatedly!) cloned Hitler (*The Boys from Brazil*).

A suburban housewife discovers that many of the women in her new suburban community have been replaced by submissive androids, and that she may be next (*The Stepford Wives*).

Levin published his first novel, *A Kiss Before Dying* (1953), when he was only 24. The novel is almost a good portrait of a greedy, socially ambitious sociopath and has twice been adapted for the screen (including a dire 1991 version starring Sean Young and Matt Dillon), despite the fact that the narrative's major highlight—a devastating mid-story plot twist that provides a master class in authorial misdirection—could only be successfully carried out in print. Though the novel was fairly successful, Levin first came to public prominence as a playwright, adapting the novel *No Time for Sergeants* (1956) for the stage, and writing the original scripts for *Drat! The Cat* (1965) and, most famously, of all, the fiendishly constructed thriller *Death Trap* (1978).

Levin made a triumphant return to popular fiction in 1967 with the publication of *Rosemary's Baby*, a taut, intelligent variation on the "paranoid woman in genuine peril" trope so often employed in the classical gothic novel. Though Roman Polanski's film version remains better known today, Levin's novel is still in print, and is highly readable. The film obsessively adheres to the source text, with Polanski replicating even minor details and descriptions on the big screen. The novel should be considered a significant precursor to the block-busting work of horror writers such as Stephen King and Peter Straub in the 1970s and '80s: without his best-selling example, it is doubtful that the supernatural thriller would have gained such traction in American genre publishing during this period. *Rosemary's Baby* helped convince mainstream publishers that there was a genuine public appetite for mass-market horror fiction.

In *The Stepford Wives* Levin was, superficially at least, treading familiar ground: once more, a trusting wife is fatally deceived by the murderously self-centered man in her life. Two factors make the basic premise of *The Stepford Wives* concept so resonant. The first is the way in which, as Robert Beuka observes in his book *SuburbiaNation* (2004), the story dramatizes contemporary anxieties regarding the changing role of women in the home and in society at large. The second is the manner in which this aspect of the novel is intertwined with a savage critique of consumerism and materialism as it relates to the suburban way of life. The novel's premise also reflects a recurring preoccupation of 1970s popular culture: people are "taken over" or "replaced" by products of man-made technology. Levin's typically sympathetic heroine, Joanna Eberhart, will, by the end of the novel, have been replaced by her own robotic double. Part blackly comic satire, part genuinely affecting mediation on the lot of the disillusioned suburban housewife, *The Stepford Wives* remains one of Levin's finest achievements, not least for the ways in which it slyly dramatizes elements of Betty Friedan's famous 1963 call to arms *The Feminine Mystique*.

Another Levin novel which sounds vaguely ridiculous in outline but was quite compelling in execution is *The Boys from Brazil*, in which, as in *The Stepford Wives*, Levin once again combined elements of science fiction and the conspiracy thriller. The film version, in which Gregory Peck starred as Joseph Mengele, and Sir Laurence Olivier starred as a similarly decrepit Nazi-hunter, is again better known, this time if only for underlining the fact that while aging Golden Age Hollywood actresses (Crawford, Davis, de Havilland) could often only find work during old age portraying homicidal grotesques (or their victims), their male counterparts could always find employment as geriatric Nazis. The disappointing effort *Sliver* (1991), while decidedly uneven, was yet another typically prescient paranoid thriller which critiqued the decade's growing surveillance culture.

As *Sliver* demonstrated, Levin's fiction could, on occasion, be below par. His follow up to *Rosemary's Baby*, the pseudo-Orwellian dystopian SF novel *This Perfect Day* (1970) is deeply derivative and mediocre. Worse still is his dreadful follow-up to *Rosemary's Baby*, *Son of Rosemary* (1997). Compounding the novel's ineptitude is the fact that it concludes with a cop out ending so insulting that the reader may be tempted to take a leaf from Roman and Minnie Castevet's book and throw it out the window of a very large building. We can only hope that Levin was at least paid well.

That aside, despite the odd slightly disreputable blip on his C.V., Levin deserves recognition for his ability to bring horror and unease into the contemporary, everyday world with a deftness and shrewdly acute sense of social observation that puts many of those who followed his lead to shame. In *Rosemary's Baby* in particular, he created a morbidly witty, yet genuinely nightmarish tale that has yet to be equaled, and the novel justifiably remains a must-read for anyone who considers themselves a true horror aficionado.

SUGGESTED FURTHER READING

Case, George. *Here's to My Sweet Satan: How the Occult Haunted Music, Movies and Pop Culture, 1966–1980*. Fresno: Linden, 2016. 21–24.
Frankfurter, David. "Awakening to Satanic Conspiracy: *Rosemary's Baby* and the Cult Next Door" in M. David Eckel, Bradley L. Herling (eds.), *Deliver Us from Evil: Boston University Studies in Philosophy and Religion*. London: Bloomsbury, 2011. 75–88.
Murphy, Bernice. "Horror Fiction from the Decline of Universal Horror to the Rise of the Psycho Killer" in Reyes, Xavier Aldana (ed.), *Horror: A Literary History*. London: British Library, 2016. 131–158.
Perry, Dennis R. and Carl Sederholm. "Evil Usher: Rosemary's Baby, Pop Culture and the Evils of Consumerism" in Poe, *"The House of Usher" and the American Gothic*. New York: Palgrave Macmillan, 2009. 131–150.
Powell, Steven. "Ira Levin" in *100 American Crime Writers*. Basingstoke: Palgrave Macmillan, 2012. 204–205.

Jeff Lieberman
(1947–)

Jon Towlson

Jeff Lieberman (perhaps best known for *Squirm*, 1976) remains a critically neglected director within the horror genre. Although not as recognized as George A. Romero, Wes Craven, John Carpenter, Tobe Hooper or David Cronenberg, his films extend and enrich sub-genres within horror cinema. *Squirm* is one of the best ecological horror films derived from Hitchcock's *The Birds* (1963); *Blue Sunshine* (1978) spans the zombie-satire gap between *Shivers* (Cronenberg, 1975) and *Dawn of the Dead* (Romero, 1978); *Just Before Dawn* (1981) develops and subverts the backwoods slasher/ family clan horror tropes of both *The Texas Chainsaw Massacre* (Hooper, 1974) and *The Hills Have Eyes* (Craven, 1977); and *Satan's Little Helper* (2004) riffs intriguingly on *Halloween* (Carpenter, 1978). Lieberman has the ability to crystallize the essence of a horror sub-genre in a single striking image. In *Blue Sunshine* we have the murderous baby sitter stalking her young charges with a large knife; her "invasion-metamorphosis" is signified by her bizarrely bald head—her possession by the visual reference to *Rosemary's Baby* (1968). In *Just Before Dawn*, Lieberman's heroine fends off her backwoods attacker by thrusting her fist down his throat—a gender subversion of the rape/violation imagery redolent in the urbanoia film (most notably the gun-in the-woman's-mouth scene in *The Hills Have Eyes*). In *Squirm*, we have three such moments, neatly encapsulating the three stages of progression in the ecological apocalypse horror film as identified by Charles Derry in *Dark Dreams 2.0: A Psychological History of the Modern Horror Film*: *proliferation*—the scene where worms infest the face of the antagonist, Roger; *besiegement*—where the worms threaten to erupt from a showerhead on to the heroine (also, a sly nod to *Psycho*—linking via *The Birds* to Hitchcock); finally, *annihilation*—when the worms invade the house and finally engulf Roger, who sinks into them like a man disappearing into quicksand.

Lieberman was born in 1947 in Brooklyn, New York, but spent his formative years in Valley Stream, a suburb of Queens. Gifted at drawing but unsure of what direction to take in his career, exposure to Antonioni's *Blow Up* in 1966 turned him on to the possibilities of film. Enrolling at the School of Visual Arts in New York, Lieberman came under the mentorship of veteran TV director, Ernest Pintoff. They collaborated on the screenplay for *Blade* (1973), a homicide thriller that Pintoff went on to direct. Lieberman cut his own directorial teeth on two commercials and a documentary on abortion, before receiving an invitation to make an anti-drug public information film to be shown in American high schools called *The Ringer* (1972).

Like other horror film directors of the era, Lieberman's experience of 1960s counterculture informed his work from the start. "I am a baby boomer," Lieberman stated in an interview with *Rue Morgue* magazine. "I was in the drug culture of the '60s and I saw everything first hand. I was at Woodstock. I did acid. Marched against the war in Vietnam. Saw *Easy Rider*. I was immersed in all that in New York. I was at the right place at the right time, at the vanguard of all that stuff. However, I have an innate cynicism so I don't ever really buy into *any*thing." It is not surprising therefore that Lieberman gravitated towards horror.

His first film, *Squirm*, about an infestation of flesh-eating worms in small-town Georgia, is a traditional creature feature, albeit it one heavily influenced by the sci-fi films of the 1950s which left a major impression on Lieberman as a child. Lieberman's films can be seen as variations on the 1950s sci-fi movie in their outward projection of fears instilled by governments. In a lecture at the Miskatonic Institute of Horror Studies in 2011, Lieberman outlined his modus operandi, stating that the atomic age fears of the 1950s gave way to fears of the effects of LSD in the early 1970s and then later the effects of manmade pollution. Throughout the years he has continued to employ the basic story telling formula of the early 1950s radiation movie, adapting it to the changing times.

Thus, the fear of ecological pollution underpins *Squirm*—be it in a satirical way. In the film, an electricity pylon collapses and "electrifies" a harvest of carnivorous bloodworms which go on to crawl amok through a backwoods Southern town, feasting on the various inhabitants. Lieberman wrote the script in a frenzied six weeks, after putting it off for two years due to family commitments. He sold the script immediately to producers Edgar Lansbury and Joseph Beruh, who, on the strength of it, allowed him to direct. Lieberman considers *Squirm* to have been his on the job training in directing, and learned how to make the film, as he said, "one shot at a time." It was his crash course in the exigencies of low budget film-making.

Reminiscent of the Melanie-Mitch plot in *The Birds*, events in *Squirm* are kicked off by the arrival of a stranger in Fly Creek who arouses the suspicion of the townies. Played by Don Scardino, Mick is a nerdish city-slicker, visiting his girlfriend Geri who lives on the outskirts. When bodies of worm victims are found, distrust falls—implausibly—on Mick. He and Geri are forced to investigate the killings themselves and then try to save the disbelieving townsfolk from the marauding polychaetes. Finally it is the small-mindedness of the Fly Creek residents, as much as the threat from the worms, which brings about the demise of the town.

Squirm was a huge financial success thanks to its positioning as superior Saturday night schlock. Although not the first of the seventies "nature attacks" films—*Frogs* (1972), *Night of the Lepus* (1972), *Phase IV* (1974) and *Bug* (1975), among others, preceded it—*Squirm*'s primacy revived this flagging cycle in the mid-seventies and inspired numerous imitators—*The Savage Bees* (1976) , *Day of the Animals* (1977), *Empire of the Ants* (1977), and *Kingdom of the Spiders* (1977). Although he described the revenge of nature films as generally less interesting and productive than other types of apocalyptic horror, Robin Wood praised *Squirm* in his seminal essay, *The American Nightmare* (1979), for its underlying familial and sexual tensions.

Fortunately, Lieberman did not have to wait long to make his second film. *Blue Sunshine* (1978) takes its title from the fictitious strain of LSD which, in the film, turns its users into psychotic zombie killers a decade after it is swallowed. A further example of Lieberman's radiation cinema, *Blue Sunshine* draws on the same government-instilled anti-drug hysteria of the early 1970s that prompted *The Ringer*. "The whole idea that LSD could cause chromosome damage, make people freak out and jump off roofs, came from the anti-drug government establishment," Lieberman told *Videoscope*'s Robert Freese in 2006. "Just saying 'what a load of crap' is not entertaining. But trying to visualize what it would look like if these bozos were right was a kick." *Blue Sunshine* is, according to Lieberman, a satire of that point of view, along with the send up of his entire generation who, in the 1970s, were right in the middle of the process of crossing over to "the other side"—the straight world of that establishment they claimed to dread during the golden hippie times.

Like *Squirm*, *Blue Sunshine* includes elements of the detective story, as the protagonist, Jerry Zipkin, goes on the lam after becoming the prime suspect in a series of murders. Zipkin discovers that old college associate Ed Flemming, now running for Congress, is trying to cover up his past as a drug dealer who sold his friends the experimental Blue Sunshine. The film builds to a confrontation between Zipkin and Flemming's henchman in a discotheque and shopping mall, symbolizing the new age of rampant consumerism that the baby-boomers—having compromised the ideals of the 1960s for their own gain—helped to usher in.

Blue Sunshine was an immediate hit at Cannes. It was invited to the London Film Festival and Edinburgh Film Festival. However, it was poorly distributed in the States and quickly disappeared. Then, in the early 1980s, *Blue Sunshine* began to enjoy a growing cult following when the legendary New York nightclub CBGB featured it regularly as background footage on its screens. Lieberman attributes its subsequent popularity among the underground hardcore punk scene to the discotheque sequences, which "shit over disco."

Despite the growing cult status of *Blue Sunshine*, Lieberman had all but given up horror by the time he was offered the script that would become *Just Before Dawn* (1981). Even if this backwoods horror film does not quite live up to the promise of *Squirm* and *Blue Sunshine*, Lieberman brings his customary intelligence and genre savvy to the run-of-mill premise: campers in the woods are terrorized by a machete-wielding killer; only one of them survives, by drawing on her own animal instincts. Borrowing heavily from *Deliverance* (1972), Lieberman highlights the survivalist aspects of the story, emphasizing the conversion to savagery of the heroine, Connie. While perhaps not his most interesting or original film, *Just Before Dawn* is Lieberman's best executed. Showing greater film-making chops than he did in *Squirm* and *Blue Sunshine*, Lieberman uses the Oregon locations masterfully to build suspense and create atmosphere.

Although some reviewers of the time appreciated the director's skill and artistry, *Just Before Dawn* was doomed by its marketing as a slasher. Demoralized by the state of horror in the 1980s, Lieberman started to write in other genres, including science fiction and comedy. Eventually he would write for the studios, including the screenplay for *NeverEnding Story 3: Return to Fantasia* (1994). By his own admission he made more money for scripts that didn't get made than for the horror movies that did.

In 1988 Vestron Video financed Lieberman's self-reflexive sci-fi thriller *Remote Control*. Again harnessing contemporary fears in the style of the '50s radiation movie, *Remote Control* satirizes growing concerns in the eighties about the phenomenon of home video, about its influence on youth behavior and its effects on society. In the film a videotape clerk stumbles upon a plot by space aliens to brainwash people using a source signal impregnated in the actual videotape of a bad sci-fi movie, and attempts to stop the tape from being distributed worldwide. A film-within-a-film commenting on the media's moral panic about home video, *Remote Control* takes a satirical sideswipe at the sociologists and media effects theorists of the day and invites comparisons with Cronenberg's *Videodrome* (1983) in its depiction of video as a modern folk devil.

In 2004, buoyed by a revival of interest in his work, Lieberman finally returned to the horror fold with *Satan's Little Helper*. By then, according to him, "people had thought that I had either dropped out of the business or died." *Satan's Little Helper* is more self-reflexive social comment and another variation on the radiation cinema theme: "an allegory of our times," according to Lieberman, "the characters and violence in video games and movies are bombarding our youth constantly, and the line between fantasy and reality is blurred like never before." A small boy obsessed by a video game called Satan's Little Helper encounters a serial killer dressed as Satan on Halloween night. The boy enlists "Satan" to kill his sister's boyfriend (of whom he is insanely jealous). The killer obliges and the boy thus becomes the "Satan's little helper" of the title. Shot on HD for a low budget, Lieberman returned to grassroots and the result was one of the freshest horror films in years.

The films of Jeff Lieberman are conscious satirical commentaries on American culture. Horror cinema, as Lieberman has stated, operates outside the boundaries of society, where neither laws nor society's accepted standards of behavior need apply. For nearly forty years Lieberman has positioned himself in a genre whose audience is open and receptive to his quirky, subversive ideas on society, politics and religion. Recognition of the full extent of Lieberman's contribution to the sci-fi/horror genre is long overdue. With remakes of *Squirm* and *Blue Sunshine* currently in the works, Lieberman's inclusion in this volume is both timely and welcome.

SUGGESTED FURTHER READING

Crawley, Tony. "Blue Sunshine." *House of Hammer*, vol. 2, no. 3 (December 1977): 16–18.
Derry, Charles. *Dark Dreams 2.0: A Psychological History of the Modern Horror Film from the 1950s to the 21st Century*. Jefferson, NC: McFarland, 2009.
Freese, Rob. "Filmmakers in Focus: Jeff Lieberman–Cult Cut Up!" *Videoscope* 57 (Winter 2006): 46–49.
Hutchings, Peter. *The A-Z of Horror Cinema*. Lanham, MD: Scarecrow, 2009.
Jones, Alan. "Just Before Dawn." *Starburst* 53 (January 1983): 14–15.
Newman, Kim. *Nightmare Movies: Horror on Screen since the 1960s*. London: Bloomsbury, 2011.
Towlson, Jon. *Subversive Horror Cinema: Countercultural Messages of Films from Frankenstein to the Present*. Jefferson, NC: McFarland, 2014.
Wood, Robin. *Hollywood from Vietnam to Reagan*. New York: Columbia University Press, 1986. Reprint, 2003.

Stephen Mallatratt
(1947–2004)

Madelon Hoedt

I have been a fan of the genre for many years now, but it is in live performance that horror has really been able to capture my imagination. Encountering horror on the stage offers a unique experience of scares and thrills. As Peter Brook has stated in his seminal 1968 work *The Empty Space*, "the theatre is the arena where a living confrontation can take place. The focus of a large group of people creates a unique intensity." More so than in literature or on film, horror in performance creates, in the words of Brook, a confrontation between actor and audience, between monster and potential victim. The meeting between live humans results in an experience that is more personal, more direct, and as a result, more frightening. Although examples of performance horror abound, one production in particular stands out: Stephen Mallatratt's stage adaptation of *The Woman in Black*.

Mallatratt enjoyed a successful career in the dramatic arts for most of his lifetime. He is known as an actor, most notably for his collaborations with Alan Ayckbourn, as well as a TV scriptwriter, with credits for several adaptations and a run as a writer on long-running British soap opera *Coronation Street*. All of these successes, however, seem far removed from what Mallatratt is arguably best known for. His name does not conjure up instant associations with the horror genre, despite the fact that he is responsible for bringing one of the most famous Christmas ghost stories on the British stage. Adapted from the novella of the same name by Susan Hill, *The Woman in Black* was staged for the first time in Scarborough, during Christmas 1987. Intended as a small production, a stocking filler, if you will, *The Woman in Black* transferred to London's West End in 1989 and at the time of writing, the production is still being performed in London and during tours around the United Kingdom.

The Woman in Black exists as part of a rich tradition of horror on the stage. The classic Gothic dramas of the eighteenth and nineteenth century were often adaptations of existing novels, which used new technologies and special effects to create a spectacle on the stage. Regarded as one of the forerunners of melodrama, these plays are often typified by heightened plots and excess. By contrast, the French *Grand-Guignol*, which emerged around the beginning of the twentieth century and enjoyed a run of 65 years in its own theatre in Paris, is best known for its tales of blood and gore. Focusing on one-act plays, the theatre offered a new type of horror on the stage, as is described by Richard Hand and Michael Wilson in *Grand Guignol: The French Theatre of Horror* (2002): "[a]lthough the Grand-Guignol steers well clear of all things supernatural, it pushes the human subject into monstrosity, extrapolating, as it were, *la bête humaine* into *le monstre humain*." Rather than drawing on the old ruins and older ghosts of the Gothic tradition, the Grand-Guignol concerned itself with plots that were more modern in nature, and were often based on real events.

By contrast, *The Woman in Black* finds itself firmly in the tradition of the classic British ghost story, both in the novella and on the stage. Hill's original contains a framing narrative in which Arthur Kipps, the narrator, finds himself asked by his stepchildren to join in with the telling of ghost stories at Christmas. This event prompts a number of unwelcome memories as Kipps proceeds to tell the reader of his younger days as a lawyer when he was sent to the village of Crythin Gifford and the old Eel Marsh House, the estate of the late Mrs. Drablow. Here, he will be attending her funeral and dealing with her affairs after her passing. Forced to stay in the old house, which is cut off from the nearest village for most of the day as the road disappears when the tide is in, Kipps finds himself steeped in the tragic history and the secrets of the eponymous Woman. With its opening a clear nod to the Dickensian tradition, Hill's novella contains numerous references to classic authors such as M.R. James and H.G. Wells.

Mallatratt's adaptation remains faithful to Hill's original story in terms of its plot, yet the way in which the play is structured adds something distinctly theatrical and uncanny. The theatre is a space that is familiar but which can conjure up new locations and incredible events in the blink of an eye. It is a place where one sits in the dark, observing and perhaps spying on the lives of others as they play out on the stage. It is a place where imagination becomes reality, where sets, costume and props mimic reality, and it is exactly these qualities that Mallatratt draws attention to in his writing.

The opening of the play is a prime example of this. As the production begins, the audience finds an older man on the stage. He is reading from a book, his voice a constant drone, until there is a shout from the back of the auditorium where a young man has appeared, who is here to help the other in his endeavors on the stage. This older man is Kipps, who has found his way to the theatre in an attempt to exorcise his demons, to tell his story and thus get rid of his demons. The younger man is an actor, here to help the other to turn this into a reality. Rather than viewing a "finished" piece, the audience has been brought to a theatre in worker state, to a space that is prepared for rehearsal rather than performance. The stage is bare apart from a few basic props and spectators openly see the Actor and Kipps reading from the script, getting ready, getting in and out of costume and character.

The effect is one similar to Orson Welles' famous 1938 *War of the Worlds* radio play: every person in the auditorium is aware of the fiction, yet they are dragged headfirst into the story all the same. A change of coat and scarf suggest a different character; a wicker basket stands in for a train carriage, or a pony and trap. The existence of Spider the terrier is simply mimed by the actors, yet the moment the little dog sinks into the quicksand and is saved with only moments to spare is still likely to illicit a strong response from the audience. Locations and persons flit between fact and fiction as the actors step in and out of their roles and the play becomes as intangible as its ghosts. The more one tries to understand the events and occurrences of the play, the more they appear to be just out of reach. The world that Mallatratt creates onstage can best be described as uncertain, and it is something he himself draws attention to in the production notes to the play: "There are anachronisms and geographical inconsistencies within the text. These are not mistakes, but indications of the neverland we inhabit when involved with the Woman in Black." Mallatratt deftly draws attention to just how ghostly and unsettling the theatre is by its very nature, and in doing so enhances the effect of the ghost story, a story that is, indeed, ghostly and unsettling.

Ultimately, *The Woman in Black* has been highly influential for horror productions made in the United Kingdom. This has been exemplified by further adaptations of Hill's novella, both for screen, such as the 1989 version for TV by Nigel Kneale and the 2012 film starring Daniel Radcliffe, and for radio, with a four part adaptation broadcast in 1993 on BBC Radio 5 and an hour-long play for BBC Radio 4 in 2004. In addition, numerous other ghost plays (both adaptations and original work) have graced British stages, most notably Hugh Janes' Dickens adaptation *The Haunting* which saw performances between 2010 and 2012, and *Ghost Stories* by Andy Nyman and Jeremy Dyson, which enjoyed a run in London in 2010 and 2011, with a revival in 2014. It is, however, difficult to find a review which does not mention *The Woman in Black* in its appraisal of these pieces. Ultimately, it is not the first play to offer a ghost story onstage, nor is it presenting something which is ground-breaking in terms of dramaturgy. Similarly, I do not wish to argue that every ghost play made since 1987 is deeply indebted to Mallatratt's brilliant adaptation. However, horror in this form is not often addressed in scholarly writing and is often unfairly dismissed by theatre critics, with its success measured only in terms of scares. What *The Woman in Black* offers is a different take on this issue. Beyond its scares is a carefully constructed narrative which expertly uses the nature of its medium, the theatre, to further unsettle the spectator, even calling into question the possible consequences of telling such a story on the stage. As Kipps states near the end of the play, "You asked for my story. I have told it. Enough," yet it is a story to deserves to be told time and again.

SUGGESTED FURTHER READING

Hand, Richard J., and Michael Wilson. *Grand Guignol: The French Theatre of Horror.* Exeter: University of Exeter Press, 2002.
Hill, Susan. *The Woman in Black.* London: Mandarin, 1994.
Janes, Hugh. *The Haunting.* London: Nick Hern, 2011.
Mallatratt, Stephen. *The Woman in Black: A Ghost Play.* London: Samuel French, 1989.

Carl Mayer
(1894-1944)

Jim Rockhill

Robert Wiene's Expressionist nightmare *The Cabinet of Dr. Caligari* (*Das Cabinet des Dr. Caligari*, 1920), Lupu Pick's domestic tragedy *New Year's Eve* (*Sylvester: Tragödie einer Nach*t, 1924), Walter Ruttmann's fusion of sound and image in *Berlin: Symphony of a Metropolis* (*Berlin: Die Sinfonie der Großstadt*, 1927), Friedrich Wilhelm Murnau's psychological portraits of humiliation in *The Last Laugh* (*Der letzte Mann* aka *The Last Man*, 1924), hypocrisy in *Tartuffe* (1925), and reawakened love in *Sunrise: A Song of Two Humans* (1927), and one of Robert Aickman's favorite films, Leni Riefenstahl's blend of fairy tale, mysticism and celebration of mountain life in *The Blue Light* (*Das blaue Licht*, 1932) all have two things in common: all stand as landmarks within their respective genres, influencing many of the films that have followed in their wake, and all owe their existence, at least in part, to one man.

In a film review published in the 8 January 1925 issue of the *Frankfurter Zeitung*, the Austrian journalist and novelist Joseph Roth focused his greatest praise not on the film's director or its famous leading man Emil Jannings, but its screenwriter:

> The great, artistic German film this year is *The Last Man*. Its author is Carl Mayer, the only German Film-Poet. I stress the word "Poet" because whereas we have others capable of writing a well-crafted script, Carl Mayer composes films like another composes poems, stories or plays: i.e. he takes the crass "stuff" of our ephemeral, mundane, and coincidental plane of existence and transmutes it into an atmosphere that is metaphysical, unique, graceful and essential.... His is a poetry not of words but of images....*The Last Man* is without a doubt ... one of the best films not only of Germany but the world.

Mayer was born on 20 November 1894, the eldest son of a Jewish businessman who had left Vienna for Paris as a penniless teen, became rich playing the stock market, then committed suicide after losing everything through poor investments and attempts to regain his riches at the gaming table. Forced out of school and into the street as a teenager, Mayer was called upon to support himself and his three brothers with a variety of jobs worthy of a character out of Dickens or one of Fritz Lang's Mabuse films, including stints as a secretary, barometer salesman, portraitist, and actor. Surviving these lean times placed him within the reach of military conscription during the First World War, a conflict Mayer evaded by engaging in a protracted battle of wits with a psychiatrist intent upon declaring him fit for battle.

Forming a friendship with the Czech writer Hans Janowitz on furlough from the German army in Berlin during June 1918, Mayer found himself collaborating on a screenplay that combined a series of unsolved murders his friend recalled reading about in 1913 with his own contempt for the psychiatric profession into what would become Robert Wiene's *The Cabinet of Dr. Caligari*. His first solo screenplay, written for Wiene's film *Genuine*, concerning a vampiric femme fatale, failed to impress the public in 1920 and continues to confuse audiences to this day.

What both films offered was a kind of storytelling that relied just as much, if not more, on the images that propelled the narrative than on the story itself, a focus that Mayer continued to refine throughout the next 12 years, as his interest in the technical capabilities of film went in stride with his exploration of psychological states and the evocation of atmosphere. Among the dozens of films for which he wrote screenplays during these years, the purely pictorial aspect reaches its peak in the great visual and musical poem in celebration of Berlin he created with Walter Ruttmann and cinematographer Karl Freund in 1927; but his collaborations with Murnau juxtaposed nightmarish images with naturalistic settings in a manner that plumbed psychological depths rarely before encountered in film. The confrontation of sympathetic characters with the darkness of their own fears and desires in the best of these films produces a terrifying poignancy. Unfortunately, Mayer refused to follow Murnau when he travelled to America to film *Sunrise*, preferring to work in familiar surroundings at home in Germany, and the last known copy of their final collaboration, *4 Devils* (1928), has been lost for decades.

Life proved equally unkind to Mayer. He found the talkies less congenial than silent film, his remaining screenplays in Germany often written in collaboration, and in the case of Riefenstahl's *Blue Light*, not even credited. His greatest collaborator, Murnau, died in an automobile accident in the United States in 1931. He accepted an invitation to join exiled friends in the United Kingdom in 1932 to participate in a film distribution agreement with Germany presided over by Alexander Korda, but when the agreement fell through in 1933, he returned to an increasingly tense homeland. After months of silence, his friends received word from him in desperate straits in Prague, from which he was eventually delivered to London, a poor man with a suspicious accent and unrecognized talents. Accepting gifts and whatever assignments came his way from friends in the British film business, he was able to eke out a living acting as script supervisor on filmed adaptations of George Bernard Shaw by producer-director Gabriel Pascal, and then documentary filmmaker Paul Rotha. He was planning a film about London along the lines of *Berlin: Symphony of a Metropolis* when he fell ill with abdominal pain in 1943, and died on July 1 the following year of pancreatic cancer. His friends described him as a short, modest man with a noble head, and a perpetual smile, always eager to learn more about the craft he loved so dearly and served so well.

Note: Passages quoted from Joseph Roth's review of "Der letzte Mann" were translated by the author of this article from Joseph Roth, *Werke 2: Das journalistische Werk, 1924–1928*, edited by Klaus Westermann (Köln: Kiepenheuer & Witsch, 1990), pp. 324–7.

SUGGESTED FURTHER READING

Unfortunately, neither Rolf Hempel's classic *Carl Mayer: Ein Autor schreibt mit der Kamera* (Berlin, Henschelverlag Kunst und Gesellschaft, 1968), nor Jürgen Kasten's *Carl Mayer, Filmpoet: Ein Drehbuchautor schreibt Filmgeschichte* (Berlin: Vistas Verlag, 1994) have been translated into English. The splendid bilingual collection of essays devoted to Mayer edited by Michael Omasta, Brigitte Mayr, and Christian Cargnelli— *Carl Mayer. Scenar(t)ist. Ein Script von ihm war schon ein Film* (Vienna: Synema, 2003)—offers many new images and much new information, but is problematical for non–German readers, as it does not translate all of the German texts in full. Therefore, in addition to the excellent essays published by the BFI devoted to individual films, the following sources are among the most reliable and insightful currently available in English:

Eisner, Lotte H. *The Haunted Screen: Expressionism in the German Cinema and the Influence of Max Reinhardt*, rev. 2d ed. (Berkeley: University of California Press, 2008).
Eisner, Lotte H. *Murnau*, rev. and enlarged ed. London: Secker & Warburg, 1973.
Luft, Herbert G. "Notes on the World and Work of Carl Mayer." *The Quarterly of Film Radio and Television*, vol. 8, no. 4, revised 2d ed. Berkeley: University of California Press, Summer 1954, pp. 375–392.
Mayr, Brigitte. "Carl Mayer: Years of Exile in London." *Destination London: German-Speaking Emigrés and British Cinema, 1925–1950*, edited by Tim Bergfelder and Christian Cargnelli. Oxford: Berghahn, 2008), pp. 195–203.

Robert R. McCammon
(1952–)

Neil McRobert

The 1980s were a boom-time for horror fiction. A new generation of writers saturated the market, led by Stephen King and backed by unprecedented publishing capital. The post-millenial contraction of the market has meant that only a handful of these authors have retained their best-seller status. Robert McCammon, unjustly, has been forgotten by all but the initiated. McCammon's anonymity is puzzling. He has won five Bram Stoker Awards, a World Fantasy Award and over a dozen other prizes. His novels regularly charted on the *New York Times* bestsellers list. Yet mention his name today and you will likely draw a blank. This may be due, in part, to a self-imposed exile from writing since 1992. This temporary retirement may have alienated readers who, considering him to be writing at the peak of his abilities, felt he owed them more. Indeed, his development as a writer up until the hiatus makes his decision frustrating, but it does not detract from a worthy body of work.

Robert Rick McCammon was born in Birmingham, Alabama, on 17 July 1952. He was raised and remains in the South. However, despite his lifelong links to the area commentators have remarked that McCammon's early work contains little acknowledgment of a southern heritage. Indeed, his first novel, *Baal* (1978) is a jet-setting narrative of good versus paradigmatic evil. McCammon himself commented that "you always hear this said to young writers, write about what you know. I wanted to write about things I didn't know, so I consciously set *Baal* in locations as far from the South as possible."

Baal was McCammon's first attempt at a novel after repeated failure in the short-fiction market. It is an ambitious first effort, if clearly indebted to other, more acclaimed works. The rape of the heroine and the ensuing birth of a demon-child mimics the central conceit of Ira Levin's *Rosemary's Baby* (1967) and the international pursuit of a supernatural antagonist is reminiscent of *Dracula*. That said, the novel is a solid contribution to the genre and like King's more-successful *Carrie* (1974) it benefits from the urgency of its composition. McCammon himself said: "I think that in Baal you can feel the friction of shoulders being squeezed by iron walls: my shoulders, pressing against the walls of a dead-end job." While *Baal* and the subsequent *Bethany's Sin* (1980) and *The Night Boat* (1980) garnered some good reviews, they are unrepresentative of McCammon's oeuvre. Each of them is derivative of other, more successful fiction by more established authors.

It is with *They Thirst* (1981) that McCammon begins to distinguish himself and it is ironic that his most original fiction to that point deals with that most overcooked figure: the vampire. There are many novels from this period that recontextualize and rehistoricize the vampire, but McCammon's depiction of the glitz and grime of Los Angeles is the perfect backdrop to a tale of vampirism as social disease and infection of the most sordid kind. As the novel emphasizes, the Los Angeles of the 1980s was so outré that *anything* could (and would) go unnoticed until it was too late. McCammon has confessed that he finds LA a terrifying place. This anxiety is enshrined in the *They Thirst*'s nightmarish urban scene.

As would become a trend in his career, McCammon followed this relative success with an abrupt change of focus. Rather than continuing with urban horror, he turned his attention to his southern roots, in the process consolidating his own authorial voice. *Mystery Walk* (1983) employs a quieter, more ruminative tone than the bombastic prose of his earlier work. It seems that by bringing his fiction home to the South he is able to better catch the essence of nature and voice.

Mystery Walk is a picaresque tale of a young Alabama boy with psychic powers. Again there are references to other authors, most notably Ray Bradbury, but for the first time they feel purposeful rather than derivative. The towns of Hawthorne in *Mystery Walk* and Zephyr in *Boy's Life* (1991) are homages to Bradbury's Green Town, yet unlike Bradbury's southern idyll, McCammon's south is presented ambivalently at best. The romance of a southern childhood is undercut by an adult awareness of social tensions: racial, sexual and economic. The Klan is foregrounded, as are the general prejudices and racial intolerance of small American communities. McCammon refuses to resort to a simple polarization of good and evil, however. The father of the Mystery Walk's protagonist, himself a sympathetic character, is affiliated with the Klan. He is ultimately redeemed but his initial collusion illustrates McCammon's refusal to portray the social landscape of his youth as simple or untainted. He offers a mythical South that is more than usually absorbing in its patchwork of overlapping codes and moralities.

His next four books all appeared within five years. Taken together this period demonstrates McCammon's awareness of genre and an emerging, confident playfulness. *Usher's Passing* (1984) takes the premise that Poe's famous family did not end with Roderick and Madeleine. Instead, another branch of the Usher's flourished into a powerful dynasty. What develops is a gloriously ludicrous plot involving a mythical panther called Greediguts, Pumpkinhead—the local bogeyman who steals children, and so many overt Gothic trappings that it is clear that McCammon knows his own genre inside out.

If *Usher's Passing* is indebted to Poe, then *Stinger* (1988) is a paean to 1950s B-movies, involving a battle between aliens in a small Texas town. *The Wolf's Hour* (1989) is an historical oddity concerning a werewolf employed by the allied powers to infiltrate and undermine the Third Reich. McCammon again makes clear his debt to genre, referring as much to James Bond as to the werewolf trope. As in *They Thirst* the novel takes an exhausted horror theme and both reconfigures and revitalizes it. *The Wolf's Hour* was McCammon's biggest success up until this point and fans have clamored for a sequel. They finally got their wish in 2011, with the publication of *The Hunter from the Woods*. The fact that this sadly went to press almost unnoticed is perhaps the greatest illustration of McCammon's popular decline.

In another about-turn, McCammons followed these playful page-turners with his bleak and grandiose masterpiece: *Swan Song* (1987). At over a thousand pages in length it is clearly part of the 1980s' trend for outlandish horror "epics." Unlike many of them, however, it doesn't feel bloated or mutated by marketing demand; the story *requires* a grand canvas. While comparisons with King's *The Stand* (1978) are generally cosmetic and a result of shared epic scope, both novels do contain a similar premise: a conflict being fought between two groups of survivors in a post-apocalyptic to protect or possess the titular Swan—a young girl with the power to heal. Her supernatural ability, and the disciple-like following that she gathers, may sound suggestive of *The Stand*'s Christian allegory but, in actuality, McCammon eschews Christian overtones and Manichean dualism to present an alternative vision of late-Cold War apocalyptic anxiety.

After *Swan Song*, McCammon moved away from straight horror towards less easily classifiable work. His next, *Mine* (1990) is in direct contrast to its predecessor. A sleek thriller in which a woman pursues the ex-revolutionary who has abducted her child, *Mine* has a lot to say about the death of the 1960s ideology and the transformation of political and economic life in America. It is McCammon's first novel to forego supernatural elements yet it won him a second Bram Stoker award and secured his standing among the premier contemporary horror novelists.

After a collection of short stories, *Blue World* (1990) he continued his breakneck pace with *Boy's Life* (1991). Here, in this elegiac tribute to childhood, the allusions to Bradbury are made overt and make most sense. Similar in both tone and form to Bradbury's *Dandelion Wine* (1957), the episodic plot involves no less than a lake monster, escaped war criminals, a haunted road, a witch, a wild-west gunfight, race problems, a resurrected dog and a dinosaur running amok through town. It is essentially unclassifiable, in turns picaresque, bildungsroman, boys-own adventure and magic realism. The novel won him his third Stoker Award but its inclusion within the contest is demonstrative of the marketing machinery that surrounded horror writer's in this period of literary history. Like Stephen King, McCammon had been forcibly categorized as a *horror* writer regardless of what he wrote.

If *Boy's Life* is a eulogy for McCammon's own youth and Southern heritage, then *Gone South* (1992) is its dark twin. It follows Dan Lambert, a Vietnam vet on the run for murder. Like much Southern Gothic Lambert's journey into the swamplands and bayous adopts the overtones of fable. The first line makes clear that this is a very different south than that of his previous work: "It was Hell's season, and the air smelled of burning children." The novel is terse and efficient, a visceral a view of the South that stands alongside William Faulkner, Cormac McCarthy or James Dickey. *Gone South* presents a more mature McCammon, probing at the confines of genre pigeonholing. With three recent Bram Stoker Awards and enviable sales records he seemed to be at the peak of his career. Then he stopped.

The issue that brought about his impromptu retirement was a disagreement with publishers over his next novel *Speaks the Nightbird* (2002). Again McCammon had tried to change tack, this time delving into the history of the seventeenth century witch trials. McCammon had a disagreement with a publisher about the novel. *Nightbird* is already a vivid piece of writing, yet, according to McCammon, the editor in question wanted to change the plot to something akin to lurid romantic fiction. The imposition of marketing and commerce was too much, and McCammon retired from writing.

A decade passed. Then in 2002 McCammon was overheard reading parts of *Nightbird* to students by a representative from River Press. They approached him with the offer of publishing the novel his way. It was an opportunity he took. Since then he has published four more novels in what has become known as the "Matthew Corbett" series. In his own words McCammon is now "absolutely unretired." In addition to the forthcoming (sixth) Matthew Corbett novel, there is also a return to contemporary fiction, in 2013's rock 'n' roll horror-show, *The Five,* and the science-fiction/horror hybrid, *The Border.* It remains to be seen whether McCammon will claim a place in the vanguard of twenty first century horror writing (and the understated release of his most recent work suggests not) but none of this detracts from his value within the field.

McCammon's oeuvre is to be celebrated. It spans almost the entire period in which horror was big business in the publishing world. His career allows the reader to chart the development of a horror writer who was unafraid to strain at the rules and resist the entrapment of genre-classification. Unlike the majority of his contemporaries, he avoids pomposity and his work offers a contemporary, yet nostalgic, trip back into the relative simplicity of early twentieth century "pulp" horror. It is certainly low-brow, even trashy in parts, but gloriously so. Importantly, what it possesses is a vitality and clarity of intention lost in some of the more grandiose tomes of the 1980s and early '90s. McCammon deserves to be remembered as an original voice in an era when repetition and overindulgence threatened to reduce horror to a bloated, repetitive exercise in profit. Within the renewed commercial pressures of contemporary horror, maybe McCammon's minor renaissance can help the genre resist another period of nullifying corporate stranglehold.

SUGGESTED FURTHER READING

McCammon, Robert R. *Blue World*. New York: Pocket Books, 1990.
McCammon, Robert R. *Boy's Life*. New York, Simon and Schuster, 1991.
McCammon, Robert R. *Mystery Walk*. New York: Simon and Schuster, 1992.
McCammon, Robert R. *Swan Song*. New York: Pocket Books, 1987.
McCammon, Robert R. *The Wolf's Hour*. New York: Pocket Books, 1989.

Shinji Mikami
(1965–)

Eóin Murphy

My heart is thumping. I can feel the beat in my wrist where skin brushes the plastic gripped between my fingers. Worse than that, my hands are sweating, my grip loose and uncomfortable. I want to stop, wipe my hands clean, take a breath. Maybe even get a drink of water.

But I can't.

There's something ahead in the corridor and the last typewriter was ten minutes ago. A moan reverberates down the hall. A zombie, I think. Easy prey.

But something isn't right. It's too easy. I approach, cautious. Stepping slowly around the corner I see it. Slow moving, rotting where it stands.

I ready my shotgun, aim at its head and step out.

The wall on my left shatters. Monstrous hands batter me down. It's Nemesis. I back away, firing. Rounds vanish into the creature's chest. I keep firing.

It isn't enough.

It's never enough.

Jill Valentine dies for the fourth time that night and, heart thumping in shock, I finally put the controller down. Damn videogames.

Resident Evil is a series that many people who used games consoles in the 1990s and 2000s will be familiar with. The most influential survival horror game of all time has since been spun off into almost a dozen sequels, a long-running film series, and a host of books and comics, and played a crucial role in the revival of zombies in popular cinema, books and games. It was developed by Shinji Mikami, whose name that has become synonymous with the survival video game horror genre. Mikami played a central role in the rise of "Survival Horror" style games, with many of the innovations he introduced into the genre still in use today.

Born in 1965, Mikami attended Doshisha University in Kyoto. With a passing interest in video games and in need of work, Mikami applied for a job at Capcom, a game development studio, following a suggestion from a friend. This chance application would lead to him developing many of the studio's biggest hits over the next twenty years. Starting as a game planner in 1990, Mikami worked on the likes of *Who Framed Roger Rabbit* (1991), *Aladdin* (1993) and *Goof Troop* (1994), a terrifying tale of a father and son facing pirates, kidnapping and the odd alligator. Oddly enough, it was while he was a game designer for *Goof Troop* that Mikami first experimented with the resource management systems that would help make *Resident Evil* unique among horror themed games of the time. In *Goof Troop*, the player had access to a limited inventory—they could only carry a single item at a time, forcing them to choose between carrying one piece of equipment or another (in this case a grappling hook, a bell or a shovel).

In 1994, Mikami was asked to work on a sequel to *Sweet Home*, a 1989 horror game based on the film of the same name. *Sweet Home* involved a group of five people searching a haunted mansion for an artist's lost paintings. Of course, things don't quite work out to plan. While working on the initial build of the game, Mikami took the idea of a group of people trapped in an isolated mansion, removed the ghosts and replaced them with monsters. As he said later: "Thinking about it, though, in the capacity of a game, there wouldn't be any real feeling of exhilaration if you were shooting at, or attacking, ghosts." Inspired by George A. Romero's *Dawn of the Dead* (1978), Mikami introduced zombies to the story and *Resident Evil* (originally titled "Biohazard" in Japan–Mikami has called the name *Resident Evil* "Stupid") was born.

In a familiar take on an old trope, an elite group of police officers known as S.T.A.R.S. (Special Tactics And Rescue Squad) are dropped off by helicopter in the forest surrounding Raccoon City to investigate the disappearance of hikers on mountain trails. Attacked by a pack of (apparently) feral dogs they take refuge in a seemingly abandoned mansion. Pretty soon after this it becomes apparent that sticking with the wild dogs would have been a better idea. Filled with zombies, "Hunters" (monsters reminiscent of H.P. Lovecraft's sea dwelling residents of Innsmouth) and spiders so big they would give an arachnophobe a heart attack, the mansion becomes a death trap only the strong would survive.

The game was a huge success, selling 2.75 million copies worldwide. A sequel quickly followed, racking up a further 4.96 million sales: in this instance, the T-virus (a bio-weapon developed by the amoral Umbrella Corp which caused the initial outbreak) had spread to nearby Raccoon City. Mikami oversaw the production of *Resident Evil 2* (1998) and a number of its sequels before going on to develop other projects. Some of these further developed and refined the survival horror genre. For example, in a foreshadowing of what Mikami would do with later iterations of the *Resident Evil* series, *Dino Crisis* (1999) (which essentially replaced zombies with dinosaurs) introduced faster paced action than the more slow and steady pace of the *Resident Evil* games.

Later games saw Mikami work in other genres but continuing to innovate. *God Hand* (2006) for instance is a beat 'em up, which, rather than rely on button mashing, made use of the analog sticks on the control pad to add depth to the traditional game set up. *Vanquish* (2010), contrastingly, is a sci-fi shooter that involves out of control Soviet robots in a world in which the Cold War never ended. *Vanquish* plays with the standard approach used in these types of games (which generally involves the player entering a new area, shooting everything that moves and then moving to the next area) instead making heavy use of cover mechanics (much like *Gears of War*). However, this cover quickly disintegrates while the player is under fire, forcing them to engage the enemy closely using a dash and slide attack rather than taking the occasional shot from behind an impregnable barricade.

Mikami returned to the *Resident Evil* franchise in 2005 with *Resident Evil 4*. Still using the survival horror tropes that made the original games so successful, Mikami introduced a faster pace, updating the game for modern audiences that had become used to games such as *Call of Duty*, yet retaining the unsettling "body horror" elements that were part of what had made the original game so appealing in the first place. Indeed, *in Resident Evil 4* Mikami manages to outdo the unpleasant sight of rotting, flesh-eating corpses by introducing a brand new (but slightly familiar) enemy, Los Ganados ("The Cattle").

The game is set in an unnamed European country (although the fact that the residents all speak Spanish is a bit of a giveaway), where villagers infected with a parasite wreak havoc and sinister forces manipulate the situation from behind the scenes. The plot also involves the daughter of the President of the United States, a cult and prehistoric parasites. With both new and old foes making an appearance, *Resident Evil 4* was a huge success, revitalizing the franchise. Indeed, the *Resident Evil* series is still going strong. *Resident Evil 6* was released in March 2013, another film began production in July 2015 and several of the older games are being updated and rereleased on the current generation of consoles.

Mikami left Capcom in 2004, starting a series of games companies including Clover Studio and Seeds Inc., following Clover's dissolution in 2006. Seeds Inc. went on to be reconfigured as Platinum Games, with Mikami leaving to form Tango Gameworks. It was there that Mikami started work on his most recent foray into survival horror with *The Evil Within*. Released in 2014, *The Evil Within* marks a return to traditional survival horror for Mikami, moving away from the more action oriented elements of the most recent *Resident Evil* games. Using psychological horror rather than jump scares, the player must grapple with limited resources and a host of monsters dredged from the darkest recesses of the mind. *The Evil Within* carries on Mikami's tradition of introducing new elements to the genre. For instance, some enemies need to be killed and then set on fire to be fully vanquished, or, in a Michael Myers–esque fashion they will rise to attack you again and again. An unreliable narrator and an ever-shifting game environment works to keep the player uncertain of just what is around the corner. Or if that even *is* a corner in the first place….

While the *Evil Within* has been the subject of a number of criticisms (a Kotaku review praised its creature design, atmosphere and sound but suggested that the control system and poor characterization let the game down), it is clear that Mikami continues to push the boundary of horror games, adding to the body of work he has developed over the past three decades. It can only be hoped that he carries on developing games that continue to take both the survival horror genre, and players themselves in a host of terrifying new directions.

Until then, turn off the lights, put on *Resident Evil* and try not to scream when *something* jumps through the window…

SUGGESTED FURTHER READING

Farghaly, Nadine. *Unraveling Resident Evil: Essays on the Complex Universe of the Games and Films*. Jefferson, N.C.: McFarland, 2014.
"The Making of Resident Evil." Now Gamer. http://www.nowgamer.com/the-making-of-resident-evil/, 4 May 2010.
Parkin, Simon. "Meeting Mikami." Eurogamer. http://www.eurogamer.net, 19 October 2014.
Reed, Charley. "Resident Evil's Rhetoric: The Communication of Corruption in Survival Horror Video Games." *Games and Culture* (2015): 1555412015575363.
Rouse, Richard, III. "Match Made in Hell: The Inevitable Success of the Horror Genre in Video Games." *Horror Video Games: Essays on the Fusion of Fear and Play* (2009): 15–25
"Shinji Mikami." Giant Bomb. http://www.giantbomb.com.
Stuart, Keith. "Shinji Mikami: The Godfather of Horror Games." *The Guardian*. http://www.theguardian.com/technology/2014/sep/30/shinji-mikami-evil-within-resident-evil, 30 September 2014.

Joseph Minion
(1957–)

GEORGE TOLES

Nicolas Cage's Peter Loew, in the early stages of his mental breakdown in *Vampire's Kiss* (1989), angrily flags a waiter strolling past the booth he occupies at Munson's, a late night New York City diner. Loew informs the server that no one has taken his order in fifteen minutes, and that he'd like to be waited on *today*! "Right away, sir, right away," the server (played by the film's screenwriter, Joseph Minion) assures Loew, unpersuasively, before leaving the frame, and the movie. Before Minion has time to return, Loew finds further cause for outrage when a young woman in the booth behind him tells a friend about her recent acceptance of a marriage proposal, which took place during a romantic carriage ride. As though the woman's desire to proclaim her happiness was too much for any civilized person to bear, Peter grabs his briefcase, rises to full height in his imposing Paul Smith business suit, and bellows "Fucking greasehole" to the crowded diner's clientele. He then strides out of the restaurant, accompanied by somber soundtrack music, which seems to affirm both the gravity of the situation and his right to his offended dignity. No sooner, however, does Loew vacate the premises than he feels neck pains from a recent (imaginary) vampire bite, whose telltale holes he has cunningly masked with a bandage. His jaws begin to spasm, his teeth to clack, and his facial muscles violently contort as he rebuffs the efforts of an elderly male passerby to help him.

Joseph Minion's cameo in this brief scene is modest and inconspicuous, as befits the screenwriter's usual function in the filmmaking process. His character's job is to take orders and provide satisfaction—a minion, if you like—and in the short time we observe him he fails to do both. The screenwriter is spotted and then berated by someone several times larger than life whom he happens to have created. Peter Loew not only is unable to recognize

Minion, but instantly feels his own superiority to this incompetent menial. The server deserves a good public dressing down. He must be put in his place. In the scene immediately preceding the diner episode, Loew is shown taking sadistic pleasure in torturing one of his office employees, Alva (Maria Conchita Alonso), demanding that she locate with the utmost speed a meaningless missing book contract that is (possibly) lurking somewhere in a Kafkaesque sea of files. A portrait of Kafka in Loew's office (let's regard it as an anonymous gift from Minion) no doubt supplies some inspiration for his indecipherable brutality. One is tempted to read the diner scene then as a turning-the-tables reversal, where another worker in the vast community of underlings does not bend to Loew's abuse or respect his position. The fact that Loew's demands are disregarded contributes in some small way to his crack-up when leaving the restaurant. The screenwriter-as-harried waiter, affiliated with the concerns of ordinary life that Loew is cut off from, might very well wish to use his brief dramatic turn to pass judgment on his creation's escalating monstrosity. But further consideration of this conflict makes it clear that we are firmly aligned here with the deplorable Loew, and meant to be. Courtesy and generosity are not the issue. A spectator attuned to the tone of *Vampire's Kiss* is instead captivated by the prospect of Peter Loew descending still further into the no man's land of his dementedness, where all bonds of normal kinship are snapped asunder. It is, after all, a comedy of madness.

But suppose Minion called upon his prerogatives as creator, and arranged a second meeting with Loew, one in which he shed some light on the freakish nature of Peter's predicament and explained his own relationship with him more fully. Taking a brief coffee break from his colossal self-absorption, Loew could be forced to listen to the man who dreamed up all his agonies. It would be the first time Loew had ever genuinely listened to anyone. Minion might begin by talking about the dead bat that he had discovered one evening on his apartment balcony. He wondered where it had come from, and whether it carried some strange infection. He then recalled that horror films were often commercially successful, and that he had the germ of an idea for one, lying on his floor. A raven had once paid a propitious visit to Edgar Allan Poe, and a "never more" bat had ended its final flight at Minion's lodgings. Within two and a half weeks, in one wild torrential gust, Minion informed Loew, he completed the screenplay of *Vampire's Kiss*. Its central character imagines that he has been infected during casual sex with a female vampire lover. He pursues the delusion that he is turning into a vampire himself with ever-deepening conviction. He believes he has been singled out, with a terrible arbitrariness, for Promethean suffering, and that he must heroically struggle—in isolation—to preserve his humanity and selfhood. The central joke of *Vampire's Kiss* is that Peter Loew lacks even a rudimentary conception of what humanity and selfhood are. The vampire takeover is the one mode of being that he has authentically experienced. It is his first feverish brush with the feeling that he actually exists. Instead of the fraudulent urban identity that he has concocted, catch as catch can, for his "unreal" job and "unreal" pursuit of sex, there is—at last!—a compelling, hallucinatory logic to his days and nights.

Minion and Loew sat together in awkward silence, allowing the paradox time to sink in. Then, rather cavalierly, Minion changed the subject to *After Hours* (1985), another comedy of madness screenplay that he had written while a student in a Columbia University scriptwriting class. His unlikely teacher was wild man director Dušan Makavejev, who gave it a grade of A. The script became, with remarkable swiftness, a film by Martin Scorsese, who was desperate to get ANY project going after the collapse of funding for *The Last Temptation of Christ*. Some of the details of the *After Hours* narrative "set up" were borrowed, without authorization, from an NPR Playhouse monologue by Joe Frank entitled "Lies." And Scorsese made a number of changes to Minion's script, far more than director Robert Bierman required for *Vampire's Kiss*. One of Minion's discarded ideas for *After Hours'* ending involved its main character, Paul Hackett (Griffin Dunne), hiding out in the womb of a female character, who grew larger and larger, like Lewis Carroll's Alice, to accommodate him, while Paul's pursuers banged on the door screaming, "We'll kill him." Scorsese eventually decided that this finale was too unrealistic.

In spite of the borrowings and director-dictated revisions, *After Hours* bears "MY unmistakable imprint," Minion insisted to Loew. The film's premise, characterization, overall tone of paranoid phantasmagoria, and antic, high wire verbal dazzle resemble the world of *Vampire's Kiss* far more strongly than they do any other film of Scorsese's. Making this claim, Minion allowed himself one fist pound of the diner table for emphasis.

Paul Hackett, eavesdropping from a nearby booth, couldn't resist raising the question of whether the AIDS epidemic was the cultural incubator of both screenplays. He had a theory that all the time-honored mechanisms for seduction and the pursuit of nocturnal, big city sexual adventure in romantic comedy were de-familiarized by the sudden arrival of this plague, and its covert, relentless advance. "Doing what comes naturally" opened up wide new vistas of fear and mistrust. AIDS, like a terrifying magician, turned every erotic impulse, with a wave of its wand, into a poisonous bloom. Replying obliquely, Minion reminded Paul of the bed surrounded by mousetraps in *After Hours*. The woman who set them intended them as safeguards against death-dealing intruders. Minion hinted that the frantic cacophony of this multitude of traps snapping shut in rapid succession could be the new lethal soundscape for sexual surrender.

Minion concluded his chat by introducing Paul to Peter, and telling both characters that they were best understood as mirror images of each other. They are casualties of sexual exploits for which they were psychically ill-equipped. Peter is one of those creatures whose spectacular mental unraveling is, to a remarkable extent, invisible to those around him. When he misbehaves as a man cushioned by privilege, his air of abandon has the cachet of an eccentric rock star. His out-of-controlness is one of the expected perks of wealth, so even to his victims he doesn't appear to be violating the system's rules. When he later acquires the look of one of the homeless mental patients set loose from hospitals in the late 80s to roam the streets, unsupervised, he is invisible in another away, and generally shunned while doing "expected" crazy things. Paul Hackett, the diffident computer processor of *After Hours*, is, by contrast, hyper-visible at all times. From the moment he ventures late at night into the Soho district in search of a "close encounter," his entire social identity (as much a counterfeit as Peter's) is suddenly magnified, submitted to "hot lights" grilling from every quarter. The garden-variety bad faith of Paul Hackett's papier-mache existence guiltily gleams through every behavioral crack, and is a magnet for everyone's suspicion. His anxious, fumbling "innocence" seems an utterly unconvincing pose, and makes him—even to the spectator—a plausible source of the urban plague and its swirling dread. As Peter and Paul gazed at each other with growing fascination and resentment, Joseph Minion quietly slipped away.

SUGGESTED FURTHER READING

Baker, Aaron. *A Companion to Martin Scorsese*. Oxford: John Wylie, 2014.
Ferguson, Kevin L. "The Yuppies and the Yuckies: Anxieties of Influence" in Ferguson, *Eighties People: New Lives in the Cultural Imagination*. New York: Palgrave Macmillan, 2016, pp. 79–108.
Grist, Leighton. "Yuppies in Peril: After Hours and Cape Fear" in Grist *The Films of Martin Scorsese, 1978-99*. Basingstoke: Palgrave Macmillan, 2013, pp. 122–152.

Paula Modersohn-Becker
(1876–1907)

WENDY MOONEY

Expressionism emerged in Germany in the early twentieth century. A reaction against realism, the drawing technique of Expressionists was crude and interpretation was seen as entirely subjective: art now came from within and was not a mere record of what lay without. Its influences are found in both primitivism—particularly in the work of Paul Gauguin—and in the paintings of artists like Vincent van Gogh, James Ensor and Edvard Munch, who distorted form, allowed bold colors to convey emotion and the inner angst and turmoil of man. Such works as James Ensor's "The Intrigue" (1890), for example, and Edvard Munch's "The Scream of Nature" (1893), were to influence the later Expressionism of German silent film—including *The Golem* (1915), *The Cabinet of Dr. Caligari* (1920) and *Nosferatu* (1922)—these silent horror movies in turn giving birth to American horror and *film noir*. Similarities can thus be found at times between the figures of early Expressionist art and the characters of American horror movies. What surprises in the work of the German Modernist and early Expressionist painter Paula Modersohn-Becker (1876–1907), however, is her anticipation of Southern Gothic and the way she uses landscape and light to emphasize the grotesque and expose the female threat and power inherent in the backwoods female child or adolescent who, in a time of development and progress, remains one with nature.

On 29 February 1900, Paula Modersohn-Becker, remembered first and foremost nowadays for her bold colors, naked self-portraits and naked nursing mothers (Diane Radycki, in *Paula Modersohn-Becker: The First Modern Woman Artist*, tells us she was the first female artist to paint herself naked), wrote to her sister, Milly, from Paris:

> My art is going well. I have a feeling of satisfaction about it. Afternoons I stroll around the city taking a good look at everything and trying to absorb it all [...] I went back to Notre

> Dame again. Such wonderful Gothic detailing, those monstrous gargoyles, each one with its own character and face [...] Directly behind Notre Dame, almost encircled by the Seine, lies the morgue. Day after day they fish corpses from the river here, people who don't want to go on living, or sometimes someone who was robbed and thrown into the water.

The passage reads more like an excerpt from a Gothic novel than from a letter. The Gothic Notre Dame, with its individualized gargoyles, is associated in Paula's mind with the morgue and with a river of death. Every day in Paula's Paris, corpses are fished from the river. "Under the colorful surface of this laughing city there lies a great deal that is black and horrible," she adds. "I sometimes fear it will tear my heart to pieces." That may well have been so, but getting under "the colorful surface" of life is, in fact, what Paula's work is all about. The naked nursing mother in her mother-child portraits exerts a female power akin to the Empress of the Tarot Cards; close to nature she is a life-giving force. Similarly, Paula's backwoods children likewise bear the same close relationship to nature and appear to take their power from it. However, had they not been created in a small German village, and some twenty years earlier, they might well be the progeny of Grant Woods's sinister-looking couple in *American Gothic* (1930), or the young inhabitants of Gatlin in Stephen King's later *Children of the Corn* (1977) and the movies of the same name.

In *Paula Modersohn-Becker: Her Life and Work*, Gillian Perry has noted the artist's "fascination with the more unusual or freakish characteristics of the people she saw around her in Worpswede," the artist colony where Paula lived much of her short life, and her preoccupation with "physical disability or illness." This fascination with the freakish and with "disability or illness" is also ironically to be found in the work of James Dickey and John Boorman, in *Deliverance* (novel 1970, film, 1972), and Tobe Hooper and Kim Henkel in *The Texas Chain Saw Massacre* (1974).

Surrounded by cornfields and birch trees amid the relentless flatlands of Lower Saxony and boasting the only hill for hundreds of miles—together with a poorhouse, filled with demented elderly and impoverished children—Worpswede was an ideal location for an artist captivated by the Gothic and by the darker elements of human life and nature. Paula quickly set about capturing her rural neighbors in paint, using the ancient peasant women of the poorhouse for models. These witch-like peasant women, with their watery eyes and soil-colored skin call to mind the vindictive servants or peasants of fairytales or Gothic novels (with her malevolent eyes, the elderly peasant woman of *Head of an Old Woman in a Black Scarf* (1903), for example, might have stepped straight out of Ann Radcliffe's *The Italian*). For all that, these workhouse women are fully human and contemplative and do not create the same feeling of unease in the viewer as do Paula's turn of the century portraits of backwoods girls and children.

The unease inherent in these paintings perhaps springs from the stillness and watchfulness that is depicted in the artist's rural subjects. No longer sentimentalized and prettified, as in mid-nineteenth century paintings, Modersohn-Becker's young rural females are secure in their ugly, ordinary or deformed selves and one with the landscape from which they have sprung. This backwoods otherness, with its primitiveness and closeness to nature, at times seems to challenge progress and change with its female power—perhaps standing for the artist herself, close to nature and painting against a realist mainstream from the countryside and counter to her artist husband's, Otto Modersohn's, style. "Paula hates to be conventional," he writes disgruntledly in September 1903 in his journal, "The expression! Hands like spoons, noses like cobs, mouths like wounds, faces like cretins ... and children at that!"

Paula Modersohn-Becker, *Two Girls with Birch Tree Trunk* (1902) (courtesy Museen Böttcherstraße, Paula Modersohn-Becker Museum).

Otto may well have had in mind the sinister children of *Two Girls with a Birch Tree Trunk* (c.1902). Here two girls, staring straight at the viewer with their dark slashes of eyes and indistinct faces, in their stillness and watchfulness anticipate the children of a Southern Gothic horror movie. The silver trunk of the birch emphasizes the blacks and grays in the dress of the child to the forefront and the black stockings and banded hat of the child in the clown-like blue spotted dress to her rear. Although giving the impression of being rooted in the moor itself, there is an intensity about their stillness, as if both are determined to pursue the artist/viewer no matter what. This haunting quality is likewise found in the earlier *Portrait of a Girl in a Landscape* (1897).

Zombie-like and perhaps semi-bald, the girl stands as a ghostly figure on a deserted landscape, one side of her face apparently corrupted by sunlight. For all that, however, and despite her doll-like eyes, she exudes a backwoods female power as she offers herself to the light and claims the blank landscape for her own.

Both these and other of Paula Modersohn-Becker's paintings of children—including *The Sick Girl* (1901), *The Blind Sister* (1903) and *Girl in a Red Dress by the Birch Tree* (c. 1905)—seem to anticipate the physically disabled or threatening child characters of Southern Gothic movies such as *Deliverance* and *Children of the Corn* (1984). The threat here, however, is in a female rustic power that demands recognition. Close to nature and cut off from the city and its ideas of progress, it is a power that can be said to reside in Paula herself as she sets out, in her own words, to "be granted the ability to express in my art that little message that is my whole being."

Paula Modersohn-Becker, *Portrait of a Girl in a Landscape* (1897) (courtesy Museen Böttcherstraße, Paula Modersohn-Becker Museum).

Paula Modersohn-Becker died, aged thirty-one, on 21 November 1907, following an embolism after the birth of her only child. In her unsentimental self-portraits of the naked female body and breast-feeding mother, who seems the source of life and nature, she proved herself an original and innovative artist. In her later child portraits of imperfect local children, however, she demonstrated the threat of female otherness and power that resides in deserted rural areas where difference and alienation from society proves an advantage and not a hindrance.

SUGGESTED FURTHER READING

King, Averil. *Paula Modersohn-Becker*. Woodbridge: Antique Collectors' Club, 2009.

Modersohn-Becker, Paula. *The Letters and Journals*. Eds. Günther Busch and Liselotte Von Reinken, trans. Arthur S. Wensinger and Carole Clew Hoey. Evanston: Northwestern University Press, 1990.

Perry, Gillian. *Paula Modersohn-Becker: Her Life and Work*. London: Women's Press, 1979.

Radycki, Diane. *Paula Modersohn-Becker: The First Modern Woman Artist*. New Haven: Yale University Press, 2013.

Fitz-James O'Brien
(1828–1862)

Kevin Corstorphine

At the height of his fame in the 1850s, the Irish-born Fitz-James O'Brien came to be known as the "Celtic Poe" among his American peers. The comparison between the two is not without validity. Like the American master, O'Brien produced works that moved between horror and science fiction, and combined biting cynicism with a capacity for whimsy. He produced dozens of short stories that we know of, although others were published anonymously and have yet to be rediscovered. Many of these were published in the most popular magazines of his day, including *Harper's Weekly*, *Putnam's Monthly Magazine*, and *Vanity Fair*. This is not to mention many successful plays and poems which are now largely forgotten. As Wayne R. Kime notes in his 2012 collection *Thirteen Stories by Fitz-James O'Brien: The Realm of the Mind*, O'Brien was at one point "acknowledged to be one of America's most talented young authors." Despite having had such a promising writing career, no collected edition of his work appeared until nineteen years after his death, when the task was undertaken by his friend William Winter. In this 1881 collection, Winter attempts to explain this with the intimation that "his character and his way of life had made him a difficult subject to treat." O'Brien, in fact, had led a short but full life, one that contained no small degree of notoriety.

Born Michael Fitz-James O'Brien in County Cork, he was raised in Limerick as part of a landholding family. He seems to have lived the idyllic life of horse-riding, hunting, and fishing that was usual for a young country gentleman until famine struck in 1845. The young O'Brien sent poems to the nationalist newspaper *The Nation*, attacking English tyranny and calling for relief for the poor. For some of these, and also for later pieces in the United States, he used the pseudonym "Heremon," naming himself for the mythical High King of Ireland. He then spent time in Dublin, claiming to have attended

Trinity College, although no record exists of his matriculation, and a certain degree of fabrication was not unusual for O'Brien. Another rumor connects him with the British army, and he may have spent time in France, certainly gaining a command of French in this period. What is known is that he then moved to London, where he managed to spend his sizeable inheritance in two and a half years of high living before leaving for New York. The impetus to leave was rumored to be the return of an English army officer who had been stationed in India, with whose wife O'Brien had apparently been conducting a love affair. Francis Wolle, in his 1944 biography *Fitz-James O'Brien: A Literary Bohemian of the Eighteen-Fifties*, points out that "The relish of gossip is in these stories; but, whatever the discrepancies as to detail, the main point of the intrigue would be thoroughly in keeping with the life and character of Fitz-James as Aldrich and Stoddard knew him in America." These were the writers Thomas Bailey Aldrich and Richard Henry Stoddard. O'Brien sound found himself at home in such literary company, and later with other famous artistic figures including Henry Clapp and Edwin Booth, with whom O'Brien frequented the famous beer cellar at Pfaff's, located on Broadway. Something of the atmosphere of the establishment is captured by another famous regular, Walt Whitman, in an unfinished poem from the early 1860s, where he writes of, "The vault at Pfaff's where the drinkers and laughers meet to eat and drink and carouse."

O'Brien and his group of friends were at the heart of literary life in New York, and also at the forefront of a burgeoning bohemian spirit. As Albert Parry notes in his 1933 book *Garretts and Pretenders: A History of Bohemianism in America*, O'Brien "fought friends and strangers with his tongue, pen, and fists. He had reckless but obscure love affairs. He played the gentleman by returning loans whenever magazines paid him for his news-topic poems, by pressing money, when he had it, into the palms of needy friends even if they did not ask for it, by con-

Fitz-James O'Brien (from William Winter, ed., *The Poems and Stories of Fitz-James O'Brien*, Boston: Osgood & Co., 1881).

cealing the names of his amours, and by shaking hands with his adversaries when the bouts were over." He was even made infamous by William North's 1855 novel *The Slave of the Lamp*, which caricatured O'Brien as the ludicrous dandy "Fitzgammon O'Bouncer." At the outbreak of Civil War in 1861, O'Brien joined the Union army, soon becoming an enthusiastic recruiter for the Seventh Regiment of the New York National Guard. He caricatured again, this time in a cartoon printed in *Vanity Fair*, which depicts a heavily mustached O'Brien dragging reluctant men in service. He later served at the front line, and in 1862 was wounded by a gunshot to the shoulder. He died less than two months later of a tetanus infection following surgery.

Jessica Amanda Salmonson, in her 1988 book *The Supernatural Tales of Fitz-James O'Brien*, calls O'Brien "the most important figure after Poe and before Lovecraft in modern horror literature." Indeed, the latter writer acknowledges O'Brien in his 1927 essay "Supernatural Horror in Literature," where he regrets that "O'Brien's early death undoubtedly deprived us of some masterful tales of strangeness and terror." His reputation is largely founded on his popular 1858 story "The Diamond Lens." The narrator, Linley, is obsessed with perfecting the microscope and resorts to consulting a spiritual medium, who puts him in communication with the spirit of the Dutch scientist Antonie van Leeuwenhoek, "the great father of microscopics." The summoned "Leewenhoek" reveals that the perfect microscope can be created through the use of a one hundred and forty-carat diamond. Seemingly by chance, Linley's friend has in his possession such a diamond, which he acquires by murdering him, justifying it to himself in terms of the necessary pursuit of science. Linley constructs his microscope and examines a drop of water. The magnification made possible by the lens reveals the internal structure of the very atoms of the water. Once he has "penetrated beyond the grosser particles of aqueous matter" he discovers an entire world filled with forests of brilliant light, and in this tiny world discovers what appears to be a woman. He falls in love with this "sylph," naming her Animula, but is struck with misery at the impossibility of communicating with her. On returning from a night at the theatre, he is horrified by her tragic (and grotesque) death when the drop of water finally evaporates on the slide and descends into a life of bitter regret. The story clearly shows the influence of Poe with its monomaniacal narrator meeting an ironic fate, but here O'Brien shows that he could be equally skilled at blending the scientific with the supernatural to produce an unsettling yet wondrous imaginative world.

A keen interest in spiritualism shows through in ghost stories such as "The Pot of Tulips" (1855). O'Brien's protagonist, Harry Escott, sets out to discover the truth behind so-called hauntings. In his era's spirit of rational investigation he sets out to show how "none of these apparent miracles are *super*natural, but all, however singular, directly dependent on certain natural laws." These stories can be seen as documenting their times, as they are clearly inspired by the case of the Fox sisters, who reported mysterious rappings in their house in Hydesville, New York, in 1848, and went on to cause a public sensation with their séances. The same year, the influential writer Catherine Crowe published her own views alongside various stories of "real" hauntings in a book called *The Night Side of Nature; or, Ghosts and Ghost Seers*. As she says of these events, "I do not propose to consider them as supernatural; on the contrary, I am persuaded that the time will come, when they will be reduced strictly within the bounds of science." Through the character of Escott, O'Brien shows that his finger was on the pulse of contemporary debates, and fictionalizes them in the form of chillingly entertaining stories. Even more interesting is the later Escott tale "What Was It? A Mystery" (1859), which is notable for displaying the first depiction of an invisible creature in a scientifically grounded story, predating H.G. Wells' *The Invisible Man* (1897) by almost four decades. Escott spends an evening smoking opium with a friend in his house in New York which is reputed to be haunted. That night, he is attacked in his bed by a "breathing, panting, corporeal shape." When he manages to wrestle it into submission, the true horror is revealed, or rather not, as he sees absolutely nothing. Told through this somewhat unreliable first-person narration, the story displays the trickery and evasion typical of Gothic fiction, yet O'Brien does something quite unexpected in having the reality of the creature validated within the narrative. Harry and his companions cover the captive creature in plaster of Paris, revealing a small yet muscular form which is distorted, yet clearly "shaped like a man." When it has later died, seemingly of starvation, the cast is taken away and is soon, we are told in a footnote, to be put on display in a museum.

Not all of O'Brien's stories deal with scientific matters so directly. His 1859 melodrama "The Wondersmith" deals with the maniacal gypsy Herr Hippe and his plot to murder children *en masse* by delivering murderous animated toy soldiers as Christmas gifts. He is eventually foiled by a Christian girl he has previously kidnapped, who is aided by a heroic hunchback and a trained monkey. "A Dead Secret" (1853) is a paranoid conspiracy narrative where the protagonist steals another man's identity and is subsequently pursued across Europe by a secretive cabal without ever finding out why. "The Child That Loved a Grave" (1861) is a poignant story about a young boy who is obsessed with tending the grave of a young nobleman. The boy himself dies when the bones are disinterred for a grand reburial abroad. Here, the poetic morbidity of O'Brien's writing places him among the great authors of the Gothic tradition. O'Brien's stories are entertaining and thought-provoking, and bear witness to the culture of his era in continually surprising and fascinating ways. His life was short, but his importance in the development of horror, science fiction, and American literature looms large.

SUGGESTED FURTHER READING

Kellermeyer, M. Grant, ed. *What Was It? & Others: Fitz-James O'Brien's Best Weird Fiction & Ghost Stories*. Madison, IN: Oldstyle Tales, 2013.

Kime, Wayne R. *Thirteen Stories by Fitz-James O'Brien: The Realm of the Mind*. Newark: University of Delaware Press, 2012.

Salmonson, Jessica Amanda. *The Supernatural Tales of Fitz-James O'Brien, Volume One: Macabre Tales*. New York: Doubleday, 1988.

Wolle, Francis. *Fitz-James O'Brien: A Literary Bohemian of the Eighteen-Fifties*. Boulder, CO: University of Colorado Studies, 1944. Reprinted in Kessinger Legacy Reprints.

Sandy Petersen
(1955–)

RACHEL MIZSEI WARD

Sandy Petersen is an American games designer who has worked in both table-top and computer-gaming companies. His most famous horror work is the design of the 1981 table-top roleplaying game *Call of Cthulhu* for Chaosium Games.

Starting in U.S. university campuses in the 1970s, role-playing games are fantasy gaming experiences where players portray characters in a communal narrative. The players can choose how their characters react to events, and what actions they take. Unlike other games, role-playing games are not about winning or losing, rather they are about playing an interesting character and creating a good story. The fantasy role-playing game *Call of Cthulhu* is based on H.P. Lovecraft and other genre writers' weird fiction.

In 1981 *Call of Cthulhu* was a unique product in the roleplaying game industry. It was the first horror game and one of the earliest licensed adaptions of an existing world. Unlike previous fantasy games such as *Dungeons and Dragons*, the *Call of Cthulhu* game emphasized eldritch horror and investigation which were the new genres in the field. Players could portray a range of what were in 1981 non-typical roleplaying characters such as antiquarians, dilettantes and professors, while mundane skills such as "Library Use" or "Anthropology" were essential, in contrast to other games where combat skills were paramount.

The unique nature of the *Call of Cthulhu* game was due to the approach taken by Sandy Petersen. Lovecraft's Mythos was very important to him and in Petersen's dedication to the *Call of Cthulhu* game he explains that he was introduced to Lovecraft's stories by his father, who lent him an Armed Services Edition. He goes on to admit that the game was "a work of love by the author." This means that some parts of the broader Cthulhu mythos were left out, and in Petersen's designer's notes he explains that he deliberately chose to leave out elements that he felt were not in keeping with Lovecraft's "original concept." This included Brian Lumley's idea of a war in heaven because it weakened the cosmic horror of an uncaring universe that is so vital to the horror inherent in Lovecraft's work. Another leap in design that Petersen led was that *Call of Cthulhu* was the first game to include flavor text and quotes from many of the Cthulhu Mythos authors and fiction, specifically the H.P. Lovecraft short story *The Call of Cthulhu* (1928), something that is now normal in modern games. Flavor text is writing that enhances the reader's experience of reading game rules by highlighting aspects of the genre, and creating atmosphere. It can be pieces of short fiction, relevant quotes, song lyrics and sections of dialogue. This flavor text style has also been incorporated into the material that comes with computer role-playing games such as *Final Fantasy*.

Over time, Chaosium, the publisher of *Call of Cthulhu*, has provided a platform for new work in the genre, as well as republishing old, often out of print, stories, under the *Call of Cthulhu* branding. Chaosium's weird fiction line is frequently not easily available from traditional booksellers because they use different distributors to fiction publishers. Instead the books are usually sold in gaming shops and specialty science fiction shops such as Forbidden Planet in London. The experience of Chaosium was that there was a distinct split between fans of weird fiction and fans of Chaosium's *Call of Cthulhu*, with the two groups having discovered Lovecraft's work in very different ways. As a result the game has been helpful in creating an alternative audience for Lovecraft and weird fiction in general.

After the critical and commercial success of *Call of Cthulhu* Petersen would be involved in designing other table-top role-playing games including a game adaption of the family comedy-horror film *Ghostbusters* (1984) for West End Games. *Ghostbusters* (1986) had an innovative rules set which was designed to be as simple and easy to learn as possible to encourage new players to engage with role-playing games.

In the late 1980s Petersen would then move on to work in the computer games industry full time. Over the next ten years he worked for several companies, including MicroProse, id Software and Ensemble Studios, and worked on key games such as *Sid Meier's Pirates*, *Civilization*, and *Age of Kings*. At id Software Petersen worked on the horror themed first-person shooter game *Doom* (1993). *Doom* was originally planned as a licensed game based on the film *Aliens* (1986), but there were problems over control of the intellectual property. As a result the game retained the concept of patrolling a maze of corridors, but replaced H. R. Giger's Alien with demons from hell. Despite the loss of the original intellectual property *Doom* has been one of the most influential first-person shooter games and was critical in popularizing the genre. The first-person-shooter is a genre specific to computer games, where the action takes place in a first-person perspective, and the player uses their quick reflexes to dispatch multiple enemies with a range of attributes. In *Doom*, the player moves his character around a maze, running and jumping to reach the goals and equipment that the game offers. The character is rated with health and armor, and carries a variety of weapons and their ammunition. The monsters that the player-character encounters in *Doom* have a variety of power levels and abilities to provide a range of challenges.

This kind of computer game is quite common today, but at the time *Doom* was unusual. What made it particularly unique was that the game was not for sale—instead it was developed as a free downloadable shareware game with additional levels (or episodes) available for purchase, predating "freemium" games by some 20 years. It has been estimated that *Doom* was downloaded and installed on 10 million computers within two years of release.

The other thing that *Doom* possessed was the social aspect of traditional table-top role-playing games. The multiplayer systems available in 1993 were primitive compared to the internet based options of today. It was not uncommon for players to have to take their expensive personal computer gaming systems to a central location such as a friend's house and physically link the computers using cabling, creating Local Area Network parties of like-minded computer gamers.

Petersen was instrumental in developing this aspect of the game. Again, using the skills he had developed in table-top role-playing game design, he was able to design new levels for the game and helped create and name popular monsters such as the Hellknight and the Cyberdemon. The look and feel of these monsters was inspired by H.P. Lovecraft's weird fiction.

Petersen has continued to work on projects inspired by H.P. Lovecraft. In 2011 he was the executive producer for the independent film *The Whisperer in Darkness*, created by the H.P. Lovecraft Historical Society. This black and white production was inspired by Universal horror films of the 1930s and based on Lovecraft's short story of the same title. Petersen also created the new board game *Cthulhu Wars* (2013) the production of which was funded by a massively successful Kickstarter campaign. In 2015, Petersen returned to Chaosium to work on the seventh edition of *Call of Cthulhu* after a change in leadership at Chaosium. Sandy Petersen has been influential in both table-top role-playing and the computer game industry. His success in computer game design was based on the skills that he developed as a table-top gamer, and he has been one of the first of many to move between these related industries.

SUGGESTED FURTHER READING

Appelcline, Shannon. *Designers and Dragons*. Swindon, England: Mongoose, 2011.
Call of Cthulhu. Chaosium, www.chaosium.com/.
Call of Cthulhu Quick Start Rules for 7th ed. http://www.chaosium.com/the-call-of-cthulhu-quick-start-pdf/.
Sandy Petersen's games company, Petersen Entertainment: https://petersengames.com/.

Leonora Piper
(1857–1950)

Dara Downey

> I feel as if something were passing over my brain, making it numb, a sensation similar to that I experienced when I was etherized [...]. I feel [...] as if a cold breeze passed over me, and people and objects become smaller until they finally disappear, then, I know nothing more until I wake up, when the first thing I am conscious of is a bright, very very bright light, and then darkness, such darkness. [...] I see, as if from a very great distance, objects and people in the room; but they are very small and very black.

This is how Leonora Piper, a highly successful medium from Boston, Massachusetts, described the process of falling into and then out of the trance state in which she claimed, during her career which spanned the final decades of the nineteenth century and beginning of the twentieth, to be able to contact the spirits of the dead. So uncannily accurate were Piper's "sittings" with relatives of the deceased that the American Society of Psychical Research (ASPR) paid her a retainer, insisting that she devote herself entirely to their enquiries into the existence of life after death. She remained with the Society (both the ASPR and the Society for Psychical Research [SPR] in England) for well over a decade, during which time she served as the conduit for messages that often reproduced so exactly the memories and personalities of the researchers' own departed friends and relations that even some of the most skeptical, hyper-rational scientists were convinced.

Piper was born in New Hampshire in 1857, and displayed psychic abilities from the age of eight, when she was experienced what the SPR came to term a "crisis apparition": the feeling of a sharp blow to the head, and a hissing voice in her ear, telling her that her Aunt Sara was dead. She told her mother, who recorded the incident carefully, and only a few days later, the family received a letter informing them of Sara's death. It was not, however, until she turned 22, while expecting her first child, and working and living as a shopkeeper in Boston, that her powers manifested themselves fully, when Piper visited one J.R. Cocke, a popular local psychic healer, and a pioneering hypnotherapist who had been blind since a very young age. During her second visit, his touch sent her into an immediate trance, during which she scribbled down a message which, it transpired, was from the dead son of an attendee named Judge Frost, a message that Cocke pronounced "remarkable" in its verisimilitude. Piper soon found herself bombarded with requests from neighbors to contact departed relatives, and it was around this time, about 1885, that she was first visited by Eliza Gibbens, the mother-in-law of William James, brother of novelist Henry James. While William was initially dubious, a later visit with his wife left him less certain in his disbelief. James, a philosopher and early psychologist who was involved with the ASPR, was intrigued and began visiting Piper regularly, later encouraging other scientists and psychical researchers to join him in his sittings with her, before ultimately offering her a position with the Society.

Like many of her contemporaries, such as the considerably more famous Florence Cook, she was best known for her series of "controls"—spirits who served as go-betweens, managing and aiding more recently deceased or weaker spirits to communicate effectively through the medium. Over the course of her career, Piper was "controlled" by a series of different personalities, the first being Dr. Phinuit, who claimed to have been a medical doctor who had lived in France during the late eighteenth and early nineteenth century. According to (A)SPR reports, Piper's manner would become more abrupt and domineering when Phinuit took over her body; her voice would change, acquiring a suitably masculine timbre and a French accent. However, some investigators were unconvinced by the accent, insisting that Phinuit's knowledge of French and indeed of medicine was patchy at best, and that "his" answers to questions of this nature were extremely evasive. Indeed, neither Society ever succeeded in finding any record of his having ever lived.

As this implies, Piper was subjected to very strict standards of investigation. Richard Hodgson, for example, who travelled from England to Boston with the express purpose of debunking her as a medium, had Mrs. Piper followed by private investigators in 1887, though with no success. Indeed, she was almost impossible to disprove—there was clearly no way that she could have gained access to private, personal information about her sitters, and yet in her trances, the details that she provided about relationships and past events was, by all reports, startlingly accurate. In particular, Piper was very skilled at psychometry, reading objects in order to determine who the owner was and to communicate details about that owner, or about significant or traumatic events that had taken place in relation to an object or within a particular place. In other words, psychometry was, in the nineteenth century, seen as one possible, quasi-scientific "explanation" for phenomena such as haunted houses.

Of course, as with all mediums, there were sittings that were far less successful, due to illness Piper's part; the spirits proving incoherent or difficult to contact; or "negative energy" from the sitter or surroundings. Spirits who claimed to have died by suicide or other traumatic means were generally the least clear in their communications, and the most likely to make what seemed to be mistakes. When she was spot on, however, even William James himself could become somewhat unnerved, though he and his fellow (A)SPR members strove to remain as objective and as scientifically detached as possible. In the spirit of scientific rigor, the SPR brought Piper to England with her two daughters in 1889 to continue the investigations in a location which they could control as fully as possible, though she was extremely reluctant at first—with good reason, as it turned out. While there, her trance was harshly tested, as the men pinched her, pricked her with pins, burnt her skin with matches, and placed all kinds of noxious-smelling, often toxic substances under her nose and even in her mouth. None of these tests succeeded in waking her from her trance, though she would complain of strange tastes and mysterious bruises upon returning to full consciousness.

In the early 1900s, the rigid skepticism of the Societies began to break down, primarily because Phinuit was gradually being replaced as a control—specifically, by now-dead friends and indeed members of the (A)SPR. The first of these was George Pellew, who had joked cynically at one meeting that if there was indeed life after death, then he would come back and tell them all what it was like. The "G.P." or "George Pelham" control, as he was known in the reports, for reasons of privacy, did indeed provide a startling amount of "information" on the conditions of the afterlife, while also stressing his own authenticity via personal details and remembered conversations with other members that only he could have known. He was soon apparently joined by other (A)SPR members who passed away over the year, including such prominent figures as Fred Myers, Edmund Gurney, and the once-disbelieving Richard Hodgson himself. The pressure and constant testing, however, ultimately proved too much for Piper, and, in 1901, she announced the end of her career as a medium, via a voluntary interview with the *New York Herald*. When the *Herald* misrepresented her announcement as a confession in which Piper recanted on her entire career and everything to do with mediumship, she was appalled, and, a few days later, conducted another interview with the *Boston Advertiser*, in which she announced that she would be returning to work with the ASPR. Even here, however, she maintained (as she had in the first interview) that she had no idea who or what was speaking though her, even implying that she may have been somehow unconsciously producing the phenomena herself. As she stated, "Spirits may have controlled me and they may not. I confess that I do not know."

Nonetheless, while the "confession" did irreparable damage to her career, and to that of the Societies' members, Piper was never actually debunked as such, despite ongoing tests, including one brutal set of experiments carried out by G. Stanley Hall and Amy Tanner in 1909, from which they published a book entitled *Studies in Spiritualism*, which further undermined Piper's and her investigators' reputations. Around this time, "G.P." was largely superseded as Piper's control by a spirit called "Imperator," one of a group of forty-nine "higher," supposedly far older spirits (including "Rector," who claimed to have also acted as a control for William Stainton Moses, an English cleric and SPR member). Imperator and his fellow spirits were notably clearer and more formal in their communications than Phinuit because, they insisted, they were further removed from the dulling influence of recent habitation in earthly bodies, and therefore were also able to convey extensive and detailed descriptions regarding the structures and functioning of the spirit world. Nonetheless, perhaps as a result of the various damning exposés that dogged this stage of her career, in 1911, Imperator announced that he was withdrawing from "the machine" as he called Piper (somewhat chillingly), and that she would no longer be a medium. By 1915, plagued by ill health, she found that she could once again conduct some automatic writing, but was unable to fall into a trance. Leonora Piper died in 1950, at the age of 93, still quietly working as a private medium, but no longer at the height of her powers.

Despite the somewhat ignominious latter stages of her career, and the often strangely brief descriptions of her mediumship in academic works (when her name is featured at all), she remained central to the (A)SPR's mission and to their investigations, and indeed to psychical research generally. As William James put it in his final Presidential address to the Society in 1895, "a universal proposition can be made untrue by a particular instance. If you wish to upset the law that all crows are black, you mustn't seek to show that no crows are; it is enough to prove one single crow to be white." He continued, in a statement that exemplifies the cautious empiricism which characterized the Societies for Psychical Research, and which Leonora Piper was so instrumental in allowing them to maintain,

> My own white crow is Mrs Piper. In the trances of this medium, I cannot resist the conviction that knowledge appears which she has never gained by the ordinary waking use of her eyes and wits. What the source of this knowledge may be I know not, and have not the glimmer of an explanatory suggestion to make; but from admitting the fact of such evidence I can see no escape.

SUGGESTED FURTHER READING

Beloff, John. *Parapsychology: A Concise History*. London: Athlone, 1993.
Blum, Deborah. *Ghost Hunters*. London: Arrow, 2007.

James, William. *Essays in Psychical Research*. Cambridge, MA, and London: Harvard University Press, 1986.
Melechi, Antonio. *Servants of the Supernatural: The Night Side of the Victorian Mind*. London: Arrow, 2009.
Oppenheim, Janet. *The Other World: Spiritualism and Psychical Research in England, 1850–1914*. Cambridge: Cambridge University Press, 1988.
Piper, Alta L. *The Life and Work of Mrs Piper*. London: Kegan Paul, Trench, Trubner, 1929.
Richardson, Robert D. *William James: In the Maelstrom of American Modernism*. Boston and New York: Houghton Mifflin, 2007.
Tanner, Amy E. *Studies in Spiritualism*. New York and London: D. Appleton, 1910.
Tymn, Michael. *Resurrecting Leonora Piper: How Science Discovered the Afterlife*. Guildford: White Crow, 2013.

Edogawa Rampo
(1894–1965)

Colette Balmain

Edogawa Rampo (also written as Ranpo) is the pseudonym of one of the most influential Japanese writers of horror and detective fiction of all time, Hirai Tarō. Yet, surprisingly enough given the West's penchant for all things Japanese which can be traced back to Japanism—the name for the European trend for collecting Japanese art which was at its height from around the mid-17th century through to the beginning of the 18th–Rampo is rarely recognized by literary and gothic scholars and his contribution to both detective and gothic fiction and other media forms including manga and television has been largely ignored by Western academics and fans alike. While Rampo is accredited with being the inventor of modern Japanese detective fiction (*tantei shosetsu*), it is, however, his erotic grotesque nonsense (*ero-guro-nansensu*) stories with their deformed, demented protagonists and their lack of moral boundaries whose influence can be most clearly seen in contemporary Japanese horror fiction and film.

In addition to being a prolific fiction writer, Rampo was also was a screenwriter and playwright, a regular radio guest and was frequently consulted by newspapers and magazines based on his knowledge of crime. Hirai began his writing career while at Waseda University by translating the works of Arthur Conan Doyle. His first foray into fictional writing was the short story "The Two-Sen Copper Coin" ("Nisen Doka") which was published in the magazine *Shin Senien* in 1923. A prolific writer, with 67 (including books for children most notably *The Boys Club* Series) and seventy-six short stories (Shreiber, 2006, p. xvi); many of which have been adapted for the small and big screen, few them ever officially distributed outside of Japan. To date, there is not a complete list of either his big or small screen works available in English at this time: MUBI only has 14 films listed, less than a quarter of films directly based on his writings. Perhaps this is because very little of his work has been translated into English until fairly recently, outside of the nine stories published in *Japanese Tales of Mystery and Imagination* in 1956 by Charles E. Tuttle, which took five years for the translator, James B. Harris, and Rampo, to finalize due to the difficulty in communicating meaning across two very disparate and etymologically different languages. His continuing influence on Japanese popular culture can be seen in manga, anime, TV and film. Indeed, I would argue that the current wave of "erotic gore" cinema which includes films such as *Big Tits Zombie* (Kyonyū doragon: Onsen zonbi vs sutorippa 5, dir. Rei Mikamoto: 2010), *Tokyo Gore Police* (Tokyo Zankoku Keisatsu, dir. Yoshihiro Nishimura: 2008) and *X-Cross* (dir. Kenta Fukasaku: 2007) owe much to the "ero-guro" writings of Rampo.

While much has been made of the fact that his penname is a transliteration of Edgar Allan Poe, and thus taken in homage to one of his literary idols (the other being Arthur Conan Doyle), critics have pointed out that this intertextual reference would have been mainly lost on his Japanese readers. Instead, the literal translation of "Edogawa Rampo" is "chaotic steps along the river Edo" which is a direct reference to the Edo River, or Edogawa.) This sense of doubleness, signified by the double meanings of his nom-de-plume, permeates his work, from the literal twins in his short story "The Twins: A Condemned Criminal's Confession to a Priest" (Sōseiji: 1924) to the metaphorical twins in "Two Crippled Men" ("Ni Haijin," 1924)—the first of which has more than a hint of Poe's "William Wilson" (1839) about it. "The Hell of Mirrors" ("Kagami-jigoku," 1926) similarly has a disturbed protagonist, Tanuma, whose craze for constructing complicated reflective surfaces calls to mind the tortured Nathanael in Hoffman's "The Sandman" (1816) whose obsession with the mechanisms of vision also leads to madness. However such similarities should not be overestimated and detract us from Rampo's originality and his importance to an understanding of contemporary Gothic as a global rather than a specifically national or even Western phenomenon. Rampo was first and foremost a Japanese writer whose contribution to Japanese literature and detective fiction in particular is considerable, and needs to be properly contextualized. Rampo was writing at a time of turmoil during which Japan's Imperial ambitions constructed narratives of nationalism which stressed Japan's civilization and modernity viz-a-viz other Asian nations. While many Western critics ascribe Japan's modernity to the U.S. Occupations, in fact the beginning of the first Showa Period (1926–1989) saw a rapid modernization of Japan and with it capitalist consumerism and a medicalization of "deviant" sexualities as part of the project of Social Darwinism for which the period is noted. In these terms, erotic grotesque nonsense's focus on so-called deviance and difference was a reaction to such dominant narratives of social superiority and inferiority associated with "abnormal" sexualities and "inferior" ethnicities and nationalities.

For these reasons, Rampo's detective fiction has been constructed by many Japanese critics as superior to his sensationalist ero-guro narratives (Angles: 2008, 101–141). In Rampo's 1930 novel, *The Fruits of Curiosity Hunting* (*Ryōki no hate*), the protagonist is a "curiosity seeker" (*ryōki*) whose ennui can only be assuaged by wandering the streets and watching strange happenings and encounters brought about by the ultimate unknowability of the modern city. This sense of ennui alleviated by watching the "deviant" actions of another permeates Rampo's work. In "The Human Chair" ("Ningen Isu" 1925), a master cabinet maker who describes himself as "ugly beyond description" constructs a luxury chair in which he is able to hide his "deformity." This is placed in the lobby of an expensive hotel by which he can "experience" the Other and "touch all desirable creatures": most of whom are European. Finally, he manages to fulfill his utmost desire when he is placed in a Japanese home where he falls in love with the wife of a high-ranking official. In another, "The Walker (Stalker) in the Attic" ("Yaneura no sanposha," 1925), the narrator's boredom is such that he wanders the streets dressed in a variety of disguises, including that of a woman, in search of something to combat his ennui. He eventually moves into a boarding house where he spies on the other tenants through gaps in the floorboards of his attic room and decides to commit the ultimate crime by dropping poison into one of the other tenant's mouth while he is asleep. There have been multiple cinematic versions of "Walker in the Attic": *Watcher in the Attic* (dir. Noboru Tanaka, 1976, dir. Akio Jissoji: 1993, dir: Mitsuhiro Mihara, 2007). "The Twins: A Condemned Criminal's Confession to a Priest" was made into a film by one of Japan's most noted directors, Shin'ya Tsukamoto in 1999 (*Soseiji/Gemini*.) "The Human Chair" and "The Hell of Mirrors" are two of the four short stories which make up the low-budget compilation film, *Rampo Noir* (2005) which also has a version of Rampo's most disturbing short story "The Caterpillar": the subject of Kôji Wakamatsu's final film of the same name (2010). However, my two favorite films are early ones: *The Horrors of Malformed Men* (*Kyôfu kikei ningen: Edogawa Rampo zenshû*, dir. Teruo Ishii: 1969) and *Blind Beast* (*Mōjū*, dir. Yasuzô Masumura, 1969).

It does seem that there is a renewed (or even "new") interest in Rampo as recent English translations and compilations of both his detective and eroguro stories such as *Edogawa Rampo: The Early Cases of Akechi Kogoro* (trans. William Varteresian, illustrator. Mike Dubisch, Kurodahan Press: 2014) and *The Edogawa Reader* (trans. Seth Jacobowitz, Preface by Takayuki Tatsumi, Kurodahan Press: 2008) suggest. It is to be hoped that that these translations reach a wide audience, as Rampo deserves to be better known, and the richness of his work appreciated, outside, as well as inside, of Japan.

SUGGESTED FURTHER READING

Angles, J. (2008). "Seeking the Strange: 'Ryōki' and the Navigation of Normality in Interwar Japan." *Monumenta Nipponica,* 63(1), 101–141.

Igarashi, Yoshikuni. "Edogawa Rampo and the Excess of Vision: An Ocular Critique of Modernity in 1920s Japan." *positions: east asia cultures critique* 13.2 (2005): 299–327.

Jacobowitz, Seth. *The Edogawa Rampo Reader: Stories and Essays.* Kurodahan Press, 2008

Reichert, Jim. (2001). "Deviance and Social Darwinism in Edogawa Ranpo's Erotic-Grotesque Thriller Kotō no oni." *Journal of Japanese Studies,* 27(1), 113–141.

Shreiber, Marc. Introduction. In *The Black Lizard and Beast in the Shadows*, by Edogawa Ranpo, trans. Ian Hughes. Fukuoka, Japan: Kurodahan, 2006.

Charlotte Riddell
(1832–1906)

Clare Clarke

Although she is now relatively unknown, in her lifetime Irish writer Charlotte Eliza Lawson Cowan Riddell (Mrs. J. H. Riddell)] was a successful, prolific, and popular author of popular fiction, the consummate Victorian literary "woman of letters" (Peterson 99). At a time when female authors were increasingly dominating the literary marketplace, particularly popular genres, Riddell's career produced over fifty books—including 40 novels and seven short story collections, with countless more anonymous contributions to Victorian magazines and periodicals as yet unattributed or undiscovered. Her body of work falls largely into two categories—novels and stories of London commercial life and supernatural stories. The two, however, often overlap in more ways than one might expect.

Riddell was born at The Barn, Carrickfergus, the daughter of James Cowan (d. 1851), flax mill owner and High Sheriff of County Antrim, and his second wife, Ellen Kilshaw (d. 1856). Despite its lowly title, The Barn was a luxurious villa with extensive gardens, as befitting her father's high status, and Charlotte enjoyed a privileged early childhood. Reading and writing were her passions: "In my very early days I read everything I could lay my hands on.... I never remember the time when I did not compose. Before I was old enough to hold a pen I used to get my mother to write down my childish ideas" (Black 19–20). This childhood idyll was to shatter, however, after her father's death in 1851, when the majority of his estate went to the family of his first wife, reducing 19-year-old Charlotte and her mother to near poverty. Much of Charlotte's adult life was to revolve around largely unsuccessful attempts to recapture the comfortable lifestyle of her early childhood.

In 1855, Charlotte and her gravely ill mother moved to London, where Charlotte struggled to support them working as a journalist and author. After countless rejections from reputable publishing houses, however, Riddell's first book, *Zuriel's Grandchild* (1856), was taken on by Thomas C. Newby, the down-market printer best known for his "shady dealings" with Emily and Anne Brontë (Peterson 161). It was published pseudonymously as R.V. Sparling. Nonetheless, this breakthrough signaled the start of Riddell's long career as a professional writer. Charlotte's mother died in December 1856, however, before she had a chance to benefit from her daughter's burgeoning literary success.

For Charlotte, professional success did not equal financial security, however. The year after her mother's death, she met and married Joseph Hadley Riddell, a charming but foolish would-be entrepreneur and inventor, who was to become bankrupt and burden his wife with his debts throughout their marriage. Over the course of the next decade Riddell's literary work supported the couple while simultaneously paying off her husband's numerous creditors. Her first significant commercial and critical acclaim came with *George Geith of Fen Court* (1864). The novel, bought by mid-market publisher Tinsley Brothers for the then huge sum of £800, tells the story of an unwittingly bigamous Anglican vicar. Despite this sensational sounding subject matter, however, it is less a sensation novel than a fiction about commercial city life, in the mode of Anthony Trollope. So successful was the novel that it went through several volume editions, was dramatized in the 1870s, and remained on stage in Great Britain, the United States, and Australia until the 1880s. It was thus as a novelist of London commercial life—"*the* Novelist of the City"—that Riddell secured her reputation and became best known in her own lifetime, although she would never repeat the success of *George Geith of Fen Court* (Kelleher 119). Indeed, despite her hard work and literary productivity, her life seems always to have been beset by financial precariousness—a result of her husband's continuing ineptitude with money.

Margaret Kelleher has observed that Riddell changed publishers and genres with increasing frequency towards the end of the nineteenth century, doubtless a strategy to remain commercially viable in an increasingly crowded literary marketplace (118–9). Indeed, from the 1870s onwards, Riddell changed direction from novels of the city, producing instead a large number of supernatural stories. At this time, and most likely a result of the enduring influence of Charles Dickens's *A Christmas Carol* (1843), ghost stories were seasonal, appearing in special Christmas editions of periodicals like Dickens's own *Household Words*. If Riddell was indeed increasingly desperate to remain commercially successful, her supernatural fictions were doubtless produced strategically to cater to the predilections of the lucrative annual Christmas periodical market.

Indeed, Riddell's corpus of supernatural fiction includes four novels, *Fairy Water* (1873), *The Uninhabited House* (1875), *The Haunted River* (1877), and *The Disappearance of Mr. Jeremiah Redworth* (1878), all of which first appeared in *Routledge's Christmas Annual*, with the subtitle "A Christmas Story," before their subsequent publication in volume form. Alongside these four Christmas ghost novels, Riddell also authored at the very least 14 supernatural short stories. All of these were most likely published in periodicals at Christmas—although recovery work has not yet been undertaken to identify the magazine locations in which they first appeared. Six of these supernatural stories were collected as the volume *Weird Stories*, published by James Hogg of London in 1882.

Pleasingly, the year that *Weird Stories* was published was also the year that the Society for Psychical Research was founded in London. The appearance of both in the same year attests to the widespread interest in the paranormal at this juncture in the late-Victorian era. The SPR conducted empirical research on haunted houses (for which they coined the marvelous term "phantasmogenetic centres") and investigate the claims of contemporary fads such as Mesmerism and Spiritualism, envisioning that these might eventually be understood within scientific discourse. They placed advertisements in British periodicals of the type that featured fictional ghost stories, asking readers to send in reports of supernatural experiences in order that they might be investigated. The second annual report from the society showcases the perceived discrepancy between the ghosts of fiction and fact:

> In the magazine ghost stories, which appear in such numbers every Christmas, the ghost is a fearsome being, dressed in a sweeping sheet or shroud, carrying a lighted candle, and squeaking dreadful words from fleshless lips. It enters at the stroke of midnight, through the sliding panel, just by the blood stain on the floor, which no effort could ever remove.... These are the ghosts of fiction, and we do not deny that we now and then receive, apparently on good authority, accounts of apparitions which are stated to exhibit some features of a sensational type. Such cases, however, are very rare and must for the present be dismissed as exceptional [Gurney 23].

Readers would struggle to discover many sweeping shrouds or indelible bloodstains in Riddell's ghost stories, however. Rather, they are almost exclusively haunted house tales that fit in with the codifications of the Victorian ghost story outlined by Michael Cox and others—these haunted properties reveal secrets, they avenge wrongs, they help to morally improve the living (xi). As Melissa Edmundson notes, female-authored ghost stories "frequently used the motif of the haunted house to comment on property, class, and economic issues (51)." Indeed, in *Weird Stories* Riddell repeatedly revisits the grand mansion of her childhood, transforming it into a decaying and destitute symbol of changing fortunes. The eponymous "Walnut-Tree House," for instance, stands "grim and lonely in the mournful twilight, look[ing] more than ordinarily desolate and deserted ... the shutters were closed—the rusty gates were fast locked—the approach was choked up with grass and weeds—through no chink did the light of a single candle flicker (Bleiler 148)."

Riddell's abandoned homes are haunted by the ghosts (both literal and metaphorical) of greedy capitalists, bankrupts, and misers. These haunted homes are feared and abandoned by their owners and local community. No one will cross their paths. The banishment of the supernatural is normally undertaken by a young man of lowly status and limited financial means, who stays in the house as a paid investigator or because he has no better option. In "The Open Door," for instance, Phil Edlyd's investigation of a haunted door at Ladlow Hall, is taken on in order to free him from the shame of telling his family that he has lost his ill-paid and uninspiring work as a city clerk. His dispatching of the ghost reifies his masculinity, earning him the respect of the lord of the manor, a tidy financial reward, and the heart of a good woman. In "The Old House at Vauxhall Walk," narrator Graham Coulton, an aristocratic young man who has quarreled with father because he won't join the army, is left "Houseless, homeless, hopeless!" (Bleiler 85) As a result, Coulton is forced to spend a night in the Vauxhall Walk property, a house so malevolent that even his lowly former servant has abandoned it. In these young men, brought low financially by family and work difficulties, Riddell herself is clearly paralleled. The haunted house story, then, extends the financial preoccupations and modern settings of Riddell's realist novels, and "transfers her interest in inheritance, debt, ownership, and tenancy to the suburbs and the countryside ... exploring the ethical responsibilities of wealth" (Margree 66–67). Her ghost stories are haunted by a deeply personal reflection on the instability of financial and job security and the difficulties of becoming a "woman of letters" in late-Victorian Britain.

SUGGESTED FURTHER READING

Black, Helen C. *Notable Women Authors of the Day* (1893). London: Maclaren, 1906.
Bleiler, E.F., ed. *The Collected Ghost Stories of Mrs. J. H. Riddell*. London: Dover, 1977.
Cox, Michael, and R.A. Gilbert, eds. *The Oxford Book of Victorian Ghost Stories*. New York: Oxford University Press, 1991.
Gurney, E., F.W.H Myers, and W.F. Barrett. *Proceedings of the Society for Psychical Research, 1884*, vol. II. London, 1884.
Edmundson, Melissa. "The 'Uncomfortable Houses' of Charlotte Riddell and Margret Oliphant." *Gothic Studies* 12.1 (2010): 51–67.
Kelleher, Margaret. "Charlotte Riddell's *A Struggle for Fame*: The Field of Women's Literary Production." *Colby Quarterly* 36.2 (2000): 116–131.
Margree, Victoria. "(Other)Worldly Goods: Gender, Money, and Property in the Ghost Stories of Charlotte Riddell." *Gothic Studies* 16.2 (2014): 66–85.
Peterson, Linda H. "Charlotte Riddell's *A Struggle for Fame*: Myths of Authorship, Facts of the Market." *Women's Writing* 11.1 (2004): 99–115.

Philip Ridley
(1964–)

Douglas Keesey

As a painter, photographer, playwright, filmmaker, and author of children's books, Philip Ridley is an artist whose work has sometimes been overlooked as confusing in its variety and confounding in its refusal to meet critics' expectations that it fit neatly within an individual art-form. Yet Ridley himself has said that, regardless of the medium in which he happens to be working at the time, all his art is about "the power of storytelling, how the stories we tell make sense of our lives." And most of these stories have elements of dark fairytale or gothic horror. In *Modern British Playwriting: The 1990s*, Aleks Sierz calls Ridley "the poet of the uncanny, whose work spawns new images of the strange, the weird, and the wonderful." Indeed, these images have proven to be too strange and disturbing for some. In the UK *Telegraph*, drama critic Charles Spencer accused Ridley of being "turned on by his own sick fantasies" and argued that his work "positively revels in imaginative nastiness." Such critics, Ridley has claimed, are "blinder than a bagful of moles in a coal cellar." Comparing his works to the dark rides at amusement parks, Ridley has said, "I like putting people on a ghost train, but I guide them safely through the other end."

The light at the end of the tunnel is certainly clearer in Ridley's works for children and young adults. In *Moonfleece* (2004)—the fourth play in his youth-oriented Storyteller Sequence—Ridley alludes to the times when, as a child, he would "mix fantasy up with real life" and invent "fairy stories" about "dragons" to calm his younger brother's fears and help him fall asleep. One such story seems to have been the source for the children's novel *Krindlekrax* (1991), in which nine-year-old Ruskin, a nerd in glasses, has to contend with a wild boy named Elvis, whose window smashing terrorizes the entire neighborhood. By imagining that Elvis is a giant crocodile named Krindlekrax who can be tamed if confronted and befriended, Ruskin is able to get a mental grip on the problem, conquering his fear of the other boy and, by understanding what has caused his delinquency, soothing Elvis and bringing him back into the community. Similarly, in the first Storyteller play *Sparkleshark* (1997), Jake, a fourteen-year-old geek in glasses, is faced with a macho bully named Russell and an angry, oversized misfit called Finn. Jake binds and redirects the other boys' negative energies by telling a spellbinding fairytale in which "hard" and "horny-as-hell" Russell plays a prince who finds the courage to express his tender feelings for the girl he loves, and in which Finn, cast as a dragon named Sparkleshark, can express his fury through roaring and then have his meanness tamed by others' compassion.

Although they started out as stories for children, Ridley's first two films take a darker turn toward more adult material. In *The Reflecting Skin* (1990), a prairie gothic which Ridley has called "my *Blue Velvet* with children," eight-year-old Seth decides that his neighbor, Dolphin, is a female vampire sucking the life out of his older brother. Under the influence of his father's horror fiction, Seth misidentifies Dolphin as the cause of his brother's mysterious illness and misunderstands her sexual relationship with him as predatory. In one scene, Seth blows air into a frog, which then bursts in Dolphin's face. Here again, just as he followed his father's horror fiction, Seth is acting out scripts he learned from his parents. As a form of punishment, Seth's mother would pour water down his throat until he felt like bursting. In addition, Seth sees his father, who has been falsely accused of murdering some local boys, swallow gasoline and then light himself on fire. Seth is entranced by the flames, having learned from his parents how to take pleasure in violent punishment, how to scapegoat individuals as the sole cause of all the pain. Originally described as "somewhere between innocence and heartlessness," Seth finally tips toward the latter, becoming complicit in the murder of Dolphin. But this attempt to lay all the blame on her does not save his brother, who is now grief-stricken as well as mortally ill. A guilt-ridden Seth is left screaming in the fiery rays of the setting sun, as if going up in flames like his father.

In Ridley's second film, *The Passion of Darkly Noon* (1995), the title character is a young man lost in a dark forest. Unfortunately, the stories that influence him only take him deeper into that darkness rather than offering him a way out. When Darkly meets a sensual woman named Callie, he follows his parents' fanatical religious teachings and blames her for exciting the desire in him that he considers a sin. Seeing Callie with Clay, the man she loves, Darkly scapegoats her for his own jealousy, which is exacerbated when Clay's mother Roxy, blaming Callie for taking her son away, labels her "the monster of the forest" and a "witch." Callie attempts to tell a different story, casting Darkly as the "prince" who can save her as the "princess" from the "witch" Roxy, but Darkly is still under the sway of the old narrative. In a fit of self-righteous fervor, he tries to set fire to Callie in order to watch the "witch" burn. She momentarily halts him by stating "I love you," but whether or not her compassion for his suffering could serve as an effective counter-narrative, we will never know, for at that point he is shot to prevent him from doing any further damage. The lyrics to the song written by Ridley to end the film suggest that Callie's words have brought Darkly to a belated realization of the role he has actually played in this dark fairytale. Too late to benefit from his new self-understanding, Darkly dies in the flames he had set to kill Callie, a conclusion which Ridley has described as "*Beauty and the Beast* meets *Apocalypse Now*: the language of the fairy tale and of the horror film come together for this explosive ending."

Ridley's third and most recent film, *Heartless* (2009), though set on the streets of East London rather than in the woods of America, is still another fairytale "labyrinth" in which "Jamie, the lead character, is lost." The film was inspired by Ridley's collaborative work with bi-polar young people on the Storyteller plays, "kids and teenagers" whose world "makes no sense" because "they can't get a grip on their story in it." When his mother is burned alive, Jamie cannot understand how the gang members who did it could be so heartless, so he imagines that they are literal monsters rather than teens wearing reptile masks. Jamie, who has a heart-shaped birthmark over half of his face, also fears that others see him as monstrous. He believes that he must get rid of this birthmark or he will never be loved. Following the bad advice of gang leader Papa B., Jamie acts out the terms of a dark fairytale. As Ridley has explained, like Cinderella, Jamie "has something to do by midnight": he must "cut someone's heart out (the proposed fate of Snow White)," or the birthmark, which has magically vanished, will come back. But after he commits this terrible act, Jamie realizes it was entirely pointless. In fact, his birthmark had never disappeared, and his girlfriend had loved him anyway. Undeterred by how he looks, she fell in love with his "beautiful heart." But by cutting out the heart of that other young man, Jamie has turned himself into a heartless monster. According to Ridley, Jamie "has found the center of the labyrinth," which is "his own dark heart"; "he's taken himself on a journey to show ... that he's got as much evil in him as the people that he failed to understand." The dark fairytale that Jamie mistakenly believed in and acted out led him to commit a terrible crime, but it also enabled him to understand that the gang members are humans like him, kids fooled into believing that by taking from others they could strengthen themselves, that by killing others they could make themselves less afraid.

The recognition of one's own potential for evil could help stop the scapegoating of others as "monsters." But Jamie's self-realization comes too late for him to make a difference in the world, as it occurs while he is being burned alive by members of the gang. As is often the case with Ridley's more adult works as opposed to his plays for children, there may be a light at the end of the tunnel, but the main character is not brought safely through to the way out. On some of Ridley's dark rides, it is only we as the audience who make it out enlightened *and* alive in the end.

SUGGESTED FURTHER READING

Izod, John. "The Polycentred Self: *The Passion of Darkly Noon*." *Myth, Mind and the Screen*. Cambridge University Press, 2001. 143–159.

Ridley, Philip. "Author's Note." *The American Dreams: The Reflecting Skin & The Passion of Darkly Noon*. London: Methuen, 1997. vii–xxix.

Ridley, Philip, and Aleks Sierz. "'Putting a New Lens on the World': The Art of Theatrical Alchemy." *New Theatre Quarterly* 25.02 (2009): 109–117.

Urban, Ken. "Ghosts from an Imperfect Place: Philip Ridley's Nostalgia." *Modern Drama* 50.3 (2007): 325–345.

Regina Maria Roche
(1764?–1845)

CHRISTINA MORIN

Little-known or read today, the Irish novelist, Regina Maria Roche (1764?–1845), was immensely popular in her own day. She shot to fame in 1796 with the publication of her third novel, *The Children of the Abbey*, a gothic tale of intrigue, sexual predation, and sublime scenery set in England, Scotland, Wales, and Ireland, and featuring several ruined castles, monasteries, and convents. Reprinted approximately eighty times by the end of the nineteenth century, *The Children of the Abbey* propelled Roche into a brief literary stardom rivaled only by that of the "mother" of the gothic novel herself, Ann Radcliffe (1764–1823), whose works she was often seen to imitate. Throughout the nineteenth century, Roche remained in the public consciousness primarily in the figure of a gothic novelist, publishing a long list of widely read, if also critically condemned, gothic tales, including *Clermont* (1798), *Nocturnal Visit* (1800), *The Discarded Son; or, Haunt of the Banditti* (1807), *The Houses of Osma and Almeria; or, Convent of St. Ildefonso* (1810), *The Monastery of St. Columb; or, the Atonement* (1813), and *Trecothick Bower; or, the Lady of the West Country* (1814). Her popular success as a gothic novelist was so pronounced that Jane Austen could include *The Children of the Abbey* as among Harriet Smith's ill-advised reading in *Emma* (1815) and *Clermont* as one of the "horrid" novels in *Northanger Abbey* (1817) without questioning her readers' familiarity with these texts. While, however, Roche's novels might have been said to be "in the hands of every novel reader in Europe and America" in the nineteenth century, they are all but forgotten today (*The New England Weekly Review*, 10 November 1828).

Why this should be has much to do with Roche's publishing choices. From the publication of *The Children of the Abbey*, Roche maintained an exclusive working relationship with William Lane and his infamous

Leadenhall-Street-based Minerva Press. Synonymous with circulating library trash, hack authorship, and the proliferation of low quality, popular gothic fiction, the Minerva Press was clearly not a choice designed to win Roche favor with the critical establishment. Contemporary concerns with the rapid expansion of the literary marketplace and the changing demographic of readers, in fact, made the Minerva Press and its publications a particular focus of ire. According to reviewers, Roche's novels were nothing more than the vile products of "the pig-stye of literature in Leadenhall Street" (*The Critical Review*, 4th ser. 5 [January 1814]: 99). Negative critical assessments of her works as Minerva Press publications notwithstanding, Roche's decision to produce all thirteen of her novels in the period 1796 to 1834 with Minerva was arguably strategic. Lane's renowned entrepreneurial spirit and skills ensured that Roche's works were represented in circulating libraries and bookshops across Britain and Ireland, as well as in Continental Europe and North America, not to mention British colonies like India and Jamaica.

Had Roche not run into severe financial difficulties owing to contested land ownership as well as personal and familial illness, she may well have ignored critical condemnation in the enjoyment of her popular success. In 1802, however, and again in 1827, her husband, Ambrose Roche, was forced to declare bankruptcy, suffering, in the meantime, a stroke that left him paralyzed. His health problems were exacerbated, if not caused, by the actions of an unprincipled Irish solicitor in whom the Roches had mistakenly placed their trust, selling to him inherited properties they believed, on his representation, to be worthless. When they discovered the truth of the matter in 1820, the Roches took the case to chancery. The matter was resolved in their favor ten years later, but, by that point, the legal fees had devastated their finances, leading Roche to describe the case in a letter to the Royal Literary Fund on 7 July 1831 as "a millstone round our necks." Moreover, while Roche wrote in a letter dated 4 August 1831 that she "cherished sanguine hopes of being able to live" on patrimony owed to her after her husband's death in 1829, she never recovered either land or money. The refusal by the Irish politician Richard Martin (1754–1834) to pay the Roches £500 of rent he owed them in 1826 undoubtedly contributed to the couple's precarious financial circumstances as well as Roche's periodic depressive episodes.

Because of her continued financial difficulties, Roche was forced to publish her fourteenth novel, *Contrast* (1828), by subscription. She also wrote several moving appeals for assistance to the Royal Literary Fund in 1827, 1830, and 1831. Although her petitions were successful, Roche never regained financial equilibrium, finding herself in the position of many early nineteenth century female authors: forced to write for her daily bread. In this, her experience speaks to that of countless female writers in the period. At the same time, it underlines the precariousness of living and writing in England at the start of the nineteenth century, when many Irish authors felt compelled to migrate in order to compete successfully in the literary marketplace. Roche's fellow Irish gothicist, Charles Robert Maturin, melodramatically complained in an 1813 letter to Walter Scott, "there is no excitement, no literary appetite or impulse in this Country, my most intimate acquaintances scarcely know that I have written, and they care as little as they know." Roche herself had written her first two novels—*The Vicar of Lansdowne; or, Country Quarters* (1789) and *The Maid of the Hamlet* (1793)—from her home in Dublin, publishing them under her maiden name, Dalton, with two different London publishers. All of her subsequent novels, with the exception of her last, *The Nun's Picture* (1834), were written in London, where she moved shortly after her marriage in 1794. She returned to Ireland in 1831, without "a guinea in the world to support herself," as her lawyer recorded in a letter of 9 November 1831. Thereafter she wrote *The Nun's Picture*, publishing it with Minerva Press and bringing her writing career to a close. She died in 1845 in her native city of Waterford in circumstances of extreme want.

Today, Roche's works continue to be assessed in much the same way as contemporary critics viewed them: as derivative fictions produced by a popular—read: low brow—publisher directly responsible for the debasement of literature at the close of the eighteenth century and the beginning of the nineteenth. Typically, what little attention Roche's novels have received in the twentieth and twenty-first centuries has tended to focus on her dependence on, if not outright plagiarism of, the gothic novels of Ann Radcliffe in the first instance and, later, the national tales of Maria Edgeworth (1768–1849) and Sydney Owenson, Lady Morgan (c. 1776–1859). Scholars have, therefore, ironically replicated, often without careful analysis, eighteenth- and early nineteenth century critical condemnations of texts like *The Children of the Abbey, Clermont, Nocturnal Visit,* and *The Discarded Son* as thinly disguised, largely unsuccessful imitations of Radcliffe's style. Irish studies scholars have also emphasized Roche's apparent tendency to jump on the bandwagon of popular literary success, tracing a turn away from the gothic to specifically Irish material with the publication of *The Munster Cottage Boy* (1820), *The Tradition of the Castle; or, Scenes in the Emerald Isle* (1824), and *Contrast*. Rather than rip-offs of Radcliffe, these works are seen as attempts to harness the financial and popular success that Edgeworth and Owenson enjoyed with national tales like *The Wild Irish Girl* (1806), *Ennui* (1809), and *The Absentee* (1812).

What goes ignored in this assessment of Roche's works as unoriginal is her knowing and skillful manipulation of gothic tropes, themes, and imagery, even in her supposedly "Irish" novels, to explore the everyday world of nineteenth-century Britain and Ireland. *The Munster Cottage Boy, The Tradition of the Castle,* and *Contrast* certainly feature Irish settings, rather than the Catholic, Continental locales now associated with the gothic novel of this period, and they also engage in pointed commentaries on specifically Irish questions of absentee landlordism, political exile, and dispossession. But, they do so largely through the conventions of the gothic novel, deploying plots of intrigue, orphaned heroines, thwarted romances, power-hungry villains, hauntingly haunted landscapes, and apparently supernatural appearances in order to depict early nineteenth century Irish reality as itself fundamentally gothic. Similarly, in many of her more obviously gothic novels, Roche purposely engages with matters of literary fame, developing printing techniques, and the contemporary growth of a new transnational and transatlantic literary marketplace. Using the gothic tropes of doubles, doppelgangers, and copies, Roche self-consciously underlines the exigencies of authorship as well the dangers of popular publication and appeal in the contemporary literary marketplace.

That most of Roche's novels continue to remain available only in first editions is a very real shame, reflecting the ongoing trend to dismiss her fictions as minor literature unworthy of notice. Given Roche's enduring appeal to the eighteenth- and nineteenth-century reading public, however, it is to be hoped that growing scholarly attention to her *oeuvre* might once again make her name known to an audience as wide as the one she enjoyed in her heyday.

A NOTE ON SOURCES

For the correspondence between Roche, her lawyers, and the Royal Literary Fund, see British Library Loan 96, M1077, Reel 17.

For Maturin's correspondence with Walter Scott, see Fannie E. Ratchford and Wm. H. McCarthy, Jr., eds., *The Correspondence of Sir Walter Scott and Charles Robert Maturin, with a Few Other Allied Letters* (Austin: University of Texas Press, 1937).

SUGGESTED FURTHER READING

Burgess, Miranda, "Violent Translations: Allegory, Gender, and Cultural Nationalism in Ireland, 1796–1806." *Modern Language Quarterly* 59.1 (1998): 33–70.

Hoeveler, Diane Long. "Regina Maria Roche's *The Children of the Abbey*: Contesting the Catholic Presence in Female Gothic Fiction." *Tulsa Studies in Women's Literature* 31.1/2 (2012): 137–58.

Mandal, Anthony. "Revising the Radcliffean Model: Regina Maria Roche's *Clermont* and Jane Austen's *Northanger Abbey*." *Cardiff Corvey: Reading the Romantic Text* 3 (1999): 1–13. Available from http://www.cf.ac.uk/encap/corvey/articls/cc03_n03.html.

Morin, Christina. "'Gothic' and 'National'? Challenging the Formal Distinctions of Irish Romantic Fiction." In Jim Kelly, ed., *Ireland and Romanticism: Publics, Nations, and the Scenes of Cultural Productio*. Basingstoke: Palgrave Macmillan, 2011. 172–87.

Vincent Schiavelli
(1948-2005)

Sorcha Ní Fhlainn

I first encountered Vincent Schiavelli onscreen as the Subway Ghost in *Ghost* (1990). In this memorable performance, the Subway Ghost teaches Sam Malone (Patrick Swayze) to move physical objects in the real world. Schiavelli's short but memorable performance combines comedy and pathos, a feeling reinforced by his long features, distinctive voice and wild hair. It is clear that his character's time haunting New York's subway has rendered him a lost and embittered soul, his fate a pertinent reminder of those left stranded in the afterlife. More than anything else, when watching this briefly appearing but still important character, one becomes aware that Schiavelli imparts a lasting depth to this character. Indeed, Schiavelli frequently played characters tinged with gothic underpinnings or suggestion. Casting directors frequently capitalized upon his distinctive physical features, which also lent themselves to more overtly comedic roles, such as the wacky biology teacher Mr. Vargas in *Fast Times at Ridgemont High* (1982). He specialized in imbuing characters with a glimmer of madness beneath a kindly veneer. As the territorial Subway Ghost in *Ghost*, Schiavelli fluidly combined these characteristics, ranging from rage to empathy to madness. It would prove to be Schiavelli's most memorable role in popular cinema.

Schiavelli was born in 1948 in Brooklyn, New York, to Sicilian parents. He was born with the genetic disorder Marfan Syndrome, which affects skeletal formation and connective tissue, and hence resulted in Schiavelli's distinctive appearance—the long facial features and large brow, his drooping "sad eyes," significant height (6'6") and elongated fingers, all of which gave him a unique screen presence. Though his unusual looks left him out of place among conventional Hollywood leading men he was perfectly suited to playing unusual and memorable characters. Schiavelli's career was punctuated by a series of diverse supporting parts, and he was often cast as villains, lost souls, or eccentrics. This led to bit-part roles in Tim Burton's 1992 film *Batman Returns* (as Organ Grinder in the Penguin's dastardly Red Triangle Circus Gang) and as a member of a freak show in a classic episode of *The X Files*. "Humbug" (season 2, episode 20) capitalized upon Schiavelli's unique appearance and empathic screen presence.

Though he worked consistently from his theatre days in the 1960s, Schiavelli successfully found film and television work in the 1970s. His first sitcom role, as Peter Panama in *The Corner Bar* (1972–73) is widely considered to be the first recurring gay character in a U.S. TV series. Schiavelli's growing reputation as a character actor also meant that he regularly appeared in special guest parts in popular television shows of the 1970s and 1980s, including *Taxi*; *Starsky and Hutch*; *Murder, She Wrote*; *Miami Vice*; *Matlock*; *Moonlighting*; *Star Trek: The Next Generation;* and *MacGyver*. However, it was his enduring collaboration with director Miloš Forman that would constitute his most significant screen partnership. Under Forman's direction, Schiavelli made his film debut in *Taking Off* (1971), and was later cast alongside Jack Nicholson, Brad Dourif, and Danny DeVito as asylum inmate Fredrickson in *One Flew Over the Cuckoo's Nest* (1975). In the opening scene of Forman's *Amadeus* (1984), he played Salieri's valet, who finds and saves the elderly maestro when he has slit his throat out of guilt and self-hatred for "killing" Mozart. Later supporting roles with Forman include Chester in *The People Vs. Larry Flint* (1996) and a part as a television executive alongside the troubled Andy Kaufman (Jim Carrey) in *Man on the Moon* (1999), as well as the role of magic guru Vinovich in Clive Barker's *Lord of Illusions* (1995). Under the direction of long-time co-star and personal friend Danny DeVito, he was cast as Buggy Ding Dong, a heroin-addict and children's television host, in the black comedy *Death to Smoochy* (2002). As these roles indicate, Schiavelli had an incomparable ability to make small character parts memorable c. Following on from a small role in the unsuccessful horror film *Lurking Fear* (1994), based on a short story by H.P. Lovecraft, he secured one of his most high-profile Hollywood roles as assassin Doctor Kaufman (complete with an overstated evil European accent) in the Bond film *Tomorrow Never Dies* (1997). This was quickly followed by his short but pivotal turn as Uncle Enyos Kaldarash in *Buffy the Vampire Slayer* (1997–2003). Enyos is part of the Kaldarash gypsy tribe who cursed the vampire Angel (David Boreanaz) with a soul, which can only be lifted if a moment of happiness is experienced by the vampire. Schiavelli brings quiet gravitas to the, delivering both the back-story of Angel's curse, and meeting a grisly end at the hands of the cursed vampire.

In 2005, Schiavelli emigrated to Polizzi Generosa, Sicily, and began to focus on his second career as a gourmet—his passion for Italian cuisine won him acclaim as a culinary expert, including the James Beard Award for Newspaper Feature Writing in 2001. He also published three books on cuisine: *Brucilino, America* (1998); *The Sicilian Cookbook* (1999); *Papa Andrea's Sicilian Table* (2001); and *Many Beautiful Things* (2002) all of which include family anecdotes and recipes from his Sicilian-American childhood. Leaving Hollywood behind to return to the homeland of his emigrant grandparents, Schievelli died in December 2005 of lung cancer and was buried in Polizzi Generosa.

I consider Schiavelli a "Lost Soul" not because of his lack of personal success—his IMDB credits alone attests to his screen achievements—but due to the regrettable lack of wider recognition his work has been afforded. Whether it was his portrayal of the eccentric Mr. Vargas pulling a human heart out of a corpse in biology class in *Fast Times at Ridgemont High*, or his unforgettable depiction of the Subway Ghost who uses "hate" to move objects in *Ghost*, Schiavelli brought a distinct sense of melancholy to many of his more notably gothic roles. Though he achieved a certain quiet recognition of his standing as an excellent character actor, this sadly never resulted in him being assigned any leading roles. Described by fans as "The man with the sad eyes," Schiavelli's contribution to film today goes largely unnoticed by mainstream audiences, who rarely recall his name and are more likely to identify by his distinctive features, if at all. Throughout his career, which spanned four decades of significant contributions to film, literature, television, the stage, videogames, and the culinary arts, Vincent Schiavelli brought a unique depth to each of his roles. His more gothic roles in particular were always infused with a unique intensity that simultaneously evoked pity and yet warned of potential malevolence. For me, Schiavelli who will always be that lonely Subway Ghost and Salieri's valet; a cinematic "Lost Soul" who often played small parts, but always made them his own.

SUGGESTED FURTHER READING

Schiavelli, Vincent. *Many Beautiful Things: Stories and Recipes from Polizzi Generosa*. New York: Simon and Schuster, 2002.

Schiavelli, Vincent. *Papa Andrea's Sicilian Table: Recipes from a Sicilian Chef as Remembered by His Grandson*. New York: Carol Publishing Group, 1993.

Schiavelli, Vincent. "Special Editorial: Living with the Syndrome." *Ophthalmic Genetics*, 1996 Vol. 17. No. 1. 1–2.

William Buehler Seabrook
(1884–1945)

ROGER LUCKHURST

William Buehler Seabrook was an American journalist, travel writer to exotic locales in Africa, Arabia and the Caribbean, a pulp anthropologist, Great War veteran (invalided out as an ambulance driver by chlorine gas poisoning at Verdun), primitivist, notorious sado-masochist, alcoholic, occultist, and fellow traveler among the Modernists in New York, London, Paris and on the Riviera. He moved in the circles of famous figures like Gertrude Stein, Man Ray, Ford Maddox Ford, Georges Bataille, Jean Cocteau and Thomas Mann. In New York, he was well known among the bohemian writers and artists of Greenwich Village and the patrons of the Harlem Renaissance. Although he published some photographs in the Surrealist journal *Documents*, edited by Bataille and Michel Leiris, and a short story or two, he was principally known for his self-mythologizing travel books and his extraordinarily open accounts of his voluntary committal to a mental hospital in an attempt to cure his alcoholism (the best-selling *Asylum*, 1935) and his autobiography, which, among other things, psychoanalyzed his own sexual "kinks," his penchant for "putting chains on ladies," without shame (*No Hiding Place*, 1942). To play out this fetishism, Seabrook even employed Man Ray to photograph Lee Miller in various masochistic positions. Twenty years after his suicide, Seabrook's perversities were further examined by his second wife, the novelist Marjorie Worthington, in her memoir *The Strange World of Willie Seabrook* (1966).

If remembered at all, it is only as a footnote in other, more celebrated Modernist biographies. Yet Seabrook is worth recovering as a "Lost Soul" of the Gothic for two reasons. First: his interest in the occult. In 1940, he published *Witchcraft: Its Power in the World Today*, which detailed his life-long obsession with collecting experiences of occult practice from around the world. This included a brief friendship with the Golden Dawn magus and self-declared Antichrist, Aleister Crowley, during Crowley's time in New York when he was busy polishing his scandalous reputation by denouncing the English war against Germany. In 1919, Crowley visited Seabrook for a week of ritual experiment at his farm, in which they decided to communicate solely by various inflections of the magic word "Wow" (events retold in Seabrook's story "Wow"). On hearing of his suicide by overdose in 1945, Crowley wrote poisonously "the swine-dog W. B. Seabrook has killed himself at last, after months of agonized slavery to his final wife."

Seabrook's book on witchcraft was cast in the rhetoric of the skeptical psychical researcher, a rational man seeking final proof in an open spirit of inquiry, but bewildered at the extent of occult credulity in the modern Western world. London and its suburbs, he said "house more strange cults, secret societies, devil's altars, professional 'Sorcerers' and charlatans than any other metropolitan area on Earth." He repeated whispered stories of sympathetic magic and voodoo dolls at dinners in Paris and on the Riviera, and spoke of attending Black Masses in New York and London ("rather a bore unless one gets a kick out of blasphemy"). Seabrook remained fascinated by this subculture, however, which presumably crossed over with his sexual predilections, and he became a photo-story in *Life* magazine at the start of the Second World War when he hosted a magical ceremony to issue a hex on Hitler.

But Seabrook was cynical about magic in the West exactly in proportion to his conviction that witchcraft still exercised power in "primitive" societies. Even if mysterious events or deaths in these cultures could be explained by the effects of suggestion or auto-suggestion, it displayed the authentic power of magic. Seabrook was brought up in the South on an old plantation, with the memory of slavery still alive: he claimed that his black nurse had been a woman with knowledge of the syncretic slave religion of Obeah (often misunderstood as a form of "black magic"). This early contact led to a lifelong obsession with cultures and superstitions declared "primitive." Indeed, his bohemianism frequently refused the strangulated niceties of civilization and embraced "savage" energies. In New York, he frequented Harlem and was in Paris when a cult built around the black dancer Josephine Baker. Negrophilia, as it was sometimes called, claimed to empower blacks with lost, primal energy precisely to the extent that it locked them into powerful cultural stereotypes of "savagery."

A longing for release from his deathly white identity explains Seabrook's escapes into exotic worlds far away from the rigid racial hierarchies of the American South. In 1924, he travelled to the Middle East and wrote *Adventures in Arabia,* subtitled *Among the Bedouins, Druses, Whirling Dervishes and Yezidee Devil-Worshippers* (1927). In 1931, he was commissioned by French writer and intellectual Paul Morand to travel to the French colonies in West Africa (principally Dahomey) with the explicit aim of joining a "cannibal" cult. It turned out that the French colonial administration was so obsessed with policing the natives from this enacting this symbolic ritual that it was impossible to eat human flesh in Africa. Seabrook returned to Paris with some recipes, however, and bribed the Paris morgue for a limb from a recent corpse that he then cooked and ate. The inversion—the most primitive act is found not in the "savage" periphery but the "civilized" metropolitan center—says everything about the economy of fantasy in primitivism.

Seabrook's second and much more enduring contribution to the Gothic emerged directly from this exotic travelling. In 1929, he published *The Magic Island,* an account of his trip to the island republic of Haiti, then occupied by American forces. He pursued his typical interests: seeking initiation into the native rituals of the vodou religion, and claiming to drink blood sacrifices and feel the authentic power of the vodou pantheon of gods passing through him. Yet it is in a later chapter that Seabrook encounters another local aspect of witchery. In the chapter "…Dead Men Working in Cane Fields," Seabrook writes up local stories about zombies. The local Creole word *zombi* had appeared in some American writings since the 1880s, but Seabrook took the credit for Americanizing this term and popularizing it.

> The *zombie,* they say, is a soulless human corpse, still dead, but taken from the grave and endowed by sorcery with a mechanical semblance of life—it is a dead body which is made to walk and move as if it were alive. People who have the power to do this go to a fresh grave, dig up the body before it has had time to rot, galvanize it into movement, and then make of it a servant or slave, occasionally for the commission of some crime, more often simply as a drudge around the habitation or the farm, setting it dull heavy tasks, and beating it like a dumb beast if it slackens.

The chapter is at first merely an accumulation of local folkloric accounts, but Seabrook is astounded when his native informant happily tells him that there are *zombies* at work nearby in the plantations of the Haitian-American Sugar Corporation. Seabrook therefore comes face to face with actual zombies, and with exquisite hesitation, remarks: "I did see these 'walking dead men,' and I did, in a sense, believe in them and pitied them, indeed, from the bottom of my heart." Finding three "dead" Haitians at work, he experiences a moment of "mental panic," only to decide that these are "nothing but poor ordinary demented human beings, idiots, forced to toil in the fields." Of course, the context of slavery provides the framework for the "undead" shuffling slave, declared "dead" by the social contract, and forced to work to exhaustion. In the eighteenth century, the French colony of Saint-Domingue, before it became independent Haiti in 1804 following a slave revolt, had the highest death rates but the largest profits among slaves taken in vast numbers from West Africa. When Seabrook travelled to Haiti, the American occupiers were in the process of reinstating large-scale plantations and trying to stamp out native superstitions in the name of modernity. No wonder the workers were locally called *zombis.*

Seabrook's book was a direct influence on *White Zombie,* the 1932 film that smuggled the zombie into the major horror cycle that began that year. The focus is on Lugosi's menacing figure of the witch-doctor rather than the zombies he commands, but it was the beginning of the cinematic career of a category of the undead that has since come to dominate contemporary horror film. The memory of Seabrook is now returning often very sketchily in pre-histories of zombie culture, but his focus on the Haitian zombie is best understood in the matrix of his obsession with witchcraft, the occult and the vital energies of so-called primitive societies around the world.

SUGGESTED FURTHER READING

Archer-Straw, Petrine. *Negrophilia: Avant-Garde Paris and Black Culture in the 1920s.* London: Thames and Hudson, 2001.

Patterson, Orlando. *Slavery and Social Death.* Cambridge: Cambridge University Press, 1982.

Rhodes, Gary. *White Zombie: Anatomy of a Horror Film.* Jefferson, NC: McFarland, 2001.

Ziegler, Susan. "The Case of William Seabrook: Haiti, *Documents*, and the Working Dead." *Modernism/Modernity* 19/4 (2013), 737–54.

Sidney Sime
(1867–1941)

Maria Beville

The Gothic monsters and fantastic creatures that populate the work of artist and illustrator Sidney Sime are without doubt part of the essential fabric of the Gothic imagination as it developed in Britain during the *fin de siècle*. With their own unique style identifiable by undercurrents of Japonisme and the decadence of the art nouveau movement, Sime's popular paintings and illustrations provided an important contribution to the emergence of cosmic horror in the twentieth century.

Sidney Sime published a huge collection of fantastic and arguably Gothic illustrations in the *Illustrated London News* and in widely read late Victorian magazines such as *Pall Mall*, and *Idler*. A contemporary of Aubrey Beardsley and not dissimilar in style, nor in levels of sensationalism, his career as an illustrator has left a significant mark on the art history of the period. Although he was not born into privilege and worked as a miner in his formative years— no doubt a period wherein he became familiar with folk tales and native legends—Sime found a way to attend art school in Liverpool and to forge a path in the commercial illustration business at a time that was increasingly competitive for young independent artists.

While serving his time as a commercial illustrator, Sime held firmly on to his ambitions to become a recognized artist. He exhibited his first artwork, a portrait, at the Walker Art Gallery Autumn Exhibition in 1889 and eventually gained membership to the Royal Society of British Artists. Following this accreditation he continued to work across his trademark genres of satire and the fantastic from the late Victorian period and through the early twentieth century. He took on the role of editor at *Eureka* magazine and through this outlet made important connections with writers and artists of the same ilk.

Sime is perhaps best known for his collaborative work and in particular for his illustrations to the fantasy literature of Irish author Edward Plunkett, the 18th Baron of Dunsany, a significant literary precursor to important figures in fantasy and horror fiction including J.R.R Tolkien, and H.P Lovecraft. Dunsany was an incredibly prolific writer and published more than eighty books including hundreds of short stories dedicated to things 'far beyond the boundaries of our world' and Sime illustrated Dunsany's works from his very first publication, *The Gods of Pegāna*, in 1905.

Paul McCann has noted that Dunsany's writings, specifically those illustrated by Sime, have, at their core, "a preoccupation with wonder and imagination ... but also with the petty and insignificant nature of mankind in the face of the vast expanses of Time and Space." This is not surprising, given that Sime was an avid reader of Edgar Allan Poe, and an admirer of Goya, among other European Romantic artists, and also that he worked continuously and in creative tension with the prominent artistic movements of Symbolism and emerging Surrealism.

While Dunsany's literary achievements traversing the realms of the fantastic and horror modes are widely recognized, these are matched by Sime's artistic accompaniments to his writing, and the dynamic artistic collaboration between the two was acknowledged by Dunsany himself, insofar as his writing was openly influenced by the fantastic originality of Sime's pen and ink drawings. Dunsany said of Sime that he had "never seen a black and white artist with a more stupendous imagination" and his admiration for Sime's work was put into practice in the case of *The Book of Wonder* (1912) when author and illustrator exchanged roles: Sime creating the illustrations and Dunsany then writing his short story collection to incorporate them. Dunsany claimed that the nature of this collaboration and the interaction of Sime's images with his creative texts would add a little to the overall mystery of the final product. Not that the mystery of the works needed much more in the way of the strange or the uncanny: even before the publication of *The Book of Wonder*, the tales and Sime's drawings bore the unmistakable quality of the unreal and the disturbing, earning Sime the title in the eyes of his more modern critics of "Master of the Mysterious" (McCann).

While he created many artworks across different genres, including romantic landscapes and caricatures of local people from his hometown in Surrey, it is those works classified as fantasy, which perhaps offer the most interesting insight into Sime's contribution to the cosmic horror genre. While many of these works are untitled, they generate a definite sense of the sublime and the uncanny. Much of Sime's work is readily accessible online alongside Dunsany's original texts. However, his more independent artistic projects are to be found as part of a unique collection held at The Sidney Sime Gallery in Sime's hometown of Worplesdon and many of his illustrations belong to the Dunsany collection, housed at Dunsany Castle in Co. Meath, Ireland.

In Michael Blouin's book on the Gothic and Japanese art, Sime is recognized as one of the first to seize upon the Gothic undertones they found in Japanese art in order to react against the rigid and conservative forms of Western art. Generating weird atmospheres and a sense of the exotic in his works, he blends stylistic aspects of "oriental" art with imaginative and unreal scenes drawn from folk and fairytale in his native England.

Notable works of Sime's include the painting *Woods and Dark Animals* (oil on canvas) which is rich in dark blue tones with geometric shapes forming an image of the dark woods as an echo of the structure of the stained glass windows of a Gothic cathedral. In the foreground, the dark silhouette of a wolf-like creature lurks with its red tongue lolling, anticipating an encounter with the viewer who faces it head on. Although his paintings establish a fantastic and colorful folk imaginary, it is Sime's pen and ink drawings which resonate most acutely with the Gothic of the period. *Incubus* from Dunsany's *The Gods of Pegāna* presents a shadowy bedroom scene in which much of the characters actions are obscured by darkness. Arousing a strange curiosity in the viewer, an elongated arm, presumably of a young woman drapes down from beside the bedpost within reach of an open book highlighted by the dramatic flame of a melting candle. The scene, although obscured, carries more than a hint of satire, echoing earlier artistic incarnations of the incubus myth in relation to the Gothic tradition which had recently come back into vogue in Britain.

Sime's illustrations became less common in the print publications of Dunsany's stories after World War I, when publishers marked a quota on the number of illustrations per book due to funding problems. His paintings in oils became more widely recognized during this time, in particular his representations of the Apocalypse as inspired by the Book of Revelations. H.P Lovecraft was an ardent fan of Sime's and mentioned his work in a number of his stories, including "The Call of Cthulhu." Following his death, Dunsany wrote of Sime: "I feel now that the world has lost a unique character, a loss that is quite irreplaceable." His legacy, however, was not lost and his drawings continue to inspire the Gothic art and literature of today.

SUGGESTED FURTHER READING

Blouin, Michael J. *Japan and the Cosmopolitan Gothic: Spectres of Modernity*. London: Palgrave Macmillan, 2013.
Ford, Henry, and Simon Heneage. *Sidney Sime: Master of the Mysterious*. London: Thames and Hudson, 1980.
Joshi, S. T. *Lord Dunsany: A Bibliography*. Metuchen, NJ: Scarecrow, 1993.
Locke, George. "The Land of Dreams: Review of the Work of Sidney H. Sime, 1905–1916." *Ferret Fantasy* (1975).
McCann, Paul. "Echoes of the Decadents and Symbolists: The Fantasies of Dunsany." *English* vol. 10 (Spring 2008).
Skeeters, Paul. *Sidney H. Sime, Master of Fantasy*. London: Ward Ritchie, 1978.

Tod Slaughter
(1885–1956)

Jarlath Killeen

In 1931, the *Observer* claimed that "probably no actor in England has a bigger public than" Tod Slaughter. In 1937 the *World Film News* acknowledged Slaughter as "the last outstanding representative of the real people's theatre." Two years later, in a fulsome review of one of Slaughter's best films, *The Face at the Window* (dir. George King, 1939), Graham Greene declared him to be "certainly one of our finest living actors." In a brilliant career stretching from his stage debut in 1905 to his final performances a few weeks before his death in 1956 at the age of 71, Slaughter was one of the most successful actors on the British stage, with an enormous repertoire of about 340 plays, performing to packed crowds and affectionate audiences up and down the country. Slaughter specialized in Gothic villains, and his extraordinary theatrical appeal led to his successful translation to the screen at the age of 50, in one of his most popular roles, the Victorian murderer and lecher Squire William Corder in *Maria Marten, or The Murder in the Red Barn* (dir. Milton Rosmer, 1935), a role he had already essayed in countless stage performances, usually with his talented wife, Jenny Lynn playing poor Maria. Slaughter went on to star in seven more successful Gothic melodramas for the screen. In the 1930s and 1940s, Slaughter was a contender for the position of leading British exponent of Gothic horror, probably rivaled only by Boris Karloff.

Around Karloff, and other British horror stars like Christopher Lee and Peter Cushing there has now grown a considerable cult of understandable adulation and admiration, but Slaughter has been almost completely forgotten, except by the odd historian of cinema and melodrama. For an explanation of this relative neglect, it would be too easy to point to the supposedly negligible quality of Slaughter's films, as this would require overlooking the fact that Karloff, Lee and Cushing starred in a remarkable number of duds, and that, in fact, Slaughter's films are effective, efficient and thoroughly enlivened by his presence. While Johnny Depp's manic performance as Sweeney Todd in Tim Burton's adaptation of Steven Sondheim's musical gained rave reviews, Slaughter's wildly popular and influential variation on the same character (the best, for my money) in innumerable stage performances, and eventually in *The Demon Barber of Fleet Street* (dir. George King, 1936), has faded ignominiously into the bargain bin background. It is interesting, for example, that most guides to horror fail to even mention his name let alone recommend any of his films.

Slaughter's disappearance from the horror canon stems from the particularities of his acting style. His intensely stylized, self-conscious, gurning, grinning, leering, cackling creepiness now seems so over-the-top that it goes beyond camp into something close to embarrassment for many horror fans. Slaughter does not so much chew the scenery as devour it with considerable relish. He essentially gives the "same" performance in all his films (and—if the theatrical reviews are anything to go by—did the same in most of his stage work): playful, hedonistic, libidinous, excessive, with sufficient eye-rolling, hand-rubbing, eye-twinkling, rip-roaring, barnstorming, pithy- and amusing-one-liner-dispatching to satisfy anyone. As, *The Manchester Guardian* (24 December 1932) put it, Slaughter knew "melodrama down to

Tod Slaughter *is* Sweeney Todd (frame grab from *Sweeney Todd*, 1936).

the last drop of blood and scream of a victim," and played each role to the hilt. The horror fan and critic discomfort with Slaughter's acting, though, is telling given that the genre is hardly renowned for subtle or internalized performances. The "greatest" actors of horror history are revered as proponents of what Ernest Mathijs has called "referential acting" (*Screen* 52: 1, 2011). In other words, theoretically at least, Slaughter's acting should not look out of place beside the excesses of Lionel Atwill or Robert Englund.

A key difference between Slaughter's acting extravagance and, say, the camp affectation of Depp, Lee, Karloff and Cushing (Bela Lugosi is purposefully left out of this list as, rather like Slaughter—and for similar reasons—though less spectacularly, he has been neglected by fans), though, is that *their* over-performances appeal to a knowing audience of cult fans, an audience that, as Matt Hills has carefully explained, in his 2010 essay "Subcultural Celebrity," typically sets itself apart from, and often looks down with some distaste on the "simple" appreciation of horror by the masses. The cult fan feels s/he shares a kind of "expert" or specialist knowledge with the referential actor which distinguishes them from others consumers of the genre. This sets the cult fan—and the cult actor—apart from the "average" audience member who, in contrast, supposedly lacks agency and is being "manipulated" by the industrial film and star system.

It would be difficult to read Slaughter as a participant in cult celebrity. For one thing, while Slaughter's acting is certainly "knowing," in that he draws on a repertoire of stylistic tics and gestures, he never appeals to the "fan" over the mass audience. Slaughter's melodramatic performances are driven by profoundly political rather than aesthetic motives—or, better, his aesthetic choices are politically motivated (though he probably would never have put it precisely this way himself). In an interview with *World Film News*, Slaughter explained that "the revival of the old popular drama after the war is what I regard as my most important work. I would always play [the villain roles] straight, you know, I have never burlesqued them." His life-long commitment to melodrama has been convincingly read by Jeffrey Richards as an attempt to tap into a kind of folk memory, a "hinterland of the imagination shared by the mass of the population," populated during the nineteenth century with mythic characters like Sweeney Todd, Burke and Hare, Mr. Hyde, Ebeneezer Scrooge, Long John Silver, Bill Sikes, Jack Sheppard, and mythologized real-life criminals such as "Jack the Ripper." Crucially, Slaughter played each of these figures in some medium at some stage (and usually multiple times) during his long career. Whereas revered horror actors may appeal to a mass audience, they are appreciated as "cult figures" through their aesthetic appeal to genre-aware audience members. Slaughter, in contrast, appeals over the fan and directly to the mass audience and does so *sincerely*. His claim that he took these roles "seriously" does not mean that there are no knowing nods and winks to the audience; however, unlike the cult star, the nods and winks are to the *whole* audience, and not just the cult fans. Slaughter's acting manifests a genuinely popular art form and style, closer to pantomime than to cult horror, and understandably leaves many horror fans cold—though the disruptive energies of the pantomime and the melodrama are closer to the excessive power of horror as a genre of affect (emotion machine [Tan, 1995]) than many fans and specialists would like to admit.

The Newcastle-upon-Tyne native (born Norman Carter Slaughter in 1885) was not an obvious candidate for the role of working class organic intellectual—he went, for example to Newcastle Royal Grammar School, and was a manager of theatrical troupes as well as a jobbing actor—becoming lessee of Hippodrome Theatres in Croydon and Richmond before the First World War, and running the Theatre Royal in Chatham (1919–1922) and the Elephant and Castle (1922–25). However, he quickly succumbed to what he called the "drug" of melodrama and Gothic horror, and absorbed and incarnated its energies, recognizing its communal potential, its ability to turn dispirited communities into a kind of family. As in pantomime, these audiences became co-performers and co-producers of the drama, their participation actively encouraged.

Slaughter embodied the folklore of the popular audience in the flesh, in the sound of his voice, and the style of his performance, and while his is indeed a kind of "bottom up" celebrity, it is *not* a fan-generated one. Slaughter is a "popular" rather than a cult celebrity, and therefore fits uneasily into fan celebrations of otherwise little known sub-culture stars. That may be reason enough to carefully re-insert him back into our histories of the genre.

SUGGESTED FURTHER READING

Egan, Kate, and Sarah Thomas, eds. *Cult Film Stardom: Offbeat Attractions and Processes of Cultification*. Basingstoke: Palgrave Macmillan, 2013. 243–258.

Mathijs, Ernest. "Referential Acting and the Ensemble Cast." *Screen* 52: 1 (2011): 89–96.

Richards, Jeffrey. "Tod Slaughter and the Cinema of Excess." In *The Unknown 1930s: An Alternative History of the British Cinema, 1929–1939*, ed. Jeffrey Richards. London, New York: I. B. Tauris, 1998. 139–61.

Sweet, Matthew. *Shepperton Babylon: The Lost Worlds of British Cinema*. London: Faber and Faber, 2005. 108–09.

Tan, Ed S. *Emotion and the Structure of Narrative Film: Film as an Emotion Machine*. London: Routledge, 1995.

Lionel Sparrow
(1867–1936)

James Doig

Lionel Sparrow was an Australian journalist and newspaper proprietor who wrote more than two dozen horror and crime short stories for the national periodical, *The Australian Journal*, and for local newspapers in Victoria. Although his stories were never collected in a book, Sparrow deserves recognition as one of the first Australian writers who wrote mainly in the Gothic mode—his stories are often set in exotic locations and his plots are melodramatic, dripping with atmosphere.

Lionel Sparrow was born in 1867 in the small Murray River town of Wahgunyah, located 272 kilometers north-east of Melbourne, and was the eldest of six children, one of whom died in infancy. His father, Isaac, was American, born in Minerva Essex County in Upper New York State. Isaac was a miner, aged 37 when he married Lionel's mother Louisa Helena Brown, a domestic aged 25, who was born in London in Turleigh on 6 October 1866. He died in Walls End, NSW, 1894, and Louisa died in Melbourne. She was described a "dressmaker" and is buried in a Pauper's Grave at St. Kilda Cemetery. Lionel seems to have then been living with her at St. Kilda when she died.

Sparrow began his long association with newspapers in Newcastle where he started an apprenticeship at the age of 14, and worked in Sydney, Melbourne and Sunbury. In 1911, after working on *The Riponshire Advocate* for six years, he moved to Linton, a Victorian mining town located 149 kilometers east of Melbourne, where he lived for the remainder of his life. He bought the local newspaper, the *Grenville Standard*, and retained it until his death. He married Alice Eliza Miller, and they had one son, Geoffrey Sparrow, who followed his father into journalism and became federal president of the Australian Journalists Association.

From all accounts, Lionel was a quiet, self-effacing man. Small in stature (about 5'4") but generous and well regarded. He was very involved in the life of Linton as, among other things, a vestryman and church warden at St. Paul's Anglican Church, a founding member and president of the Linton Dramatic Club, and a founding member of the Old Lintonians Association, which first met on 9 October 1913. At the time of his death on 9 April 1936, he was described by one of the locals in *The Grenville Standard* as a "go ahead little man" always in the vanguard of progress. He had literary aspirations and apart from the stories he wrote for *The Australian Journal*, he also published poems in the celebrated literary journal *The Bulletin*, twenty-four of which were collected into a slim volume, *Poems*, under the byline "Ignotus." During the 1890s Lionel Sparrow also wrote stories and serials for the *Sunbury News and Bulla and Melton Advertiser*. Some of these were reprints from stories published in the *Australian Journal*, such as "The Wrestler of Tokio" and "The Mystery of Mervale," but others appear to be first and only publications, such as "Shadows of the Past" and "Miss Waysmith's Poems." The serials include "The Tragedy at Waritungah" and "The Loss of the 'Black Swan.'"

He was clearly influenced by the "sensational" type of fiction that was popular at the time, in Australia represented in particular by Marcus Clarke, whose *Sensational Tales* was published in 1886. It is also possible to detect the influence of Edgar Allan Poe and the residual Gothic influence found in the popular Penny Dreadfuls of the day.

Sparrow's first story, "The Jewelled Hand," appeared in the August 1887 issue of *The Australian Journal*, when he was nineteen. This story is a typical *grand guignol* gothic horror story featuring an ingenious decapitation machine that would not look out of place in a Roger Corman film. Set in Spain, the narrator reveals his increasing obsession with decapitation and whether or not will remains in the mind after severance. This leads him to construct a machine for decapitating human beings, which he uses to murder his closest friend, Don Alvaro, a man of great mind and will power who proves the theory by obtaining posthumous revenge.

A series of gothic melodramas followed, which were published in quick succession in 1888. It seems reasonable to assume that Sparrow wrote the stories as a group and then sought publication—certainly they are very similar in theme and style. In "The Torture of the Clock," set in underground vaults, presumably in Europe, the narrator is cruelly tortured by the evil Zaroni who is himself destroyed by the fate prepared for his victim. "The Tenant of the Third Cell" is about a father's thirst for vengeance against the rejected suitor who poisoned his daughter and nephew the week before their wedding. When he catches up with the murderer he is more than satisfied to discover him hideously deformed by leprosy. What is particularly striking about these stories is their excessiveness—we have violent murder, mutilation, disfiguring disease, and torture (both physical and psychological). Take for example, the following description of a swordfight in "In the North Wing," which occurs after the mad Sir Phillip Margrave has plucked out the eyes of Lady Alice Tremaine:

> It was a fight of madmen—a mutual butchery. There was no attempt at defense on either side. Each struck blindly at the other, and every blow, every thrust, took effect. In a few seconds both combatants, pierced in twenty places and bathed in blood, rolled on the marble floor. Sir Phillip Margrave, as he fell, breathed his last. But Cyril Verehurst lived some moments; that is to say, long enough to feel the last embrace of Lady Alice, who had seized the Damascus sword which her hand, groping about, had touched, and had plunged it into her breast. And then, falling upon the body of her lover, she mingled her last sighs with his.

Others may have been influenced by the decadent literature of the day. Consider the following paragraph from "Irene":

> I looked upon her as she lay, still, and white, and cold. Her beauty had always been great, but now there seemed in it a very pronounced, though indefinable, weirdness that rendered it almost superhuman to my eyes, and I shuddered as I thought how soon would this matchless handicraft of nature be the food of the worm. For many minutes I stood gazing at the motionless face, the closed lids, the heavy raven hair, the slender but exquisitely moulded arms, the delicately perfect outlines of the bosom. I had been suffering acutely, and my nerves were highly strung by excessive draughts of laudanum. It may be that I uttered some wild words, for I have an indistinct remembrance of an agitation of some sort within the room; however, I was led away, and found myself next morning in my own chamber.

Another *fin de siécle* tale is "Seagram's Manuscript," published in October 1895, which is an opium tale. In the story the narrator obtains a manuscript from a former friend within a few weeks of his death in an opium den. It reveals his intense depression after his sister's death and the terrible dreams haunting him in which he murders his closest friend, who was his sister's fiancé. In an obsessed dreamlike state he kills him and for a time finds relief because the dreams stop. However, he is soon haunted by guilt—opium gives him ease and the sleep which he once again craves.

Sparrow published stories regularly throughout the early 1890s, but after 1895 his output slowed considerably as his life became centered on his journalism and newspaper work. However, he did publish the occasional tale, such as "The Lady with the Veil," which appeared in *The Australian Journal* in June 1903. This is another curious story in which the narrator, a wealthy man, has a hereditary disease that manifests itself in an abhorrence of perfumes, particularly patchouli. He marries and for a time is happy, and his wife eschews all perfumes. However, a financial crisis causes the loss of all his wealth and part of hers, and she turns against him. She torments him by sprinkling patchouli on him and, in an uncontrollable rage, he disfigures her with a shard from a broken perfume bottle. He escapes and builds a new life in the country, adopting a young child who was orphaned during a bush fire. His wife has her revenge, however—she tracks him down and gives the unsuspecting child a bottle of patchouli; the narrator kills the child in a rage when she sprinkles it on his handkerchief.

Almost from the start of his writing career Sparrow mixed his gothic stories with adventure and crime stories, some of which had an Australian setting. The first of these was "The Glass Dagger," a crime romance about a woman who falls in love with the brother of a convicted forger who is transported to Australia. Some of these stories, like the gothic tales, have exotic locations—"A Tale of Tokio," for example, is a strange story about a failed Japanese wrestler's obsessive hatred of the narrator, a westerner, who only manages to escape his murderous intentions through the intervention of an earthquake. "The Purple Death," published in August 1906, is set in Melbourne and is an unusual melodrama. The narrator makes the acquaintance of the brilliant and saturnine Dr Wainwright, a scientist and rival for the affections of Marie Seymour. Wainwright kidnaps him and attempts to drive him insane through an experiment where he is locked in a room and continually exposed to the color purple.

His later stories were published at irregular intervals in *The Australian Journal*. He abandoned the excessive gothic trappings of his earlier tales and introduced occult/psychic elements from Eastern religions, perhaps influenced by Theosophy.

His last horror story (at least, the last I have so far found), "The Vengeance of the Dead," is a vampire story set in Melbourne, which again has a strong flavor of Eastern mysticism. Martin Calthorpe, an occultist, dies mysteriously as does his wife soon afterwards of a wasting disease. Before long, the narrator's sister, Winnie, falls ill and dies, and his other sister, Connie, starts to decline. The narrator and Connie's fiancé, Harry Thornten, an adept in the mystical arts, seek the help of Ravanna Dâs, a Hindu Brahman, who reveals that Calthorpe was a black magician whose spirit leaves its physical remains to pray on the living for sustenance. The narrator's father commits suicide and reveals in a letter that he had murdered Calthorpe. The narrator and Thornten, with the help of Ravanna Dâs, discover Calthorpe's body and decapitate it. The interesting and unusual plot is marred somewhat by being overlong with a lot of explanatory material. How were Sparrow's Gothic stories received by their readers? That the stories continued to be published suggests they were well received and that there was a demand for them. Nevertheless, at least one of the stories prompted a critical letter to the editor. The editor, William Smith Mitchell, responded to the reader's comment on "The Torture of the Clock" as follows:

> We regret that you [W. Neale] could discover neither "sense nor meaning" in the story "The Torture of the Clock," of a recent issue of the journal. The tale appeared to us as

complete, to thoroughly explain itself, and to be of a highly interesting character. The abrupt commencement to which you probably refer—where the incident is at once related without introduction—appears to be a characteristic of the author. It is suggested that you have not read the tale with care, especially as regards the opening.

Mitchell was the editor of *The Australian Journal* throughout Sparrow's literary career, and it is certainly conceivable that he encouraged Sparrow's writing and directed him into other genres, styles and plots. Sparrow's work as proprietor of *The Grenville Standard* prevented him from developing as a writer of sensational fiction. This is to be regretted as his tales are a cut above the standard popular fiction of the time, both in terms of the quality of his prose and in the often exotic and bizarre nature of his plots.

SUGGESTED FURTHER READING

Doig, James. *Australian Gothic: An Anthology of Australian Supernatural Fiction.* Maryland: Wildside, 2013.

Doig, James. "Lionel Sparrow (1867–1936): An Unknown Australian Author of Gothic Horror," *Wormwoodiana* blog, July 12, 2014. http://wormwoodiana.blogspot.ie/2014/07/lionel-sparrow-1867-1936-unknown.html

Sparrow, Lionel, "The Vengeance of the Dead" in Eighteen-Bisang, Robert, and Dalby, Richard (eds.), *Vintage Vampire Stories.* New York: Skyhorse, 2011.

Montague Summers
(1880–1948)

Frank Furedi

Montague Summers was not simply an archaeologist and editor of classic Gothic novels and essays (as evidenced by his 1936 collection *The Grimoire and Other Supernatural Stories*.) He also embraced the world of Gothic horror fiction and his life was devoted to exposing the evil of witchcraft that lurked in the dark corners of society. As far as Summers was concerned, the ideas associated with medieval demonology did not lose their salience in the modern era. That is why he felt called upon to publish in 1928 the first English translation of the *Malleus Maleficarum*.

The *Malleus Malleficarum* (The Hammer of Witches) was originally published in 1486 in Germany. It was one of the first examples of what we call today a "self-help" manual. The aim of this text was to directly challenge those who were skeptical of the existence of witchcraft. The expertise of professional demonologists could only be affirmed through discrediting and silencing those who questioned the existence of witchcraft. As today, so in the past was the skeptic the natural target of the demonologist. Montague Summers, who was particularly hostile to those who questioned the existence of Satanic forces, was almost spontaneously drawn towards this 15th century bible of the witch-hunter.

In his 1948 Preface to *The Malleus*, Summers acknowledged his debt to and affection for the manual. Pointing to the "weight and dignity" of this text, Summers explained that in a short period of time the *Malleus Maleficarum* had become the de facto handbook for witch-hunters and Inquisitors throughout Europe. According to him, "the *Malleus* lay on the bench of every magistrate." It was the ultimate, "irrefutable, unarguable authority" he argued, accepted not only by Catholic but by Protestant legislature. What was significant about the *Malleus* was that it provided a theologically acceptable framework through which traditional popular prejudices about witches could be reframed through an intellectually coherent doctrine. Moreover the way that witches were represented lent them an intensely sinister dimension. Witches were no longer portrayed as mere individuals practicing sorcery and magic. They were now depicted as heretics who were actively assisting the work of Satan.

Summers was one of a tiny band of believers who in the 20th century still took arguments and sentiments outlined in the *Malleus* seriously. He was convinced that the perils of Satanism continued to pose a threat to the moral order. He railed against the skeptics whose "flat denial" of witchcraft was, according to him, a manifestation of "their own narrow prejudice." As outlined in his 1926 tome *The History of Witchcraft and Demonology*, he promised to rectify this state of affairs by showing once and for all the witch as "she really was":

> an evil liver; a social pest and parasite: the devotee of a loathly and obscene creed; an adept at poisoning, blackmail, and other creeping crimes; a member of a powerful secret organization inimical to Church and State; a blasphemer in word and deed; swaying the villagers by terror and superstition; a charlatan and a quack sometimes; a bawd; an abortionist; the dark counselor of lewd court ladies and adulterous gallants; a minister to vice and inconceivable corruption; battening upon the filth and foulest passion of the age.

Sadly, for Summers, his vivid portrayal of the threat posed by demonic forces was not taken very seriously in the 1920s. People and communities during his time did not feel threatened by creeping blasphemers practicing their dark art during the middle of the night. They had other problems to worry about. The fear of unemployment and of economic insecurity provided a more pressing focus for people's anxieties during this period.

Montague Summers was all too conscious of the fact that his conviction that witchcraft was a serious, ongoing threat to European civilization lacked any official support from the authorities. With a hint of frustration he stated in the *History*, "what matter the logical and reasoned belief of centuries, of the most cultured peoples, the highest intelligences of Europe" who believed in witchcraft. But he knew that appealing to the "highest intelligences" of the Middle Ages would provide little authority for his thesis in the 1920s. Rounding on his doubters, he asserted "any appeal to authority is, of course, useless, as the skeptic repudiates all authority—save his own."

This devotee of the Gothic therefore devoted most of his adult life to pointing to a danger that others did not appear to comprehend. He was a fervent collector of rumors and anecdotes that hinted at Satanic practices and plots. His conspiratorial imagination led him to interpret every scrap of gossip as yet another piece of evidence supporting this belief regarding the ongoing practice of the dark arts. As he concluded his *History*, "Yet, if what is whispered be true, and seem strong confirmation enough, the shedding of blood is not unknown among the devil worshippers today in London; in Brighton and Birmingham; in Oxford and Cambridge in Edinburgh and Glasgow, and in a hundred cities more of the British Isles."

Moral crusaders always reserve their most venomous rhetoric for their critics. Medieval witch-hunters who regarded incredulity in the malevolent forces of demons as a crime as bad as devil-worship itself systematically pursued this line of reasoning. Anyone who questioned the existence of demonic forces could be denounced as an associate of Satan. Such was the power and influence of this that few were prepared to question the existence of witch-craft. Summers wholly internalized this orientation towards the skeptic. In his writings he associated skepticism with the power of the demonic force of witchcraft and a sinister hidden agenda. As far as he was concerned, there were "solid facts which cannot be ignored":

> save indeed by the purblind prejudice of the rationalist, and cannot be accounted for, save that we recognize there were and are individuals, devoted to the service of evil, greedy of such emotions and experiences, rewards the thralldom of wickedness may bring [sic].

From this perspective it was not genuine doubt, but malevolent intent that motivated the behavior of those who insisted on voicing skepticism about witch-craft.

The anti-skeptical fear of the forces of darkness continues to excise the contemporary imagination. In the early twenty-first century, modern witch-hunters continue to castigate the skeptic. During the outbreak of the Satanic Ritual Abuse panic in Britain during the 1980s, zealous campaigners claimed that an "insidious and dangerous" disease was sweeping the country— incredulity in the existence of ritual abuse. As Judith Dawson noted in the British current affairs magazine *New Statesman* in October 1990, "this contagion takes the comforting form of skeptical and rational inquiry, and its message is comforting too: it is designed to protect "innocent family life" against a new urban myth of the satanic abuse of children." Paradoxically, in the 21st century skepticism continues to be condemned –but now by secular moral crusaders. Climate skeptics, Euroskeptics, or those who are skeptical of recovered memory syndromes are often described through a narrative of evil. Montague Summers would approve.

SUGGESTED FURTHER READING

Furedi, F. *The Power of Reading: From Socrates to Twitter*. London: Bloomsbury, 2015.
Newman, P. *A History of Terror: Fear and Dread Through the Ages*. Stroud, Gloucestershire: Sutton, 2000.
Montague S. *The History of Witchcraft and Demonology*. London: Routledge & Kegan Paul, 1969.

Team *Silent Hill*

Ewan Kirkland

As a boy growing up in the 1970s I was among the first generation for whom videogames were part of everyday popular culture. I remember playing monochrome tennis on my family's television set, the thrill of early arcades with their space invaders, colorful cartoon characters and pervasive cigarette smoke, heated arguments in the playground concerning the virtues of the ZX Spectrum over the Commodore 64. As a young man I was one of the first to enroll for a Media Studies degree, and later, as a postgraduate, I was given the opportunity to contribute to the program and develop the field as an academic. At university I studied, taught, and researched film, television, radio, newspapers, magazines and literature. But not videogames. Never videogames.

By now it was mid-1990s, the era of the PlayStation 1 (1994), *Tomb Raider* (1996), and *Grand Theft Auto* (1997). As a habitual gamer I sought to engage academically with these electronic experiences, in the same way as contemporary scholars wrote about soap opera, situation comedy and action cinema. But the interactive medium of the videogame seemed too different a form of culture, its extent too expansive, its mode of engagement too elusive, its pleasures too alien. Moreover, videogames appeared to lack the materiality required for productive textual analysis. I saw no way to incorporate the games I played into the existing structures of media and cultural studies. Until I played *Silent Hill 2* (2001).

A number of aspects make this title, a survival horror sequel with little connection to its 1999 predecessor, particularly appropriate for academic analysis. It has an intriguing storyline. A man receives a mysterious letter from his dead wife, Mary, telling him to come to the town of Silent Hill where she is waiting for him. The game has a particularly cinematic aesthetic, overlaid with a misty, grainy visual effect which produced a uniquely creepy sensation of contamination, decay and delirium. There is an intertextuality to the title, including allusions to the films of David Lynch, *Jacob's Ladder* (1990), the legend of Orpheus, *Vertigo* (1958) and *The Silence of the Lambs* (1991).

But what made the game so compelling for a student of media and culture is a quality rarely associated with videogames: ambiguity.

The game starts unsettlingly enough. Following a brief monologue, players take control of James Sunderland in following the costal path from the car park to the town which is his destination. The journey takes the player deeper and deeper down the narrow misty pathway, surrounded by fog which seems filled with strange creatures existing just out of view, snuffling and snarling at James as he makes his way down, down, down. Most disturbing of all, throughout this protracted opening sequence... nothing happens. This opening sequence makes it clear. This is not a game about killing zombies, negotiating elaborate action set pieces, or wielding explosive weaponry. Rather, this is a game about one man's descent. Into precisely what remains unclear.

Similar moments of isolation, inaction and monotony are represented in James' architecture-defying trip to the Silent Hill Historical Society, or his journey across the Styx-like Toluca Lake to the hotel where James and Mary spent their honeymoon. The game is full of unsettling moments, all the more discomforting for remaining unresolved. Soon after arriving at the town James encounters a tailor's dummy wearing the exact dress as his wife in the photograph he carries. Later James meets Maria, a dead ringer for his dead wife, who even shares some of her memories. Other characters the player engages with, a woman who murdered her abusive father, a young girl who shared Mary's hospital ward, seem confused or engaged in experiences of the town very different from that of the protagonist. The first time players see Pyramid Head, the game's main monster, a contorted figure dressed in a slaughterhouse apron with an enormous triangular contraption bolted to its head, the beast is engaged in violent activity involving a manikin-styled creature. Is it an act of murder, rape or birth which the player and protagonist witness? The collapse of these three possibilities into a single scene makes this one of the most disturbing moments in videogame history.

As the game progresses, small details suggest that James may not be as innocent as he appears. Our nondescript hero has a drinking problem, appears implicated somehow in his wife's death, and is experiencing a sense of guilt-induced amnesia. The game's climactic battle, on a ruined hotel rooftop, represents a repetition of the murderous act that may have brought James here in the first place.

What is Silent Hill, the small lakeside town around which the on-going series revolves? A haunted ghost town? A limbo? A beacon for lost souls seeking some kind of redemption? A hell where hapless individuals are tormented for their crimes? A place of the psyche, a dreamscape, a world of madness and hallucination. Is James dead? Is he in purgatory? Is he insane? This ambiguity is never resolved. It is this profound and pervasive sense of uncertainty which makes *Silent Hill 2* an eminently gothic experience.

Videogame production represents a collaborative process, but this does not invalidate the collective artistry involved in the design process. A number of videogame auteurs have already emerged within the canon: Sid Meier (*Civilization*), Will Wright (*Sim City*), Shigeru Miyamoto (*Donkey Kong, Mario, Legend of Zelda*), and Hideo Kojima (*Metal Gear*), as well as Sandy Petersen and Shinji Mikami, who are also discussed in this volume. The release of *Silent Hill 2* in 2001 was accompanied by a documentary identifying three key individuals as central to the game's design: producer Akihiro Imamura, CG and character director Takayoshi Sato, and sound director Akira Yamaoka. The interviews and commentaries that comprise this video show how the creatives involved in game production are influenced by art, philosophy and psychology. The tension between repulsion and attraction built into the game's visual aesthetic, the monster designs' uncanny combination of human and inhuman qualities, the melancholy aspects of the musical themes, the sound designer's use of silence, and the ambiguity and ambivalence which is a recurring quality across the game, are all foregrounded and discussed in detail by its creators.

The team behind this title, those honored in the accompanying documentary, and mentioned in the credits which roll upon the game's completion, are authors of a masterfully gothic text which deserves critical attention for its creative and artistic achievements. *Silent Hill 2*, conspicuously working within a Gothic tradition, confronts the player with a profoundly unsettling experience, in which they are implicated in the narrative, despite their lack of control or certainty over what is actually happening. This is a melodramatic story of murder, deception, love, betrayal and madness. As the game unfolds we sense a growing disconnect between ourselves and the unreliable amnesiac protagonist who we control. By the end we are unclear exactly what has happened, an ambiguity exacerbated by the game's numerous endings. In *Silent Hill 2*, and across the long-running series, we see the translation of traditional tropes of the uncanny, the supernatural, terror, suspense and the fantastic, into a new digital medium. Scholars of the gothic would do well to look at videogames, particularly of the survival horror cycle, for evidence of contemporary transformations and continuations in gothic themes, tropes and characteristics.

SUGGESTED FURTHER READING

Kirkland, Ewan. "Restless Dreams in Silent Hill: Approaches to Video Game Analysis." *Journal of Media Practice* 6.3 (2005): 167.
Kirkland, Ewan. "Discursively Constructing the Art of Silent Hill." *Games and Culture* (2010).
Perron, Bernard, ed. *Horror Video Games: Essays on the Fusion of Fear and Play*. Jefferson, NC: McFarland, 2009.
Perron, Bernard. *Silent Hill: The Terror Engine*. Ann Arbor: University of Michigan Press, 2012.

Peter Van Greenaway
(1929-1988)

EDWARD O'HARE

If Peter Van Greenaway tried to ensure that the details of his life remained a mystery he certainly succeeded. Even though he only died twenty-eight years ago, hard facts about this writer are impossible to come by. And yet, for over two decades Van Greenaway was among the most prolific of popular novelists. He was also one of the most unusual, intelligent, and skillful British horror writers of the 20th century who, when at the height of his abilities, produced a genuine genre masterpiece, *The Medusa Touch* (1973).

What do we know for sure? According to one brief biography Peter Van Greenaway was born in London in 1929. As no person of that name was ever listed in a census it's safe to assume that it was an alias. Van Greenaway never gave interviews or publicized his work, and only one photograph of him exists. Apart from reviews of his novels, the only occasions when Van Greenaway's name appeared in newspapers was when his engagement was announced in 1949 and when he attended a memorial service in 1951.

Van Greenaway's books also state that he practiced law before turning to fiction, something confirmed by the numerous convincing descriptions of legal procedure in his novels. Before long he seems to have given this up and tried his hand at a number of vocations, including commercial art and acting. In 1955 a play for radio he wrote was broadcast. He appeared in a 1957 episode of the World War II prison camp drama *Escape*. Van Greenaway's ambition to be an actor does not seem to have persisted and by the late 50s he had moved the other side of the camera, writing scripts for such "play of the week" series as *Thirty-Minute Theatre*, *ITV Playhouse*, and *Saturday Night Thriller*. The intermittent nature of his contributions suggests that this line of work was not his forte either.

Instead Van Greenaway turned to the novel and became established as a reliable but far from conventional popular writer. In 1972 he was contracted by the publishing house Gollancz, famous for its high-quality genre fiction, and turned out a book roughly every other year until his death in 1988. His work is extremely varied, taking in detective stories, supernatural mysteries, conspiracy thrillers and science-fiction. His books are also interesting generic combinations, often defying any strict classification. However, it's Van Greenaway's talent for the macabre that most readily distinguishes his work. Nowhere is this trait more in evidence than in his finest novel, and the only one to enjoy any following today, *The Medusa Touch*.

Looking at his earliest work, it's astonishing that Van Greenaway ever had a successful writing career. His first novel, *The Crucified City* (1962), is a cheerful piece about the aftermath of a nuclear attack on London. The plot follows a group of survivors, all dying of radiation sickness, as they make a grim final pilgrimage. The book is typical Van Greenaway, neither straightforward commercial sci-fi nor a "Ban the Bomb" parable, but a mixture of allegory, horror and satire which set the trend for what followed. It also had something that would become a standard feature of Van Greenaway's novels: a final surprise that completely inverts much of what you have read. In *The Crucified City*, the only character to reach the last page alive is a deaf mute who is revealed to be the resurrected Jesus Christ.

Van Greenaway had two further stabs at writing a bestseller before hitting the jackpot with his fourth novel, *Judas!* (1972), which won him much acclaim and a wide readership. Hardly a year passed and Van Greenaway was back with the best book he would ever write. *The Medusa Touch* is a devilishly clever horror story, a disturbing, blackly comic and gripping genre classic that still reads exceptionally well.

It begins with a murder. Reclusive novelist John Morlar has been found in his London flat, his head smashed in. Inspector Francis Cherry of Scotland Yard is baffled why anyone would wish to kill a man who wanted nothing to do with the world. However, just as the mortuary wagon arrives it emerges that Morlar is still alive. Despite having literally had his brains beaten out, the writer clings to life by the merest thread and is rushed to hospital and put on a life-support machine.

With no other leads, Cherry delves into Morlar's journals. In these he encounters a man fixated with human evil who believes he is conducting a lonely crusade against corruption, hypocrisy and tyranny. Cherry's inquiries lead him to Morlar's psychiatrist, Dr. Zonfeld. Zonfeld explains that Morlar saw himself as responsible for a series of horrific incidents dating back to his childhood, that he had a "gift for disaster" which had already claimed many lives. The more Cherry learns about Morlar the more astounding the chain of deaths becomes. It seems that Morlar's nanny, parents, schoolmaster, the judge who ruined his legal career, his unfaithful wife, her lover and many others all perished in tragic circumstances after receiving the full force of his terrible, demonic gaze.

Morlar lately believed that his powers had intensified, allowing him to bring about a series of earth-shattering calamities, including sinking an atomic submarine, crashing a jumbo jet into a London tower block and sending an American lunar module hurtling into infinity. The abnormal resilience with which Morlar is keeping himself this side of the grave suggests that he has some unfinished business. Doubting even his own sanity, Cherry begins to wonder if Morlar could really be what he claimed, "The Man with the Power to Create Catastrophe."

The joys of *The Medusa Touch* are many. Prime among these is Van Greenaway's unique prose style. Elegant, allusive, full of dark jokes and wordplay, this is a popular writer with the courage to assume that his reader has a brain. He prefaces the novel with a quotation from Parmenides, "That Which it is Possible to Think is That Which it is Possible to Be" and a maxim of his own, "Reality is the Hard Core of Myth," and fills it with enough paradoxes and philosophical conundrums for a dozen books. For a piece of genre fiction the book is also surprisingly experimental. Van Greenway leaves sentences tantalizingly unfinished. He addresses questions directly to the reader. Cryptic statements emerge from the shadows to mystify. The overall effect is deeply unsettling.

John Morlar, "the disaster man," is Van Greenaway's supreme creation and like many of literature's great monsters he is also a sympathetic antihero. Gleefully vengeful and megalomaniacal one moment, full of torment and melancholy the next, his denunciations of the evil soul and brutal nature of humanity are sonnets of despair. Morlar's loathing for mankind is matched by an overwhelming self-hatred, since his telekinetic powers can only be used to destroy. The extracts from his journals are masterful examples of modern gothic writing: "There are more tears than smiles. There is more sea than earth. One day the insupportable grief of mankind will sweep over the land and an ark will float on that liquid expression of misery."

The Medusa Touch's treatment of the supernatural is also ingenious. As it progresses, Van Greenaway compels us to think more and more about the relationships between mind and matter, thought and action, good and evil. Consequently, we come to realize how little we understand ourselves or the universe in which we exist and Morlar's terrible "gift" seems less and less incredible. The novel's central debate about rational belief is encapsulated in the blazing exchanges between Morlar, a character who clearly contains more than a little of his creator, and Dr. Zonfeld, a thinly disguised Sigmund Freud. These two intellectual equals are separated only by one factor: one believes in the paranormal, the other does not. This leads to a deadly battle of wills, with the two men holding on to their theories of reality for dear life.

If H.G. Wells used his Martian invaders to annihilate what he detested about society, then Van Greenaway uses Morlar for a similar purpose. He channels his "gift" at all those he loathes, which amounts to just about everybody. The novel is a succession of barbed and witty attacks on various groups and institutions, including politicians, scientists, the church, the military, the legal system, the media, the intelligentsia, the psychiatric profession, actors and the middle classes. *The Medusa Touch* reaches its stunning zenith when Morlar unleashes the full force of his telekinetic powers to bring down the dome of St. Paul's Cathedral upon a collection of the glitterati, including the Royal family. And then, when all seems safe, there is a final Van Greenaway twist that leaves a very nauseous taste in the mouth.

Given its bleak outlook and troubling themes, it's surprising that *The Medusa Touch* was turned into a film, and even more surprising that the result is as good. Lew Grade, cleverly making the most of the late '70s fad for doomsday thrillers, brought together a fine cast, including Richard Burton, Lino Ventura, Lee Remick, Harry Andrews, Gordon Jackson, Philip Stone, Michael Hordern and Jeremy Brett and gave them a director, Jack Gold, and a script, by John Briley, worthy of their talents. No actor before or since was as perfectly suited to the role of Morlar as Burton, even though Gold had originally wanted Nicol Williamson. Burton's performance is remarkably somber and all the more eerie for it. A sudden glare, a slight sneer, a thunderous rumble in that richest of voices is enough to suggest the vast destructive powers at his command.

Despite continuing to write for another fifteen years, Van Greenaway never brought together a magic combination of dark elements in quite the same way he did in *The Medusa Touch*. He produced some highly effective works, but despite an ample amount of thrills, chills and interesting concepts they are mundane in comparison. Some, such as 1975's *Doppelganger* (involving an ancient gothic mansion, mysterious archaeological discoveries, a cast of grotesques, and a man whose double can appear *anywhere*) and *The Destiny Man* (1977) (about an actor who becomes possessed by the manuscript of a lost Shakespeare play), have their moments but lack the gnawing tension and streak of the perverse that marked Van Greenawa's *magnum opus*.

Van Greenaway came to the short story quite late, producing his first collection, *Edgar Allan Who-?*, in 1981 as an homage to the great American master who was a definite source of inspiration (and whose tales he adapted for television in the mid-'60s) and his second, *The Immortal Coil*, in 1985. By the early 1980s Van Greenaway's writing had become even more pessimistic. In his final works he concentrated his attacks on the scientific community but his creativity was clearly waning. *Manrissa Man* (1982), a *Frankenstein* simulacrum, concerned the development of a race of apes with human mental faculties who take over the world. By the time Van Greenaway wrote *Mutants* (1986), a tale of razor-toothed ultra-intelligent mice, his imagination was obviously exhausted.

If anything is certain about Van Greenaway it's that he was a man extremely ill at ease in modernity. To read one of his books is to step inside a brilliant but haunted mind which had colossal contempt for all kinds of authority, technology, political correctness and mass culture. Although he was undoubtedly capable of more, Van Greenaway stuck with popular fiction because as well as paying the bills it allowed him to pour scorn upon his chosen nemeses. The critic Christopher Fowler is correct when he writes that Van Greenaway "at his best wrote popular fiction with a rare passion and erudition" and that his "peculiar talents were suited to the period in which he wrote, but transcended them." As much as his books are about the supernatural, they are equally about the madness generated in men by the systematized madness of civilization. The symbols he chose for humanity's destructiveness over four decades ago, car wrecks, exploding power stations, planes being flown into skyscrapers and nuclear attacks, are now charged with a prophetic resonance. He was a writer with a truly apocalyptic imagination that has lost none of its persuasive force.

SUGGESTED FURTHER READING

Taylor, Anthony. *London's Burning: Pulp Fiction, the Politics of Terrorism and the Destruction of the Capital in British Popular Culture, 1840–2005.* London: A&C Black, 2012.

Van Greenaway, Peter. *The Immortal Coil: Short Stories.* London: Victor Gollancz, 1985.

Van Greenaway, Peter. *Judas!* London: Victor Gollancz, 1972.

Van Greenaway, Peter. *The Killing Cup: A Novel.* London: Victor Gollancz, 1987.

Van Greenaway, Peter. *The Medusa Touch.* London: Victor Gollancz, 1973.

Stephen Volk
(1954–)

JAMES ROSE

Born 3 July 1954 in Pontypridd, Wales, Stephen Volk has steadily become one of the key *quieter* figures in modern British horror. With a career that now spans over two decades, the writer has steadily crafted an increasingly assured and complex body of genre work across a range of platforms, including film, serialized television, novellas and short fiction as well as theatre. Of all of his work to date, Volk is perhaps best known for his groundbreaking *Screen One* drama *Ghostwatch* (Lesley Manning, BBC, 1992): presented to the viewing audience as a "live" broadcast from an alleged haunted house in contemporary London, the program functions as one of the genre's first mockumentaries, a work of supernatural fiction that presents itself as *actual* fact. As such, the program is flawless in its replication of what the audience *expects* a live broadcast to be like (real-world presenters, hand-held camerawork, a live phone-in, momentary loss of transmission, the sound levels dropping or cutting out entirely, the awkward pause before the presenter realizes they are on air) and how that can effectively blend with the supernatural to create a palpable sense of terror. So effective was this synthesis of audience expectation and deft production that, during the program's broadcast, the BBC received approximately 30,000 phone calls of complaint. It transpired that the program's greatest asset—the construction of a near-perfect false reality—actually became its downfall: such was the power of the audiences belief in "live" television that numerous audience members not only believed that the (fictional) house was indeed haunted (and they themselves had seen the ghost drifting through the background) but the occupants of the house and the program's presenter, Sarah Greene (playing herself), were actually being attacked by this malevolent spirit. With such content and impact, *Ghostwatch* has rightly become one of the defining moments in British horror.

After studying Graphic Design at Coventry College of Art and gaining a Postgraduate Certificate in Radio, Film and Television at Bristol University, Volk entered into industry as an advertising copywriter where, within the employ of Ogilvy, Benson and Mather, he would go on to win a number of awards. His "proper" entry into the genre came when his screenplay, *Gothic* (1986), was optioned and put into production with Ken Russell as its director. It is perhaps serendipitous that *Gothic* should initiate his career as the film fictionalizes Mary Shelley's visit to Lord Byron at the Villa Diodati which inspires her to write *Frankenstein* (1818). According to Volk much of his original screenplay remained intact and was committed to film, with Russell inventing sequences such as the reconstruction of Fuseli's painting *The Nightmare* (1781) "on the (cloven) hoof" (Rose, 2012) and, predictably, amplifying the dream sequences. The released film is, unsurprisingly, a riot of drug-taking, nudity, color and imagery, all infused with a delirious terror, culminating in a ninety-minute hallucination that captures the heady hysteria of the alleged events at Lake Geneva. Subsequent to its release, Volk would go on to write further produced screenplays including *The Kiss* (Pen Densham, 1988), *The Guardian* (William Friedkin, 1990) and, more recently, *The Awakening* (Nick Murphy, 2011).

Looking across the increasing body of Volk's film and television work, a series of preoccupations emerge to define the supernatural and conceptual borders of his narratives: the opposition between Believer and Skeptic; the presence of the Ghost; the Strong Female; the guilt-ridden Male. All evidence themselves across Volk's fiction, regardless of the format they take. These preoccupations function to not only stimulate the narrative's intended horrors but to also question it, to propose ways of thinking and reflecting upon the spectral and what they may mean to the audience.

Dominating this sense of an authorial stamp is the triangular relationship between the ghost, the believer and the skeptic. *Ghostwatch* has its truly terrifying ghost in the form of Mr. Pipes (an horrific manifestation who is only briefly seen as a fragment, a moment, a doubt in the increasingly fraught viewer's mind) whose actual presence is made all the more tangible (and perhaps all the more palpable) by psychiatrist Dr. Lin Pascoe (Gillian Bevan) yet thrown into doubt by skeptical British broadcaster Michael Parkinson (playing himself). Then there is Dr. Robert Bridge (Andrew Lincoln) trying to understand the apparent abilities of medium Alison Mundy (Lesley Sharp) who is, in her own way, tormented by the ghosts she sees in the acclaimed television serial *Afterlife* (ITV, 2005–2006) and séance debunker Florence Cathcart (Rebecca Hall) in *The Awakening* who not only encounters those that believe but also a potentially real ghost. Through this triangular relationship and the narrative trajectory Volk takes his characters upon, the ghost is made real and, in turn, transforms the skeptic into believer. While this may seem superficial, more complex human drama is played out: for Robert Bridge this transition becomes a painful journey of accepting his son's death and the subsequent coming to terms with the immense guilt he feels over this loss; for Cathcart the acceptance of the supernatural allows her to not only accept the grief for her lost fiancé but also allows her to confront the horror of her repressed childhood. For Michael Parkinson, the transition from skeptic to believer is far more horrific and without catharsis: possessed by the spirit of Pipes, *Ghostwatch* closes with Parkinson stumbling around the television studio, insanely muttering nursery rhymes across the transmission.

While Volk's film and television work has its own set of internal consistencies, the actual products of film and television become the source of some of Volk's fiction. This is not to suggest that all of this work is imbibed with this quality but more to suggest that there are strong and sustainable links between the three platforms, with the personalities and characters of film and television acting as starting points for a number of Volk's horror stories: for example, his novella's *Whitstable* (2013) and *Leytonstone* (2015) are fictionalized accounts of an elder Peter Cushing and a young Alfred Hitchcock respectively, while the collection of short stories *Monsters in the Heart* (2013), opens with Ann Darrow mourning the loss of King Kong. Another, *Who Dies Best*, reflects upon the effect of violence in film, while during *In the Colosseum* a picture editor is drawn into a party of TV industry elites. Further to this, Volk's fiction seeks to rework and extended the narratives of other's creations, with Volk writing a number of further adventures of Sherlock Holmes as well as adventures for Edgar Allan Poe's C. Auguste Dupin and Mike Mignola's Hellboy.

Alongside these works are Volk's first collection of short stories, *Dark Corners* (2006) and his first Novella, *Vardøger* (2009) as well as other numerous short stories that have appeared across a range of magazines and edited collections. Regardless of narrative, the majority of these fictions reflect a certain duality in that they seek to provide their physical and psychological horror in often blunt and certain terms yet, in contrast, contain a sense of poignancy and loss to negate such content. Again, Volk seeks to ask the reader to quietly reflect upon the protagonist's emotional response as much as the predicaments the narrative places them within. Volk's fiction then is both playful and terrifying, with narratives which convincingly relay dialogue and atmosphere, thought and emotion, culminating in a rich and melancholy body of fiction that both frightens and moves.

Despite this increasingly complex body of work, Volk's ongoing contribution to British horror seems to remain unexplainably enclaved. As both horror film and fiction has become overly saturated with a seemingly monotonous repetition of sanitized horror monsters and specters that seek to haunt an increasingly younger audience, the genre has potentially become diluted in form, content and meaning. Within Volk's approach and work such parameters are there to be invested in, explored, elaborated, and progressively pushed. This constant advance beyond the genre's boundaries is not to take the audience into excess but, instead, to position them into Volk's favored dynamic of believer and skeptic so they too may have their position on the supernatural questioned and, perhaps, exchanged. Volk's works then are narratives of change, capable of provoking a shift, a subtle realignment that may help us understand what surrounds us above, below and beyond.

SUGGESTED FURTHER READING

Heller-Nicholas, Alexandra, *Found Footage Horror Films: Fear and the Appearance of Reality*. Jefferson, N.C.: McFarland, 2014, pp.76-82.
Rose, James. "Stephen Volk Interview." *The Irish Journal of Gothic and Horror Studies* (June 2012). Web. 27 June 2015.
Volk, Stephen. *Dark Corners*. Whitby: Gray Friar, 2006.
Volk, Stephen. *Monsters from the Heart*. Whitby: Gray Friar, 2013.
Volk, Stephen. *Vardoger*. Whitby: Gray Friar, 2009.

Tom Waits
(1949–)

JENNY MCDONNELL

There are plenty of lost souls to be found throughout Tom Waits' work. He sings of the loners and drifters who populate the seedy, noirish worlds of the likes of "9th & Hennepin" (from 1985's *Rain Dogs*); those who wander in the apocalyptic landscapes typified by "The Earth Died Screaming" (from 1992's *Bone Machine*); and the carnies and freaks of "Circus" (from 2004's *Real Gone*), among many others. In light of this, it is little wonder that Waits has so often been affiliated with such avant-garde and counter-cultural figures as Charles Bukowski, William Burroughs (his collaborator on the play *The Black Rider*, first produced in 1990), and Jim Jarmusch (who directed him in *Down by Law* [1983] and *Coffee and Cigarettes: Somewhere in California*, the 1993 short film later included in Jarmusch's anthology film *Coffee and Cigarettes* [2003]). Like them, Waits documents those who exist at the margins of American culture, and notes in a 2009 interview with the *Guardian* newspaper that "I always liked the idea that America is a big facade. We are all insects crawling across on the shiny hood of a Cadillac. We're all looking at the wrapping. But we won't tear the wrapping to see what lies beneath." Yet his frequent exploration of "what lies beneath" also points to another tradition that runs throughout his work, one that is distinctly gothic. In depicting these "lost souls," Waits regularly draws on an American folk-history that is uncanny and macabre, populated by characters and motifs that often seem reminiscent of the Southern Gothic grotesquery of writers such as Flannery O'Connor and Carson McCullers.

Waits himself has gone through numerous iterations over sixteen studio albums (as well as additional live releases, soundtracks, and anthologies). The bluesy balladeer of his debut album (1973's *Closing Time*) has long since given way to the experimental auteur that emerged on *Swordfishtrombones* (1983), characterized by the increased experimentation with varied instrumentation and musical form that continues to endure up to his most recent studio release, *Bad as Me* (2011). This has gone hand-in-hand with the evolution of the Waitsian persona and live show, in which he spins tall tales and surrealist between-song patter, performing the role of a cabaret impresario all the while. It's no surprise, then, that Waits has not limited himself to the world of music, as is evident in his work for both theatre and film. His theatrical work on *The Black Rider*, *Woyzeck*, and *Alice* has spawned albums that rate among his most eerie (in particular the latter, which is based on Lewis Carroll's relationship with the girl who inspired the *Alice in Wonderland* series). He has also made memorable onscreen contributions to more than one gothic text. These include his 1992 turn as Renfield for Francis Ford Coppola in *Bram Stoker's Dracula*, and his distinctively Waitsian devil in Terry Gilliam's ill-fated *The Imaginarium of Doctor Parnassus* in 2009.

In each of these performances, there are clear traces of the Waits that is familiar from his musical output, characterized by his distinctive, gravelly voice, and arrangements that are at times haunting and melodic ("Dead and Lovely" from *Real Gone*), and at other times discordant and unsettling ("Shake it" from the same album). Whether spoken or sung, though, Waits' songs often find beauty in surrealist imagery. On "Kentucky Avenue," for example, from 1978's *Blue Valentine*, he recalls a childhood friend, confined by polio to a wheelchair, and imagines him taking flight in a contraption that fuses the wings of a magpie with the spokes of the boy's wheelchair.

Physical disability emerges as a recurring theme across several albums, in particular in a series of songs in which Waits draws on the iconography of the freak show. The phenomenon itself was famously discussed by Leslie Fiedler in *Freaks: Myths and Images of the Secret Self* (1978), dramatized in Tod Browning's notorious *Freaks* (1932), and recently pastiched in the fourth season of *American Horror Story* (2014–15). Waits' 2002 album *Alice* in particular utilizes this tradition, featuring songs inspired by such real-life performers as Johnny Eck, the "Half Boy" who played a key role in Browning's *Freaks*. On the incredibly catchy "Table Top Joe," Waits traces his protagonist's journey from rejection by the wider community to eventual acceptance and financial success within the world of the circus. More maudlin by far, on the same album, he laments the tale of the somewhat apocryphal "freak," Edward Mordake (or Mordrake), afflicted with a second face on the back of his head.

Elsewhere, on *Mule Variations* (1999), Waits sings of the "Eyeball Kid," who forges a similar career trajectory to "Table Top Joe" despite his entire lack of a body, coupled with an inability to speak or blink. Waits' use of freakshow and circus imagery in this way clearly sees him draw on American gothic and grotesque traditions, and at times, there is an undercurrent of violence detected in these narratives. For example, the previously mentioned "Circus" is a spoken-word piece that provides an account of a travelling show that features an array of circus and freak show acts. The song builds to an account of Funeral Wells' knife-throwing routine, and the time he accidentally injured the unfortunate Poodle Murphy, before the speaker concludes by articulating their two-fold desire: first, to fashion a bullet out of a ring, which seems ominously linked to the final (repeated) wish for whiskey and a firearm.

There's an even more overtly violent atmosphere evident in the likes of "Murder in the Red Barn" (included on *Bone Machine*) and "Don't Go Into That Barn" (from *Real Gone*), both of which combine Waits' trademark vocalization with appropriately discordant musical arrangements. But it is on the deeply creepy "What's He Building?" that these aspects combine to most memorable effect. A spoken-word piece that makes use of minimal instrumentalization, the song features a speaker who obsessively watches and records his neighbor's activities, detecting hints of unsavoriness in his magazine subscriptions, rumors about his personal and family life, and his insistence on keeping himself to himself. Certainly, his actions seem to be cause for concern, as he seems to stockpile both poison and formaldehyde. However, by the end of the song it's clear that the speaker's paranoid surveillance of his neighbor is equally (if not more) suspicious, and positions him as a figure that acts just as shiftily as the man on whom he spies so incessantly.

Certainly, it's on songs such as "What's He Building?" that Waits' gothic inclinations come most to the fore, yet his work as a whole frequently returns to such concerns. He regularly presents a world that seems off kilter, but in ways that do not necessarily inspire a sense of despair. It's worth noting that one key exception to this can be found in several recent songs about contemporary U.S. foreign policy, such as "Hell Broke Luce," in which the hellishness of war proves to be entirely horrifying. When drawing on past traditions of American folk history typified by the freak show, though, Waits tends to be far more equivocal. Speaking about his appreciation of Kurt Weill in an NPR interview first broadcast in 2002, he observed that "I like beautiful melodies telling me terrible things." Waits' own work is arguably characterized by a similar fusion of beauty and terror, but ultimately, the distinction between the two is not necessarily clear-cut in his depiction of "an American Gothic of three-time losers, lost souls, and carnival folk," as Jay S. Jacobs describes his work in *Wild Years: The Music and Myth of Tom Waits*.

SUGGESTED FURTHER READING

Fiedler, Leslie. *Freaks: Myths and Images of the Secret Self*. New York: Simon and Schuster, 1978.
Jacobs, Jay S. *Wild Years: The Music and Myth of Tom Waits*. Toronto: ECW Press, 2006
Mahar, Paul, ed. *Tom Waits on Tom Waits: Interviews and Encounters*. London: Aurum, 2011.
Montandon, Mac, ed. *Innocent When You Dream: Tom Waits—The Collected Interviews*. London: Orion, 2007.

Fredric Wertham
(1895–1981)

Sarah Cleary

Though censorship and horror fandom have had a long and tumultuous history ever since Horace Walpole penned what is considered the first Gothic text, *The Castle of Otranto* in 1764, there have been certain individuals along the way that have engendered a particular form of contempt from the genre's loyal fan base. Fredric Wertham is one such individual. As the comic book historian, Catherine Yronwode, quoted by Jeet Heer in the article, "Caped Crusader: Fredric Wertham and the Campaign against Comic Books," states "We hate [Wertham], despise him." A child psychiatrist, expert witness in murder trials, founder of the subsidized Harlem based Lafargue clinic and an anti-segregation activist, Wertham is often credited with almost single-handily bringing down horror comics in fifties America. While such a claim is not entirely true, the fact that Wertham was considered the "face" of anti-comic propaganda in the fifties was enough to secure his reputation as the "boogeyman" of EC Comics. His seminal text *Seduction of the Innocent* (1954) denounced the comic book industry so vehemently in regards to its allegedly negative effects upon children, it was deemed responsible for not only instigating federal investigations into the alleged harm but ultimately for bringing about the "Seal of Approval," dictated by the Comics Code Authority which made the production of horror comics close to impossible.

Originally from Germany, Wertham moved to America in 1922 after he was asked to join the Phipps Psychiatric Clinic in Maryland. In 1932 he became affiliated with the New York Court of General Sessions, and would examine convicted felons to determine whether they were "of sane mind" when they committed their crimes. In 1946, appalled by the inadequate facilities provided to minority groups, Wertham opened the Lafargue Clinic in the basement of St. Philip's Church in Harlem. Financed mostly by voluntary contributions, it was a low-cost psychiatric clinic specializing in young and marginalized ethnic groups. Aside from his genuine philanthropic desire to provide care to disadvantaged children and young adults, Wertham offered his services as a liberal and progressive voice of reason for the defense in many court cases. Just three years into his tenure in Maryland, having already established himself as a forthright advocate for the criminally insane, he found himself testifying for the defense in the trial of notorious child-killer and cannibal Albert Fish. Having conducted multiple interviews with Fish, Wertham concluded that he was indeed criminally insane. However, this claim was refuted in court and Fish was put to death on 16 January 1936.

While Wertham never acted alone in terms of his desire to regulate and restrict the comic book industry, he was a much more complex character than the bowdlerizing right-wing fanatic he is often portrayed as. In fact his first public denunciation of comic books came when he took the stand May in 1948 in defense of a nudist magazine called *Sunshine and Health* during the Post Office obscenity trial. Wertham argued that the magazine was "neither pornographic nor salacious" and that there was material far worse on sale to children in the United States every day. In a particularly dramatic move, Wertham pulled from his pocket issues of the magazine *Crime Does Not Pay* and slammed them down on the stand, declaring that these publications were the true agents of pornography and therefore "constituted genuine obscenity." While absolving one form of entertainment at the expense of another may not in retrospect be considered the most judicious of acts, especially when matters of taste were concerned, it did serve to highlight Wertham's complex attitude towards censorship.

Perhaps as a preamble to his seminal 1954 *Seduction of the Innocent*, in 1949 Wertham published *The Show of Violence* which was, as James Reibman, recalls in his introduction to *Seduction of the Innocent,* "an indictment against a culture that fails to act as 'its brother's keeper.'" Explaining how an individual deserted and let down by society could conceive of murderous intentions, Wertham made the erroneous deduction that *any* child may become emotionally disarmed as a result of reading comics. Setting the tone for his public stand against comics later that year, Wertham wrote in his most famous book that "Brutality in fantasy creates brutality in fact. Children's games have become more brutal in recent years and there is no doubt that one factor involved in this is the brutalizing effect of children's comics."

Though he was without doubt a genuinely compassionate medical professional who cared deeply about protecting children from violence and abuse, Wertham was also something of show man. And is so often the case with pride that was perhaps was his ultimate failing. Over twenty years earlier, his most famous mentor, Sigmund Freud, had categorically warned the young doctor that one should never write on psychiatry for the popular press and added that in America no one really cared for the often nuanced practice of psychoanalysis. Failing to adhere to his mentors warning's Wertham did the exact opposite and published *Seduction of the Innocent* in 1954. While *Seduction* was in essence a diatribe concerning the dangers posed by young people reading comic books, it was also very much a product of its times. Encapsulating the zeitgeist of fifties paranoia, Wertham sought to prove beyond reasonable doubt that somehow comic books were responsible for the moral decline of a nation's youth. While much of the research was informed by his observations at the Lafargue Clinic, his overly sensational accounts of how comics were responsible for juvenile delinquency secured his position as leading light among anti-comic crusaders. One of the most infamous of his conclusions was derived from an unsubstantiated report were "a young child hangs himself and beneath the dead child is found an open comic book luridly describing and depicting a hanging." When asked to appear as a key witness expert witness before the Senate Subcommittee on Juvenile Delinquency (led by anti-crime crusader Estes Kefauver) Wertham had finally saw his opportunity to publically denounce comic books before the nation's press. Defying his mentor once again, he also proceeded to actively court public attention. In this case at least, Freud was right. The hearings were not concerned with the complexities of analytical reasoning and a nuanced consideration of the actual facts. They wanted to draw blood, and the EC horror comics were their main target

Hot off the back of the 1951 Senate special committee to investigate crime in 1951, Kefauver used a similar framework to investigate the causes of juvenile delinquency when he devoted nearly three days of hearings to accounts proffered by high profile individuals concerning the perils of horror comics. Wertham would of course appear as the star witness. Despite his clinical background, Wertham's testimony represented a particularly sensationalized account of the menace comic books supposedly posed to society. In an era where intellectualism was often viewed with outright suspicion, Wertham had, as Amy Nyberg argues "de-emphasized the intellectual roots of his argument" at the expense of his overall scientific integrity. All comics as far as Wertham was concerned were a "betrayal of childhood."

However, regardless of how forthright Wertham was about informing the public about the apparent dangers of comic books, it should be noted that he never asked for outright censorship. Testifying before the Senate Subcommittee on 21 April 1954, he declared, "I detest censorship. I believe that what is necessary for children is supervision." Moreover, contrary to the committees' insistence upon singling out horror comics as a primary cause for alarm, Wertham was not as concerned with honing in on any particular subgenre of comic book. Be it crime, war or super hero titles, he felt it necessary to remove "these books off the newsstand and candy stores." Although

Wertham was indeed a key figure in the bid to regulate horror comics, he was also not the main force behind this cause. Having unsurprisingly declined the role of director of the Comics Magazine Association of America (CMAA), Wertham's high profile position within the hearings was arguably never anything more than that of a "Tin God" who was put on the stand as part of a wider attempt to eradicate "distasteful" elements from the mass media.

While his work would come under intense scrutiny almost thirty years after his death, as an academic investigation conducted by researcher Carol L. Tilley (2012) into Wertham's Lafargue Clinic files pointed to blatant modifications and alterations of the data cited in *Seduction*, his complex legacy endures. In the service of his career-long effort to further the rights of children, Wertham had allowed himself to become caught up in an ill-founded crusade which sought to police and regulate the tastes of youngsters. While manipulating his data in order to make his agenda more cogent was in essence a malpractice which has it could be argued plagued the so called "media effects" debate for generations, his ultimate failing was that Wertham, a medical practitioner specializing in mental ill-health had allowed a narrow and myopic assessment of juvenile culture in the 1950s dictate his research. Ironically, the root cause of Wertham's downfall was probably his vanity: he had arguably become seduced by his role as a real-life superhero championing children's causes in pursuit of his arch nemesis the comic book, to the later detriment of his academic credibility and personal reputation.

SUGGESTED FURTHER READING

Benton, Mike. *The Illustrated History: Horror Comics*. Dallas: Taylor, 1991.
Hajdu, David. *The Ten Cent Plague: The Great Comic-Book Scare and How It Changed America*. New York: Picador, 2008.
Nyberg, Amy. *Seal of Approval: The History of the Comics Code*. Jackson: University Press of Mississippi, 1998.
Rhoades, Shirrel. *A Complete History of American Comic Books*. New York: Peter Lang International Academic, 2008.
Trombetta, Jim. *The Horror! The Horror! Comic Books the Government Didn't Want You to Read!* New York: Abrams Comic Arts, 2010.

About the Contributors

Colette **Balmain** is a film critic, writer and a lecturer in media and cultural studies at Kingston University, London. She is an editor for *Gothic Studies* and is the author of the first volume of *Directory of World Cinema: South Korea* and a forthcoming book on East Asian Gothic cinema. She is writing a book on Korean horror cinema as well as updating her book *Introduction to Japanese Horror Film*.

Maria **Beville** is a lecturer in the Department of English Language and Literature at Mary Immaculate College, Limerick. Her publications include *Gothic-postmodernism: Voicing the Terrors of Postmodernity,* shortlisted for the ESSE 2010 Book award; *The Unnameable Monster in Literature*; and *Living Gothic: Histories, Practices and Legacies* (co-editor, with Lorna Piatti Farnell).

Clive **Bloom** is an emeritus professor of English and American studies at Middlesex University. His numerous publications on popular culture, cultural history and literary criticism include *Gothic Histories: The Taste for Terror, 1764 to the Present*; *Restless Revolutionaries: A History of Britain's Fight for a Republic*; and *Victoria's Madmen: Revolution and Alienation*.

Ailise **Bulfin** is an Irish Research Council postdoctoral fellow in the School of English at Trinity College Dublin. Her research is in the cultural history of the nineteenth and early twentieth centuries. She is working on the monograph *Gothic Invasions: Imperialism and Fin-de-Siècle Popular Fiction, 1890–1914*. She has published articles on fin-de-siècle popular culture, including yellow peril fiction, gothic tales of Egypt, Sherlock Holmes, and the fiction of natural catastrophe.

Clare **Clarke** is an assistant professor at the School of English, Trinity College Dublin. She has published articles on Victorian crime fiction in *Victorian Periodicals Review*, *Victorian Literature and Culture*, and *CLUES: A Journal of Detection*. Her book *Late-Victorian Crime Fiction in the Shadows of Sherlock* won the HRF Keating Award for best non-fiction crime book 2013–15.

Sarah **Cleary** earned a Ph.D. at Trinity College Dublin, researching how the horror genre has been restricted in response to its alleged influence on children. She has published on a variety of horror and pop culture subjects, has hosted screenings of *The Rocky Horror Picture Show* in Dublin for ten years and is the driving force behind Horror Expo Ireland.

About the Contributors

Mark **Cofell**'s fascination with gorilla suit actors and films led to the creation of Hollywood Gorilla Men, a now mostly dormant blog. The gargantuan labor of love is the recipient of the Bob Burns Kogar Award.

Kevin **Corstorphine** is a lecturer in English at the University of Hull. His research interests are in the Gothic, the reception of science in literature, American literature, ecology and theories of spatiality. He has published pieces on Ambrose Bierce, H.P. Lovecraft, Robert Bloch and Stephen King. He is writing a book on haunted houses in fiction and culture.

Peter **Dendle** is a professor of English at Pennsylvania State University, Mont Alto. His books include *Satan Unbound: The Devil in Old English Narrative Literature*, *Demon Possession in Anglo-Saxon England*, *The Zombie Movie Encyclopedia*, *The Zombie Movie Encyclopedia, vol. 2*, and *The Ashgate Research Companion to Monsters and the Monstrous*, co-edited with Asa Simon Mittman.

James **Doig** works at the National Archives of Australia. He has published a number of anthologies and single author collections of supernatural stories by colonial Australian authors. He has also published articles about obscure writers of horror and supernatural stories such as "Keith Fleming," R.R. Ryan and Reginald Hodder.

Dara **Downey** is a lecturer in American literature in the School of English, Drama and Film, University College Dublin. Her research interests span eighteenth- and nineteenth-century American fiction, children's literature, women's writing and gender studies, literary theory, geography, and anthropology. She is the co-editor of *The Irish Journal of Gothic and Horror Studies*.

John **Exshaw** is a freelance writer, film critic and historian whose research interests include Westerns, horror, and Italian cinema. He has written for various film magazines and is a regular contributor to *Cinema Retro*, as well as a frequent writer for the obituaries page of *The Independent*. His interviews with Peter Cushing and Christopher Lee were collected in the book, *Dracula: Celebrating 100 Years*.

Tracy **Fahey** is head of the Department of Fine Art and head of the Centre of Postgraduate Studies in Limerick School of Art and Design. Her primary research area is Gothic, with emphasis on the visual arts. She has published on medical Gothic, contemporary art, transgressive art and pedagogy and is the founder of the art collaborative Gothicise.

Katherine **Farrimond** is a lecturer in media and cultural studies at the University of Sussex. Her research focuses on the intersections of the body, sexuality and gender in contemporary popular film and television. She has published widely on representations of girlhood, femininity and sexuality, and has a forthcoming monograph, *The Contemporary Femme Fatale*.

Frank **Furedi** is an emeritus professor of sociology at the University of Kent. His work has focused on the relationship between the uncertainty of authority and fear in contemporary society. Since the publication of his *Authority: A Sociological History,* he has embarked on a study of the history of reading and the moralization of cultural consumption.

Wendy **Haslem** teaches and researches the intersections of film history and new media in the screen studies program at the University of Melbourne. She is the author of *A Charade of Innocence and Vice: Hollywood Gothic Films of the 1940s*, the co-author of *Experimenta: Playground* and a co-editor of the anthology *Super/Heroes: From Hercules to Superman*.

Madelon **Hoedt** is a part-time lecturer on the Faculty for Creative Industries of the University of South Wales. Her Ph.D. focuses on genre, performance, stagecraft and audience affect. She is also concerned with issues of narrative in live performance, specifically in relation to horror and the Gothic.

William **Hughes** is a professor of Gothic studies at Bath Spa University, England. Recent publications include *The Victorian Gothic: An Edinburgh Companion* (co-edited with Andrew Smith), *The Encyclopedia of the Gothic* (co-edited with Andrew Smith and David Punter) and *The Historical Dictionary of Gothic Literature*.

Peter **Hutchings** is a professor of film studies at Northumbria University. He is the author of *Hammer and Beyond: The British Horror Film*; *Terence Fisher*; *The British Film Guide to Dracula*; and *The Historical Dictionary of Horror Cinema* (republished as *The A-Z of Horror Cinema*). He has also published on horror cinema, British film and television, science fiction cinema and television, and the thriller.

Mark **Jancovich** is an associate dean for research at the Faculty of Arts and Humanities at the University of East Anglia, where he is also a professor of film studies for the School of Art, Media, and American Studies. His books include *Horror: The Film Reader* and *Rational Fears: American Horror in the 1950s*.

Darryl **Jones** is dean of arts, humanities and social sciences at Trinity College Dublin. His major research and teaching interest lies in popular literature, particularly horror fiction and film, and Victorian and Edwardian adventure fiction. He is the author of *Horror: A Thematic History in Fiction and Film* and editor of *M.R. James: Collected Ghost Stories* and *Horror Stories: Classic Tales from Hoffmann to Hodgson*.

Douglas **Keesey** is a professor of film and literature at California Polytechnic State University. He has published books on Catherine Breillat, Brian De Palma, Don DeLillo, Peter Greenaway, and Paul Verhoeven as well as on erotic cinema and film noir. Some of his articles on horror fiction and film can be found at http://works.bepress.com/dkeesey/.

Jarlath **Killeen** is an associate professor in the School of English, Trinity College Dublin. He is the author of *The Faiths of Oscar Wilde*; *Gothic Ireland: Horror and the Irish Anglican Imagination in the Long Eighteenth Century*; *History of the Gothic: Gothic Literature 1825–1914*; and *The Emergence of Irish Gothic Fiction: History, Origins, Theories*. He is also editor of *Bram Stoker: Centenary Essays*.

Caitriona **Kirby** is a Ph.D. candidate in the School of English at Trinity College Dublin. Her thesis explores the influence of the visual arts on late Victorian and modernist fiction, and she teaches Victorian and Modernist courses. She is a co-founder and organizer of Modest Proposals, a platform for university research to engage with public debate through workshops, seminars and blogs.

Ewan **Kirkland** is a lecturer in media and screen at the University of Brighton's College of Arts and Humanities. His interests include representations of race, gender and sexuality in popular culture. His work includes the textual analysis of videogames. His articles and book chapters range in subject from gender and race to horror video games.

Kristine **Larsen** is a professor of physics and earth sciences at Central Connecticut State University, New Britain. Her research and teaching focus on issues of science and society. Her publications include *Stephen Hawking: A Biography*; *Cosmology 101*; *The Mythological Dimensions of Doctor Who* (co-edited with Anthony Burdge and Jessica Burke); and *The Mythological Dimensions of Neil Gaiman* (co-edited with Burdge and Burke).

Murray **Leeder** has a Ph.D. from Carleton University and teaches in the Film Studies program at the University of Calgary. He is the author of *Halloween* and editor of *Cinematic Ghosts: Haunting and Spectrality from Silent Cinema to the Digital Era*. Forthcoming projects include *Horror Film: A Critical Introduction* and *The Modern Supernatural and the Beginnings of Cinema*.

Peter N. **Lindfield** is an historian of Georgian architecture and design, particularly on the Gothic Revival and its interactions with other contemporary fashionable tastes. He is also interested in antiquarianism more broadly, and the use of heraldry in the visual arts. He is a postdoctoral research fellow at the University of Stirling, working on *Writing Britain's Ruins 1700–1850: The Architectural Imagination*.

Roger **Luckhurst** is a professor in modern and contemporary literature, an assistant dean of research for the School of Arts and director of research for the Department of English at Birkbeck, University of London. His publications include *Science Fiction*; *The Trauma Question*; *The Mummy's Curse: The True Story of a Dark Fantasy*; *The Shining*; and *Alien*.

Elizabeth **McCarthy** is a lecturer in English at Dun Laoghaire Institute of Art Design and Technology Dublin. She is co-author of *Fear: Essays on the Meaning and Experience of Fear* (with Kate Hebblethwaite) and *It Came From the 1950s! Popular Culture, Popular Anxieties* (with Bernice M. Murphy and Darryl Jones). She is the co-founder and was co-editor of the online *Irish Journal of Gothic and Horror Studies*.

Jenny **McDonnell** is a lecturer in English at Dun Laoghaire Institute of Art Design and Technology Dublin. She is author of *Katherine Mansfield and the Modernist Marketplace: At the Mercy of the Public* and articles on Mansfield and Robert Louis Stevenson. She is the co-editor of the *Irish Journal of Gothic and Horror Studies* and editor of the *Katherine Mansfield Society Newsletter*.

Neil **McRobert** has written about the author-protagonist in horror fiction, zombies and the War on Terror and the rise of found-footage cinema, and is the co-editor of *Transgression and Its Limits*. He completed a doctorate in Gothic literature at the University of Stirling.

Rachel **Mizsei-Ward** graduated with her Ph.D. from the University of East Anglia in 2013. Her research looks at popular media, including reception, transmedia and licensing between film, television and games. Rachel has published an edited collection on transnational superheroes called *Superheroes on World Screens* (2015) which has been nominated for a 2016 Eisner Award.

About the Contributors

Wendy **Mooney** lives in Dublin and is a lecturer and tutor in Irish literature and poetry and has also taught Victorian studies. She has had poems published in *Poetry Ireland Review*, *Crannóg Magazine*, *New Irish Writing* and other journals. Her Ph.D. thesis focused on the Irish Victorian poet William Allingham.

Christina **Morin** is a lecturer in English University of Limerick, Ireland. Her primary area of interest lies in the literary Gothic in Romantic Ireland, Britain, and Europe, and she has several articles published and forthcoming on the subject. She is the author of *Charles Robert Maturin and the Haunting of Irish Romantic Fiction* and the co-editor of *Irish Gothics: Genres, Forms, Modes and Traditions* (with Niall Gillespie).

Bernice M. **Murphy** is a lecturer in popular literature at the School of English, Trinity College Dublin. She is the author of *The Suburban Gothic in American Popular Culture*, *The Rural Gothic*, *The Highway Horror Film* and *Key Concepts in Contemporary Popular Fiction*. She edited *Shirley Jackson: Essays on the Literary Legacy* and co-edited *It Came from the 1950s!* She is co-founder and editor of the online *Irish Journal of Gothic and Horror Studies*.

Eóin **Murphy** was new media reviews editor for the *Irish Journal of Gothic and Horror Studies*. He also writes short fiction, mainly horror and fantasy. His most recent publication was the short story "Waking the Mammy" in *The Incubator Journal* (New Short Fiction from Ireland, issue 1).

Sorcha **Ní Fhlainn** is a lecturer in film studies and contemporary American literature at Manchester Metropolitan University. She has published on gothic and horror studies and on the representation of monstrosity and subjectivity. She is the author and editor of numerous publications on popular Hollywood cinema, contemporary American politics onscreen and vampire studies.

Brendan **O'Connell** lectures on medieval literature at the School of English, Trinity College Dublin. His research focuses on the poetry of the fourteenth and fifteenth centuries, in particular the works of Chaucer and the Gawain-poet. He co-edited *Transmission and Generation in Medieval and Renaissance Literature: Essays in Honour of John Scattergood* (with Karen Hodder).

Edward **O'Hare** is completing a Ph.D. on the work of Edgar Allan Poe at Trinity College Dublin and has a master's of philosophy in popular literature. He reviews books and films for the *Irish Journal of Gothic and Horror Studies*.

Maria **Parsons** is a senior lecturer in English at Dun Laoghaire Institute of Art Design and Technology Dublin. Her teaching and research include Gothic and horror literature and film, gender and body theory, and nineteenth century literature. She has published, presented and exhibited work relating to Deleuze, queering the Gothic, and menstrual pathologies.

Anna **Powell** retired as a reader in film and English studies to become a research fellow at Manchester Metropolitan University. Her interests include Gothic and steampunk, film and philosophy and affect in film and literature, experimental film and video. She is the director of *A/V* web journal and a member of the editorial board of *Deleuze Studies*. Her books include *Deleuze and the Horror Film*; *Deleuze, Altered States and Film*; and *Teaching the Gothic* (with Andrew Smith).

About the Contributors

David **Punter** is a professor of English at the University of Bristol and author of many works on Gothic and romantic literature, as well as modern and contemporary writing, critical theory and psychoanalysis. Recent books include *Rapture: Literature, Addiction, Secrecy*; *A New Companion to the Gothic*; and *The Literature of Pity*. He is also a widely published poet.

Xavier Aldana **Reyes** is a senior lecturer in English literature and film at Manchester Metropolitan University. His books include *Body Gothic: Corporeal Transgression in Contemporary Literature and Horror Film; Digital Horror: Haunted Technologies, Network Panic and the Found Footage Phenomenon* (co-edited with Linnie Blake), *Horror Film and Affect: Towards a Corporeal Model of Viewership* and *Horror: A Literary History* (as editor).

Jim **Rockhill** is editor of volumes collecting Sheridan Le Fanu, Bob Leman, and E.T.A. Hoffmann, co-editor of Jane Rice's collected fiction, the essay collection *Reflections in a Glass Darkly*, and the anthology *Dreams of Shadow and Smoke*. He has contributed to books by Seabury Quinn and Brian Showers, *Supernatural Literature of the World, The Freedom of Fantastic Things, Warnings to the Curious*, and *Dead Reckonings*.

James **Rose** is concerned with interpretations of contemporary horror and science fiction cinema and television. He has written critical texts for a range of international film journals and magazines, including *Senses of Cinema, The Film Journal, Terrorizer* and *SCOPE*. His most recent book is *The Devil's Advocate: The Texas Chain Saw Massacre*.

Tania **Scott** completed a doctorate at the University of Glasgow in 2011. Her thesis considered the works of Irish fantasy author Lord Dunsany. She has written further on Dunsany, including a chapter in *Border Crossings: Narration, Nation and Imagination in Scots and Irish Literature and Culture*. She has reviewed contemporary science fiction and fantasy novels and stories in journals such as *Foundation*.

Catherine **Spooner** is a senior lecturer in the Department of English and Creative Writing at Lancaster University and is co-president of the International Gothic Association. Her research focuses on Gothic in literature, film and popular culture since the eighteenth century. Her publications include *Fashioning Gothic Bodies, Contemporary Gothic* and *The Routledge Companion to Gothic* (co-edited with Emma McEvoy) and numerous articles.

George **Toles** is a distinguished professor of literature and film at the University of Manitoba. He is the author of *A House Made of Light: Essays on the Art of Film* and a study of Paul Thomas Anderson. For twenty-five years, he was director Guy Maddin's screenwriting collaborator. He wrote the original story and co-authored the screenplay for *Edison and Leo*, Canada's first stop-motion animated feature film.

Jon **Towlson** is a freelance journalist and film critic and has written for *Starburst, Paracinema, Exquisite Terror, The Irish Journal of Gothic and Horror Studies, Shadowland Magazine, Bright Lights Film Journal* and *Digital Film-maker*. He is author of *Subversive Horror Cinema: Countercultural Messages of Films from Frankenstein to the Present*.

About the Contributors

Dale **Townshend** is a senior lecturer in Gothic and Romantic Studies at the University of Stirling, Scotland. He has published widely on literature of the late eighteenth and early nineteenth centuries, and is working, with Peter N. Lindfield, on *Writing Britain's Ruins 1700–1850: The Architectural Imagination.*

Bill **Warren** published his exhaustive two-volume survey of the golden age of science fiction film, *Keep Watching the Skies!* (McFarland) beginning in 1982 (volume 2 in 1986), a book that has assumed seminal status as a reference work for the genre (it was fully revised and repanded in 2010). He was a newspaper film critic, reported for a number of genre magazines, and was a regular contributor to *Leonard Maltin's Movie Guide.*

Tom **Weaver** is one of the "leading scholars in the horror field" (*New York Times*). The Sleepy Hollow, New York–based film researcher has written nearly 30 books on vintage horror and sci-fi movies (most from McFarland) and done dozens of DVD audio commentaries. He is an eight-time winner of the Rondo Hatton Classic Horror Award, and was inducted into the Rondo Awards' Monster Kid Hall of Fame in 2011.

Index

Abbott and Costello 11, 98
The Absentee (novel, 1812) 188
Adam Had Four Sons (film, 1942) 36
"The Adventure of the Six Napoleons" (short story, 1904) 13
Adventures in Arabia (travelogue, 1924) 194–195
After Hours (film, 1985) 153–154
Afterlife (TV show) 221
Aickman, Robert 139
alcoholism 35, 69, 120, 193, 213
Alice (music album, 2002) 225
Alice (stage play, 1992) 225
Alice in Wonderland (novel, 1865) 83, 153, 225
Aliens (film, 1986) 166
All Heads Turn When the Hunt Goes By (novel, 1977) 81
All in a Bustle (play, 1795) 124
Amazing Stories (comic) 31
American Horror Story (TV show) 225
Amii Toytal and the Croixroads 63
Andrews, Harry 218
Angkor (travelogue film, 1935) 97
Ankers, Evelyn 11–15
Ankrum, Morris 16–19
anti-Catholicism 108, 112–113
Antonioni, Michelangelo 131
The Ape Woman (film series) 13
Arch of Triumph (film, 1948) 36
architecture 7, 107–113
Ashton Smith, Clark 103
Asylum (novel, 1935) 193
Atwill, Lionel 119, 202
Austen, Jane 1, 116, 124, 186
Australia 7, 38, 41, 68–71, 179, 204–208
The Australian Journal (periodical) 204–208
Avant-Garde 58, 62, 63, 72–74, 224
The Awakening (film, 2011) 221
The Axeman Cometh (novel, 1989) 80

B-Movies 14, 16–19, 46–49, 115, 144
Baal (novel, 1978) 142–143

Baby Moll (novel, 1958) 80
Bacall, Lauren 24
Bad as Me (music album, 2011) 225
Ballard, J.G. 66
Banks, Iain 66
Bara, Theda 6, 20–25
Barker, Lex 14
Bat Masterson (TV show) 17
Bataille, Georges 2, 193
Batman Returns (film, 1992) 191
The Battle of Apache Pass (film, 1952) 46
Beardsley, Aubrey 60, 197
The Beatles 62, 66
Beaumont, Charles 30–33
Bedlam (film, 1946) 118
Benny, Jack 17
Benoit, Victor 20
Benson, E.F. 115
Bergman, Ingrid 7, 8, 34–37
Berlin: Symphony of a Metropolis (*Berlin: Die Sinfonie der Großstadt*) (film, 1927) 139
Bester, Alfred 81
Bestsellers 7, 39, 40, 54–57, 127, 142, 216
Beswick, Martine 28
Bethany's Sin (novel, 1980) 143
Bevan, Gillian 221
A Bid for Fortune; or, Dr. Nikola's Vendetta (novel, 1895) 38, 40
Big Tits Zombie (*Kyonyū doragon: Onsen zonbi vs sutorippa 5*) (film, 2010) 175
The Birds (film, 1963) 130, 131
The Black Rider (stage play, 1990)
Blackbeard, the Pirate (film, 1952) 118, 119–120
Blackwood, Algernon 69, 115
Blade (film, 1973) 131
Blake, Peter 62
Blast the Human Flower (music album, 1980) 63
Blind Beast (*Mōjū*, film, 1969) 176
Blow-Up (film, 1966) 131
The Blue Light (*Das blaue Licht*) (film, 1932) 139, 140

239

240   Index

Blue Sunshine (film, 1978) 130, 132–133, 134
Blue Valentine (music album, 1978) 225
Blue World (short story collection, 1990) 144
The Body Snatcher (film, 1945) 120
Bogart, Humphrey 18
Boklin, Arnold 3–4
Bone Machine (music album, 1992) 224
The Book of the Damned (collection of anomalies, 1919) 86–88
The Book of Wonder (short story collection, 1912) 198
"Boomerang" (short story, 1931) 51–52
Booth, Edwin 161
Boothby, Guy 7–8, 38–42
Borneo: The Stealer of Hearts (memoir, 1924) 50
Boston Advertiser (newspaper) 171
Botany Bay (film, 1952) 118–119
The Boys from Brazil (novel, 1976) 127, 128
Boy's Life (novel, 1991) 143, 144
Bradbury, Ray 32, 33, 143, 145
Bram Stoker Award 142, 144, 145
Bram Stoker's Dracula (film, 1992) 225
Brett, Jeremy 218
Briant, Shane 26
Bride of Frankenstein (film, 1935) 6, 12, 14
Brontë, Anne 179
Brontë, Emily 179
Browning, Tod 225
Buchan, John 7, 43–45
Buck Benny Rides Again (film, 1940) 17
Buffy the Vampire Slayer (TV show) 191
Bug (film, 1975) 132
Bukowski, Charles 224
Burne Jones, Philip 22
Burr, Raymond 17
Burroughs, William 224
Burton, Richard 218
Burton, Tim 201
Byron, Lord 108, 221

The Cabinet of Dr. Caligari (*Das Cabinet des Dr. Caligari*) (film, 1920) 139, 140, 155
Cabot, Susan 46–49
Cabot, Tim 47
Cage, Nicolas 151
Call of Cthulhu (video game, 1981) 165–166
"The Call of Cthulhu" (short story, 1928) 199
Campbell, Mrs Patrick 22
cannibalism 24, 51–52, 195, 228
Captive Wild Woman (film, 1943) 12
Carmen (film, 1915) 21
Carpenter, John 130
Carradine, John 13
Carrie (novel, 1974) 143
Carroll, Lewis 225
Carson, John 27
The Castle of Ollada (novel, 1795) 124, 125
The Castle of Otranto (novel, 1764) 111, 227

Cat People (film, 1942) 13
Catacombs (1981) 81
Catholicism 107–108
censorship 2, 84, 227–229
Chaney, Lon, Jr. 11–12
Chief Crazy Horse (film, 1955) 18
"The Child That Loved a Grave" (short story, 1861) 163
The Children of the Abbey (novel, 1796) 186, 188
Children of the Corn (film, 1984) 158
"Children of the Corn" (short story, 1977) 155
The Chimp (film, 1932) 98
A Christmas Carol (novella, 1843) 179
Circus of Dr. Lao (film, 1935) 32
Clapp, Henry 161
Clarke, Mae 12
Cleopatra (film, 1917) 21–22
Clermont (novel, 1798) 186, 188
Close, Glenn 24
Closing Time (music album, 1973) 224
Clover, Carol J. 14
The Cock-Eyed Miracle (film, 1946) 18
Cocteau, Jean 193
Coffee and Cigarettes (film, 2003) 224
Colonial Horror 41, 55–53, 67, 105–6
Colonialism, British 6, 41, 50–53, 187
Comics Industry 7, 89, 227–230
Conan Doyle, Arthur 13, 61, 114, 174, 175
Conjure Wife (novel, 1943) 32
Contrast (novel, 1828) 187, 188–9
Cook, Florence 170
Cook, Oscar 7, 50–53
Coppola, Francis Ford 225
Corelli, Marie 7, 8, 54–57
Corman, Roger 19, 32, 46, 205
Countess Dracula (film, 1971) 36
Craven, Wes 130
Creature from the Black Lagoon (film, 1954) 14
Creature with the Atom Brain (film, 1955) 14
Crime Does Not Pay (comic) 228
Cronenberg, David 130, 133, 81
"The Crooked Man" (short story, 1955) 33
The Cross of Lorraine (film, 1943) 18
Crowe, Catherine 163
Crowley, Aleister 5, 7, 58–62, 194
The Crucified City (novel, 1962) 216
Curtis, Jamie Lee 14
Cushing, Peter 27, 200, 202, 222

Dalle, Beatrice 24
Dandelion Wine (novel, 1957) 145
Dark Corners (short story collection, 2006) 222
Davis, Joan 11
Dawn of the Dead (film, 1978) 130, 148
Dax, Danielle 5, 7, 63–67
Day of the Animals (film, 1977) 132
Deamer, Dulcie 7, 72–75

Index 241

Death to Smoochy (film, 2002) 191
Death Trap (film, 1978) 128
Deliverance (film, 1972) 133, 156, 158
The Demon Lover (novel, 1927) 91
Demons and Night Visions (1926) 121
Demons of the Mind (film, 1972) 26
Denning, Richard 14
De Palma, Brian 80–81
Depp, Johnny 201, 202
Deren, Maya 6, 72–75
"A Descent Into the Maelstrom" (short story, 1841) 122
The Destiny Man (novel, 1977) 218
The Devil's Daughter (film, 1917) 21 and
The Devil's Saint (novel, 1924) 69
DeVito, Danny 191
"The Diamond Lens" (short story, 1858) 162
The Diary of a Drug Fiend (novel, 1922) 59
Dick Tracy Meets Gruesome (film, 1947) 119
Dick Tracy vs. Cueball (film, 1946) 119
Dickens, Charles 114, 140, 179
Dietrich, Marlene 24
Dinehart, Alan 105
The Discarded Son; or, Haunt of the Banditti (novel, 1807) 186, 188
Divine Horsemen: The Living Gods of Haiti (ethnographic study, 1953) 72
Dr. Jekyll and Mr. Hyde (film, 1941) 34–35, 105
Dr. Jekyll and Sister Hyde (film, 1972) 28
Doom (video game, 1993) 166
Doppelganger (novel, 1975) 218
Dourif, Brad 191
Down by Law (film, 1983) 224
Dracula (character) 11, 27, 104
Dracula (film, 1931) 104
Dracula (novel, 1897) 143
Dracula's Daughter (film, 1936) 13
Dragonfly (film, 1995) 80
Drake, Francis 12
Drat! The Cat (musical play, 1965) 128
Dyson, Jeremy 137

Eagle Rock (film, 1964) 19
Earth Versus the Flying Saucers (film, 1956) 18
Earwigs, man-eating 52
Eco Horror 43, 45, 85, 101, 130–134
Edgar Allan Who-? (short story collection, 1981) 218
Edgeworth, Maria 188
Edogawa Rampo: The Early Cases of Akechi Kogoro (short story collection, 2014) 176
The Edogawa Reader (fiction and non-fiction collection, 2008) 176
Egypt 23, 40–41
Ellison, Harlan 31, 32
Emma (novel, 1815) 186
Empire of the Ants (film, 1977) 132
Englund, Robert 202
Ennui (novel, 1809) 188

Ensor, James 155
The Erkenwald Poet 76–80
The Esoteric Philosophy of Love and Marriage (esoteric textbook, 1924) 91
The Evil Within (video game, 2014) 149
The Exorcist (film, 1973) 29, 81
The Exorcist (novel, 1971) 80, 128

The Face at the Window (1939) 200
Fairy Water (novel, 1873) 179
Fangoria (magazine, 82
Farris, John 7, 80–82
Fast Times at Ridgemont High (film, 1982) 190, 192
Fatal Attraction (film, 1987) 24
Fear of the Night (film, 1972) 28
The Feminine Mystique (feminist study, 1963) 128
Femme Fatale 23, 24, 140
Fiedler, Leslie 225
Fin-de-Siècle era 40–41, 54–57, 58–63, 121, 197, 206
"Final Girl" trope 14
Finney, Charles G. 32
Fish, Albert 228
Fisk, Nicholas 7, 83–85
Fitz-James O'Brien: A Literary Bohemian of the Eighteen-Fifties (biography, 1944) 161
Flame of Araby (film, 1951) 64
Flight to Mars (film, 1951) 16, 18
A Fool There Was (film, 1915) 20, 22
For Whom the Bell Tolls (film, 1943) 36
Ford, Ford Maddox 193
Forever Amber (film, 1947) 118
Forman, Miloš 191
Fort, Charles 7, 86–89
Fortune, Dion 7, 90–93
Fragments Towards the Chimera (art installation film, 1986) 65
Frankenstein (film, 1931) 12, 104
Frankenstein and the Monster From Hell (film, 1974) 26
Frankenstein; or, The Modern Prometheus (novel, 1818) 218, 221
Frankenstein's Monster 11
Frazer, James 45, 60
Freaks (film, 1932) 69
Frenyen, Mabel 20
Freud, Sigmund 121, 217, 228
Freund, Karl 140
Friedan, Betty 128
Fripp, Robert 63
Frogs (film, 1972) 132
From the Earth to the Moon (film, 1958) 19
The Frozen Ghost (film, 1945) 12
The Fruits of Curiosity Hunting (*Ryōki no hate*) (novel, 1930) 176
"Full Circle" (short story, 1920) 44
The Fury (film, 1976) 80–81
Fuseli, Henry 22

Gaslight (film, 1944) 34–35, 37
Gemora, Charles 5, 94–99
Genuine (film, 1920) 140
George Geith of Fen Court (novel, 1864) 179
Ghost (film, 1990) 190, 192
The Ghost of Frankenstein (film, 1942) 12
The Ghost Ship (film, 1943) 120
ghost stories 68–71, 114–116, 135–138, 160–164, 174–178, 180–181, 204–208, 220–223
Ghost Stories 137
Ghostbusters (film, 1984) 166
Ghostbusters (video game, 1986) 166
Ghostwatch (TV show) 220, 221–222
The Giant Claw (film, 1957) 19
Giant from the Unknown (film, 1958) 16, 19
Giger, H.R. 166
Gilliam, Terry 225
Girl's Town (film, 1942) 106
"The Goatfoot God" (short story, 1936) 45
The Gods of Pegāna (short story collection, 1905) 198
The Golden Bough (comparative study of mythology and religion, 1890) 45, 60
Golden Dawn, Hermetic Order of the 60, 61, 90, 91, 93, 194
Gone South (novel, 1992) 145
Gone with the Wind (1939) 3
The Gorilla (film, 1927) 96
Gorilla Men, Professional *see* Gemora, Charles
Goth fashion 63–67
Goth music 63–67
Gothic (film, 1986) 221
Gothic revival (in literature) 107–113, 124–127, 178–181, 186–189, 227
Grand Theft Auto (video game, 1997) 212
Greene, Graham 200
Gregory of Tours 100–103
The Grenville Standard (newspaper) 204, 205, 208
The Grimoire and Other Supernatural Stories (short story collection, 1936) 209
Grinny (novel, 1973) 83
"The Grove of the Astaroth" (short story, 1912) 45
The Guardian (film, 1990) 221

Hall, G. Stanley 172
Halloween (film, 1978) 14, 130
Halperin, Victor 6, 104–106
Hammer Horror 1, 26–29
Hammid, Alexander 73
Hardy, Oliver 24
Harper's Weekly (magazine) 160
Harrison High (book series, 1957–74) 80
Harryhausen, Ray 84
Hatton, Rondo 13
The Haunted Palace (film, 1963) 32
The Haunted River (novel, 1877) 179

Haworth, Jann 62
Hayworth, Rita 24
Heartless (film, 2009) 184
"The Hell of Mirrors" ("Kagami-jigoku") (short story, 1926) 175, 176
Her Double Life (film, 1916) 21
Her Greatest Love (film, 1916) 22
High Bloods (2009) 80
Hill, Susan 135–137
Hills, Matt 202
The Hills Have Eyes (film, 1977) 130
History of the Franks (historical study, c. 575) 103
The History of Witchcraft and Demonology (historical study, 1926) 210–211
Hitchcock, Alfred 34, 80, 130, 222
Hobson, Valerie 12
Hodges, Runa 20
Hoffmann, E.T.A. 175
Hold That Ghost (film, 1941) 11
Holden, Gloria 13
Hooper, Tobe 130, 156
Hopalong Cassidy (film, 1935) 18
Hordern, Michael 218
horror movies, British 26–29, 117–120, 183, 200–203, 215, 220
horror novels 30–33, 80–82, 127–129, 144, 215–220
The Horror of Frankenstein (film, 1970) 26–27
The Horrors of Malformed Men (*Kyôfu kikei ningen: Edogawa Rampo zenshû*) (film, 1969) 176
House of Dracula (film, 1945) 119
House of Horrors (film, 1946) 13
Household Words (magazine) 179
The Houses of Osma and Almeria; or, Convent of St. Ildefonso (novel, 1810) 186
How to Make a Monster (film, 1958) 19
Human Beings (novel, 1807) 124
"The Human Chair" ("Ningen Isu," short story, 1925) 176
The Hunchback of Notre Dame (film, 1923) 94, 104
The Hunger and Other Stories (short story collection, 1957) 31
The Hunter from the Woods (short story and novella collection, 2011) 144
Hutchinson's Adventure Story Magazine 51

I Don't Want to Be Born (film, 1975) 28
I Wake Up Screaming (film, 1941) 18
I Walked with a Zombie (film, 1943) 120
The Idle Thoughts of an Idle Fellow (essay collection, 1886) 114
Idler (magazine) 197
Illustrated London News (magazine) 197
illustrators 176, 197–199
The Imaginarium of Doctor Parnassus (film, 2009) 225
Imamura, Akihiro 214

Index   243

The Immortal Coil (short story collection, 1985) 218
In a Lonely Place (film, 1950) 18
In the Beginning (short story collection, 1909) 69
"In the North Wing" (short story, 1888) 206
Ingagi (film, 1930) 97
Inky Bloaters (music album, 1987) 65
Intermezzo (film, 1936, 1939) 34, 46
Invaders from Mars (film, 1953) 16, 18
The Invisible Man (film, 1933) 6
The Invisible Man (novella, 1897) 163
The Invisible Man's Revenge (film, 1944) 13, 118
The Island of Dr. Moreau (novel, 1896) 2–3, 40
The Island of Lost Souls (film, 1932) 2–3
Isle of the Dead (film, 1945) 2
Italian Mysteries (novels, 1820) 124
The Italian, or the Confessional of the Black Penitents (novel, 1797) 156
Ito, Teji 72
ITV Playhouse (TV show) 215

Jackson, Gordon 218
Jackson, Peter 117
Jacob's Ladder (film, 1990) 212
Jagger, Dean 106
James, Henry 170
James, M.R. 116, 136
James, William 170, 171, 172
Janes, Hugh 137
Jannings, Emil 139
Janowitz, Hans 140
Japanese horror fiction 174–177
Japanese Tales of Mystery and Imagination (short stories, 1956) 175
Jarmusch, Jim 224
Jerningham, Edward 107–114
Jerome, Jerome K. 114–113
Jesus Egg That Wept (music album, 1984) 63
"The Jewelled Hand" (short story, 1887) 205
Jim Henson Hour (TV show) 85
Joan of Arc (film, 1948) 36
journalism 6, 7, 23, 24, 50, 54, 60–61, 65, 68, 104, 114, 139, 178, 182, 193, 204–208
Judas! (novel, 1972) 216
The Jungle Captive (film, 1945) 13
Jungle Woman (film, 1944) 13
Just Before Dawn (film, 1981) 130, 133

Kafka, Franz 121, 152
Karloff, Boris 200, 202
Kathleen Mavourneen (film, 1919) 22
Keen, Geoffrey 27
"The Keeper of Cademuir" (short story, 1894) 43
Kenton, Erle C. 2–3
King, Stephen 81–82, 128, 142, 143, 145, 156
King Kong (film, 1933) 1, 97, 222

Kingdom of the Spiders (film, 1977) 132
Kipling, Rudyard 22, 114
The Kiss (film, 1988) 221
A Kiss Before Dying (novel, 1953) 127, 128
Kiss of Death (film, 1947) 46
Kliner, Max 122
Knaggs, Skelton 6, 117–120
Kneale, Nigel 137
Kojima, Hideo 214
Korda, Alexander 140
Krindlekrax (novel, 1991) 182
Kronos (film, 1957) 16, 18
Kubin, Alfred 121–123

"The Lady with the Veil" (short story, 1903) 206
Lane, William 186–187
Lang, Fritz 32, 140
The Last Laugh (*Der letzte Mann* aka *The Last Man*) (film, 1924) 139
Lathom, Francis 7, 124–126
Laughton, Charles 2
Laurel and Hardy 98
Lawman (TV show, 1959) 16
Lee, Christopher 27, 200, 202
Le Fanu, Sheridan 114
Lemon Kittens 63
leopard skin, use as fashion accessory 68, 70
Levin, Ira 7–8, 80, 127–129, 143
Lewis, Matthew 1, 125, 109
Lewton, Val 2, 105, 120
Leytonstone (novella, 2015) 222
Lieberman, Jeff 6, 130–134
Lincoln, Andrew 221
Live and Learn (novel, 1823) 125
Lo! (nonfiction—unusual phenomena, 1939) 87
Lobsterman from Mars (film, 1989) 19
The Lodger (film, 1944) 118
Lombard, Carole 105
"The Lone Hand" (short story, 1908) 69
Love Life of a Gorilla (documentary film, 1931) 97
Lovecraft, H.P. 32, 100, 148, 162, 165–166, 167, 191, 199
Lugosi, Bela 11, 12, 97, 104, 202
The Lure of Ambition (film, 1919) 22
Lurking Fear (film, 1994) 191
Lust for a Vampire (film, 1972) 28
Lynch, David 66, 212
Lynn, Jenny 200

MacGyver (TV show) 191
Machen, Arthur 61, 70
Machine Gun Kelly (film, 1958) 46
The Mad Ghoul (film, 1943) 12
Mad Love (film, 1935) 12
Madame Mystery (film, 1926) 24
The Magic Island (travelogue, 1929) 104, 195
Magick 58–62, 194

244 Index

The Maid of the Hamlet (novel, 1793) 188
Mallatratt, Stephen 7, 135–148
Malleus Maleficarum (treatise, 1486/1928) 209, 210
Man Ray 193
The Manchester Guardian (newspaper) 201
Mander, Miles 13
Mann, Thomas 193
Manrissa Man (novel, 1982) 218
Martians 14, 16, 18, 19, 98–99, 218
Marx Brothers 98
The Masque of the Red Death (film, 1964) 32
Matheson, Richard 31, 82
Mathijs, Ernest 202
Matinee (film, 1993) 19
Matlock (TV show) 191
"Matthew Corbett" series (novels) 145
Mature, Victor 18
Maturin, Charles 1, 188
Mayer, Carl 6, 139–141
McCammon, Robert R. 7, 142–146
McCarthy, Kevin 19
McCullers, Carson 224
mediums, psychic 3, 5, 7, 65, 81, 90–94, 105, 115, 143, 162, 169–174, 180, 194, 207, 221
The Medusa Touch (film, 1978) 218
The Medusa Touch (novel, 1973) 215, 216–218
Meier, Sid 214
Memory Hold the Door (autobiography, 1940) 43
Men and Manners (novel, 1799) 124
Meshes of the Afternoon (short experimental film, 1943) 73–74
Miami Vice (TV show) 191
Middle Ages 3, 76–79, 100–103, 209–211
The Midnight Bell (novel, 1798) 124, 126
Mikami, Shinji 147–150, 214
Mine (novel, 1990) 144
Minion, Joseph 6, 151–154
Minotaur (novel, 1985) 80
Miyamoto, Shigeru 214
Modersohn, Otto 157
Modersohn-Becker, Paula 5, 7, 155–159
The Monastery of St. Columb; or, the Atonement (novel, 1813) 186
The Monk (novel, 1796) 109
Monster Maker (novel, 1979) 84
Monsters in the Heart (short story collection, 2013) 222
Moonchild (novel, originally The Butterfly Net, [1917] republished 1929) 59–62
Moonfleece (stage play, 2004) 182
Moonfleet (film, 1955) 118
Moonlighting (TV show) 191
More Not at Night (short story collection, 1961) 31
Most Dangerous Man Alive (film, 1961) 19
Mule Variations (music album, 1999) 225
Munch, Edvard 155
The Munster Cottage Boy (novel, 1820) 188-9
Murder, She Wrote (TV show) 191

Muren, Dennis 17
Murnau, Friedrich Wilhelm 139, 140
Murray, Margaret 45
Mutants (novel, 1986) 219
The Mysterious Freebooter (novel, 1806) 124
Mystery (novel, 1800) 124
Mystery Walk (novel, 1983) 143
Mystic Events (novel, 1830) 124

Naldi, Nita 24
Nation Aflame (film, 1937) 106
Negri, Pola 24
Nelson, Lori 46
NeverEnding Story 3: Return to Fantasia (film, 1994) 133
"The New People" (short story, 1960) 31
New Statesman (magazine) 211
New Year's Eve (Sylvester: Tragödie einer Nacht, film, 1924) 139
New York Herald (newspaper) 171
Nicholson, Jack 191
Night and Day (film, 1946) 118
The Night Boat (novel, 1980) 143
Night Gallery (TV show) 52
Night of the Demon (film, 1957) 105
Night of the Eagle (film, 1962) 32
Night of the Lepus (film, 1972) 132
Night of the Living Dead (film, 1968) 106
Night Ride and Other Journeys (short story collection, 1960) 31
Nightfall (novel, 1987) 80
The Nightmare (painting, 1781) 22, 221
No Hiding Place (autobiography, 1942) 193
No Time for Sergeants (novel, 1956) 128
Nocturnal Visit (novel, 1800) 186, 188
Nolan, William F. 31
None But the Lonely Heart (film, 1944) 118
North, William 162
Northanger Abbey (novel, 1817) 124, 186
Nosferatu (film, 1922) 155
Not at Night (anthology series, 1925) 51
Notorious (film, 1946) 35, 37
The Nun's Picture (novel, 1834) 188
Nyman, Andy 137

O'Brien, Fitz-James 7, 160–164
Observer (magazine) 200
occultism 3, 5, 7, 23, 40, 58–62, 65, 86, 90–93, 104, 193–196, 207, 209–211
O'Connor, Flannery 224
O'Connor, Una 6
Ogilvy, Ian 26
The Old Dark House (film, 1932) 12
Olivier, Sir Laurence 129
The Omen (film, 1976) 81
On the Isle of Samoa (film, 1950) 46
On the Wallaby (travelogue, 1894) 38
One Flew Over the Cuckoo's Nest (film, 1975) 191
Orlando and Seraphina (stage play, 1800) 124
Orwell, George 52

Index   245

Osborne, Vivienne 105
Ouspenskaya, Maria 11
The Outcast Manufacturers (novel, 1909) 86
Owenson, Sydney (Lady Morgan) 188

paganism 43–44, 45, 60–61, 76, 78, 92
Pal, George 32
Pall Mall (magazine) 197
Pan (Greek God) 61, 69, 92
Pan Book of Horror Stories (series) 51
paranormal phenomena/abilities 80, 86–89, 126, 144, 171, 180, 217, 221–222
Parkinson, Michael 221
Pascal, Gabriel 141
The Passion of Darkly Noon (film, 1995) 183
The Pearl of Death (film, 1944) 13
penury 38, 70, 120, 139–140, 141, 178–179, 181, 187
Perry Mason (TV show) 17, 19
Persecution (film, 1974) 28
Petersen, Sandy 165–168, 214
Phantom Nights (novel, 2005) 82
Phantom of the Opera (film, 1925) 96
Phantom of the Rue Morgue (film, 1954) 99
Pharos the Egyptian (novel, 1899) 40–41
Phase IV (film, 1974) 132
Pick, Lupu 139
The Picture of Dorian Gray (film, 1945) 118
Pintoff, Ernest 131
Piper, Leonora 169–173
Pitt, Ingrid 26
Plunkett, Edward (18th Baron of Dunsany) 198
Poe, Edgar Allan 3, 32, 60, 122, 144, 152, 162, 175, 198, 205, 222
poetry 59, 68–71, 76–79, 108, 111, 160–161, 205
Polanski, Roman 128
Poldark (TV show) 29
Polidori, John 112
Pop Eyes (music album, 1983) 63, 64
"The Pot of Tulips" (short story, 1855) 162
Powell, Frank 20
Powell, Michael 3, 119
The Premature Burial (film, 1962) 32
psychiatry 7, 35, 140, 216, 218, 221, 227–230
Psychic Self-Defense (instruction manual, 1930) 91
Psycho (film, 1960) 80, 130
psychoanalysis 34, 60, 193, 229
public houses, as a stimulus to great ideas 5
publishing industry 51, 57, 70, 114, 128, 142, 145–146, 166, 179–180, 186–187, 188, 199, 205, 207, 216
The Purity Squad (film, 1945) 18
Putnam's Monthly Magazine, 160

Radcliffe, Ann 1, 72, 75, 125, 156, 186, 188
Radcliffe, Daniel 137
A Rag, a Bone and a Hank of Hair (novel, 1980) 85

Rain Dogs (music album, 1985) 224
Rains, Claude 11
Rampo, Edogawa 7, 174–77
Rampo Noir (film, 2005) 176
Rawhide (TV show) 17
Real Gone (music album, 2004) 224
Red Planet Mars (film, 1952) 18
Reeves, Michael 26
The Reflecting Skin (film, 1990) 183
Remick, Lee 218
Remote Control (film, 1988) 133
Resident Evil (video game series) 147–150
Reunion in Vienna (film, 1933) 17
Revenge of the Creature (film, 1955) 46
Revolt of the Zombies (film, 1936) 105–106
Riddell, Charlotte 7, 178–182
Ridley, Philip 6, 182–185
Riefenstahl, Leni 139, 140
"The Rime of the True Thomas" (short story, 1912) 43
The Ringer (public information film, 1972) 131, 132
The Riponshire Advocate (newspaper) 204
rites, unspeakable 50
Ritual in Transfigured Time (short experimental film, 1946) 74
Roche, Regina Maria 7, 186–90
Rocketship X-M (film, 1950) 16, 18
A Romance of Two Worlds (novel, 1886) 54–55
Romero, George A. 106, 130, 148
The Rose of Blood (film, 1917) 22
Rosemary's Baby (film, 1968) 128, 130
Rosemary's Baby (novel, 1967) 7, 8, 127–129, 143
Rotha, Paul 141
Ruttmann, Walter 139, 140

Sadsy, Peter 26, 29
Saint Erkenwald 76–78
Sallis, Peter 27
Salome (film, 1918) 22
"The Sandman" ("Der Sandmann," short story, 1816) 175
Sane Occultism (advice/instruction manual, 1938) 91
Satan/Satanism 20, 27, 31–32, 43, 57, 58, 134, 209–211
Satan's Little Helper (film, 2004) 130, 133–134
Sato, Takayoshi 214
Saturday Night Thriller (TV show) 215
The Savage Bees (film, 1976) 132
Schiavelli, Vincent 190–192
science fiction 16–19, 30, 81, 83–85, 89, 127, 129, 133, 131, 145, 160, 163, 166, 216
Science Fiction Theatre (TV show) 18
science, mad 12–13, 40, 105–106, 119
Scott, Randolph 105
Scott, Walter 188
Scream Queens 11–14

Index

Seabrook, William Buehler 7, 104, 193–196
"Seagram's Manuscript" (short story, 1895) 206
The Secrets of Doctor Taverner (short story collection, 1926) 91
Seduction of the Innocent (psychiatric, social study, 1954) 227, 228
See Here, Private Hague (film, 1944) 18
Selznick, David O. 34
Sensational Tales (short story collection, 1886) 205
Serling, Rod 32, 33, 52
7 Faces of Dr. Lao (film, 1964) 32
sex rituals 45, 59, 92, 211
Sgt. Pepper's Lonely Hearts Club Band (music album, 1967) 62
Shakespeare, William 125, 218
Sharp, Lesley 221
Shatter (novel, 1980) 80
Shaw, George Bernard 141
Shelley, Mary 1, 14, 221
Sherlock Holmes and the Voice of Terror (film, 1942) 13
Shivers (film, 1975) 130
short stories 30–33, 50–53, 69, 70, 81, 83, 91, 114–116, 122, 144, 160–164, 174–177, 218, 222
The Show of Violence (psychiatric, social study, 1949), 228
"Si Urang of the Tail" (short story, 1923) 51
The Silence of the Lambs (film, 1991) 212
silent cinema 20–25, 96, 117–120, 139
Silent Hill (video game) 212–214
Sime, Sidney 7, 196–99
Simon, Simone 1
Sin (film, 1915) 21
The Siren's Song (film, 1919) 22
skepticism 56, 87–88, 169, 171–172, 194, 209–211, 221–223
"Skule Skerry" (short story, 1928) 43
Slaughter, Todd 6, 8, 200–203
The Slave of the Lamp (novel, 1855) 162
Society of the Inner Light 90–92
Sohl, Jerry 31
Son of Ali Baba (film, 1952) 46
Son of Dracula (film, 1943) 12
Son of Rosemary (novel, 1997) 129
Son of the Endless Night (novel, 1984) 80
Sondheim, Steven 201
Soon She Will Be Gone (novel, 1997) 80
The Sorcerers (film, 1967) 26
Sorrows of Satan (novel, 1895) 54, 56
The Soul of Buddha (film, 1918) 22
The Soul of Lilith (novel, 1897) 55
Sparkleshark (stage play, 1997) 183
Sparrow, Lionel 204–208
Speaks the Nightbird (novel, 2002) 145
special effects 17, 94–99, 117, 136
Spellbound (film, 1945) 34–35, 37
spiritualism 55, 105, 162–163, 169–173, 180
Squirm (film, 1976) 130–133, 134
The Stand (novel, 1978) 144

Star Trek: The Next Generation (TV show) 191
Starsky and Hutch (TV show) 191
Steele, V.M. 92
Stein, Gertrude 193
The Stepford Wives (novel, 1972) 8, 127, 128
Stinger (1988) 144
Stone, Philip 218
The Strange World of Willie Seabrook (memoir, 1966) 193
Straub, Peter 82, 128
Stuart, Gloria 12
Studies in Spiritism (documented the tests, 1910) 172
suburbia 31, 83
Sugarfoot (TV show) 17
Summers, Montague 7, 209–211
Supernatural (film, 1933) 105
"Supernatural Horror in Literature" (essay, 1927) 100, 162
survival horror (video games) 147–150, 212–214
Swan Song (novel, 1987) 144
Swayze, Patrick 190
The Sweeney Todd: Demon Barber of Fleet Street (film, 1936) 201
Sweet Home (video game, 1989) 148
Sweets from a Stranger and Other Science Fiction Stories (short story collection, 1982) 83
Swiss Miss (film, 1938) 98
Swordfishtrombones (music album, 1983) 224–225
Symons, Arthur 22

Taking Off (film, 1971) 191
Tales of Hoffmann (film, 1951) 3
Tanner, Amy 172
Tartuffe (film, 1925) 139
Tarzan's Magic Fountain (film, 1949) 14
Taste the Blood of Dracula (film, 1970) 27, 29
Tatsumi, Takayuki 176
Taxi (TV show) 191
Taza, Son of Cochise (film, 1954) 18
Telegraph (newspaper) 182
television 17, 32, 81, 85, 89, 131, 135, 137, 174, 191
"The Tenant of the Third Cell" (short story, 1888) 205
Tennessee Johnson (film, 1942) 18
Terror by Night (film, 1946) 119
The Texas Chain Saw Massacre (film, 1974) 130, 156
Theosophical Society 59, 90
They Thirst (novel, 1981) 143, 144
Thirty-Minute Theatre (TV show) 215
The Thirty-Nine Steps (novel, 1915) 43
This Perfect Day (novel, 1970) 127, 129
Thompson, David 36
Those That Bite the Hand That Feeds Them

Sooner or Later Must Meet... (music album, 1982) 64
Three Men in a Boat, To Say Nothing of the Dog (autobiographical sketch) 114
Tokyo Gore Police (*Tokyo Zankoku Keisatsu*) (film, 2008) 175
Told After Supper (collection of short stories, 1891) 116
Tolkien, J.R.R. 198
Tomahawk (film, 1951) 46
Tomb Raider (videogame, 1996)
Tomorrow Never Dies (film, 1997) 191
"The Torture of the Clock" (short story, 1888) 205
Tower of London (film, 1962) 19
The Tradition of the Castle; or, Scenes in the Emerald Isle (novel, 1824) 188–9
Trecothick Bower; or, The Lady of the West Country (novel, 1814) 186
Trillions (novel, 1971) 83
Trollope, Anthony 179
Trouble Everyday (film, 2001) 25
Tsukamoto, Shin'ya 176
Tuner, Lana 24, 28
The Twilight Zone (TV show) 32, 89
"The Twins: A Condemned Criminal's Confession to a Priest" ("Sōseiji," short story, 1924) 175, 176
"Two Crippled Men" ("Ni Haijin," short story, 1924) 175
"The Two-Sen Copper Coin" ("Nisen Doka") (short story, 1923) 174

Under Capricorn (film, 1949) 35–36
The Uninhabited House (novel, 1875) 179
The Uninvited (novel, 1982) 81
Universal Studios 1, 6, 11–14, 31, 46–47, 95–96, 98, 104, 167
Usher's Passing (novel, 1984) 144

The Vampire (painting, 1897) 22
"The Vampire" (short story, 1894) 22
The Vampire Lovers (film, 1970) 26, 28
Vampire's Kiss (film, 1989) 151–153
vampires/vampirism 27, 77, 143, 151–152
vamps 20–25, 140
Van Gogh, Vincent 155
Van Greenaway, Peter 215–219
Vanity Fair (magazine) 160, 162
Van Thal, Herbert 51
Vardøger (novella, 2009) 222
Ventura, Lino 218
Vertigo (film, 1958) 212
The Very Eye of Night (1952–59) (film, 1952–59) 91
The Vicar of Lansdowne; or, Country Quarters (novel, 1789) 188
video games 147–150, 165–168, 212–214
Videodrome (film, 1983) 133
Viking Women and the Sea Serpent (film, 1957) 46

The Vixen (film, 1916) 21
Volk, Stephen 6, 220–223
voodoo 72, 75, 81, 104, 193–196

Waits, Tom 7, 8, 224–226
"The Walker (Stalker) in the Attic" ("Yaneura no sanposha") (short story, 1925) 176
Walpole, Horace 1, 100, 107–8, 111–112, 227
War of the Satellites (film, 1958) 46
The War of the Worlds (film, 1953) 98, 99
The War of the Worlds (radio drama, 1938) 137
Warburton, Holly 65
The Wasp Woman (film, 1959) 46
"Watcher by the Threshold" (short story, 1901) 43
Watcher in the Attic (film, 1976; 1993; 2007) 176
Weill, Kurt 226
Weird Stories (short story collection, 1882) 180
Weird Tales (magazine) 51
Welles, Orson 17, 137
Wells, H.G. 2, 40, 69, 136, 163, 218
Wertham, Fredric 7, 227–230
West, Mae 24
"When Glister Walked" (short story, 1927) 51–52
The Whisperer in Darkness (film, 2011) 167
White Stains (poetic work, 1898) 60
White Zombie (film, 1932) 104–106, 196
Whitman, Walt 161
Whitstable (novella, 2013) 222
Who Framed Roger Rabbit (video game, 1991) 148
Wiene, Robert 139, 140
The Wild Irish Girl (novel, 1806) 188
Wild Talents (non-fiction on the paranormal, 1932) 87–88
Wilde, Oscar 60
Wildwood (novel, 1986) 81
"William Wilson" (short story, 1839) 175
Williamson, Nicol 218
"Wind in the Portico" (short story, 1928) 43
The Wind in the Willows (novel, 1908) 61
The Winged Bull (novel, 1935) 91
The Witch-Cult in Western Europe (anthropological study, 1921) 45
Witch Wood (novel, 1929) 44
witchcraft/witches 44–45, 70, 87, 145, 183–184, 194–196, 209–211
Witchfinder General (film, 1968) 26
The Wolf Man (film, 1941) 11
The Wolf's Hour (novel, 1989) 144
Wolle, Francis 161
The Woman in Black (novella, 1983) 135–136
The Woman in Black (stage play, 1987) 135–137–139
A Woman There Was (film, 1917) 22

The Wonderful World of the Brothers Grim (film, 1962) 32
Wood, Robin 132
World Film News (magazine) 202
Worthington, Marjorie 193
Woyzeck (stage play, 2010) 225
Wright, Will 214

X: The Man with the X-Ray Eyes (film, 1963) 19
X-Cross (film, 2007) 175
The X-Files (TV show) 89, 191

X-Men 89

Yamaoka, Akira 214
Yeats, W.B. 60
Yonder (short story collection, 1958) 31
You Remember Me! (novel, 1984) 84
Yronwode, Catherine 227

zombies 7, 104–106, 132, 148–9, 158, 193–198
Zombies of Mora Tau (film, 1957) 19
Zucco, George 12

www.ingramcontent.com/pod-product-compliance
Ingram Content Group UK Ltd.
Pitfield, Milton Keynes, MK11 3LW, UK
UKHW041936140426
5217IPUK00014B/509